Economic Cooperation in an Uncertain World

Economic Cooperation in an Uncertain World

Economic Cooperation in an Uncertain World

Atish R. Ghosh and Paul R. Masson

BLACKWELL
Oxford UK & Cambridge USA

Copyright © Basil Blackwell Ltd 1994

First published 1994

Blackwell Publishers
238 Main Street
Cambridge, Massachusetts 02142
USA

108 Cowley Road
Oxford OX4 1JF
UK

Library of Congress Cataloguing-in-Publication Data

Ghosh, Atish R.
    Economic cooperation in an uncertain world/Atish R. Ghosh, Paul
R. Masson.
        p.   cm.
    Includes bibliographical references and index.
    ISBN 1–55786–306–7
    1. International economic relations. I. Masson, Paul R.
II. Title.
HF1359.G49   1994
337–dc20   93–29370
                                                                              CIP

British Library Cataloguing in Publication Data

A CIP catalogue record for this book is available from the British Library.

Typeset in 10 on 12 pt Times Roman
by Grahame & Grahame Editorial, Brighton
Printed in Great Britain by T.J. Press (Padstow) Ltd., Padstow, Cornwall

This book is printed on acid-free paper

Contents

List of Figures

List of Tables

Preface and Acknowledgements

This book grew out of our common interest in various aspects of policy coordination and our earlier collaboration on two papers, one published in IMF *Staff Papers* "International Policy Coordination in a World with Model Uncertainty," June 1988, and the other in the *American Economic Review* ("Model Uncertainty, Learning, and the Gains from Coordination," June 1991). These papers looked at the effects of uncertainty on the incentive of governments to coordinate their macoeconomic policies. As we studied this issue, however, it became increasingly apparent that such effects are very complex, and that a satisfactory analysis would require a more systematic treatment. To this end, we extended the scope of our previous empirical analysis and explored a variety of theoretical issues related to the design, negotiation, and enforcement of coordinated agreements when there is uncertainty. We also tried to draw some conclusions for real-world coordination, and to survey the post-war experience of international macroeconomic cooperation. This book is the result.

We are grateful to a number of people who have encouraged us, given us ideas, and read the manuscript. These include Ralph Bryant, Matt Canzoneri, Wendy Dobson, Jeff Frankel, Swati Ghosh, Joe Grieco, Anne-Marie Gulde, Randall Henning, Andy Hughes Hallett, Peter Kenen, Warwick McKibbin, David Vines, and Peter Winkler.

Finally, we would like to make clear that the views expressed in this book are personal to the authors and do not represent those of the International Monetary Fund or of any other official institution.

We would like to thank the IMF for permission to reproduce extracts from IMF *Staff Papers*, "Portfolio Preference Uncertainty and Gains from Policy Coordination" (vol. 39, March 1992).

1
Introduction

The Conference is unanimous, however, in believing that
national action is not by itself sufficient. International cooperation, of which the Conference itself is the first effort and
example, must continue and develop . . .

> From the Recommendations of the Brussels
> International Monetary Conference, 1920
> (League of Nations, 1920, p. 11)

Interest in the international coordination of macroeconomic policies has
waxed and waned ever since the Brussels Conference of 1920 first urged
cooperation among central banks. Though attempts at coordination
during the interwar years ended in spectacular failure as governments
pursued beggar-thy-neighbor devaluations, various forms of international cooperation played an important role in sustaining the Bretton
Woods system of fixed exchange rates. Interest in coordination fell in the
early 1970s with the advent of floating exchange rates, which were
purported to allow independent monetary policies. Within a few years,
however, it became clear that floating exchange rates did not eliminate
the need for international coordination. The Bonn Summit of 1978
represented one of the most important attempts at coordination, though
it is generally judged to have been a failure, in large part because the
expansionary policies envisioned at the time it was negotiated were no
longer appropriate in the aftermath of the second oil shock. More
recently, governments of the largest industrialized countries have
coordinated their efforts at stabilizing exchange rates and at correcting
external imbalances.

This book examines the case for policy coordination, paying particular
attention to how macroeconomic uncertainty affects international
cooperation. Why should governments coordinate their macroeconomic
policies? At the most general level, the case for coordination rests on the
existence of spillovers, or externalities, from the policies of one country to
the welfare of its neighbors. Governments acting non-cooperatively may

succeed only in neutralizing one anothers' policies. Through coordination, they can better achieve crucial macroeconomic goals – individual and collective.

Though the intuition behind this seems straightforward, defining coordination, and distinguishing it from what governments would do anyway, is no mean task. This distinction is not difficult to make in theoretical models of coordination. These papers assume that each government's preferences over macroeconomic outcomes can be adequately captured by an objective, or welfare function. In the absence of coordination, each government is then assumed to set its policy instruments to maximize only its own objective function. When policies are coordinated, policymakers maximize a joint welfare function which is usually taken to be an arithmetic or geometric average of the various countries' welfare functions. Of course, the national welfare functions may include what may be termed "international" objectives: exchange rate stability, for example, may be in the interest of every country. It is very unlikely, however, that all of the objectives will be common to all the countries: most governments presumably care more about unemployment or inflation at home than in foreign countries. As long as the national objectives differ in at least some respect, and as long as there are spillover effects from one government's policy instruments onto the objectives of another country, coordination will yield higher levels of welfare than would uncoordinated policies.

In the real world, however, it is virtually impossible to characterize policymaking in this way since it is hard to identify governments' true objective functions; in fact, policymaking in all countries usually represents an aggregation of various views with weights that shift over time. Is the fiscal stimulus in Japan designed to boost domestic activity or to improve the U.S. trade balance? Both considerations could have some weight; quite how much each received in the decision, though, will be impossible to tell. Policymakers themselves are unlikely to be of much help: to their domestic constituents they will present their actions as a vigorous stance against the specter of unemployment; to their trading partners it is their commitment to the common good which will be stressed. Moreover, short of abandoning sovereignty to some supranational institution, all governments have some scope for aiming at purely domestic objectives – something they usually do.

However coordination is defined, it is useful to distinguish it from cooperation, which includes other forms of interaction, including the sharing of information about the economic situation facing countries as well as the narrower concept of coordination. While governments certainly engage in some forms of cooperation, whether coordination is also involved is more difficult to determine. Some have argued that what purport to be coordinated policies among the Group of Seven (G-7) countries are really no different from the policies which would have been pursued by the national authorities of each country were they acting independently (see Feldstein, 1988b). In our view, however, there is substantive international economic policy coordination; negotiations among governments do generally lead to outcomes that would not have been reached by governments acting alone.[1] For analytical convenience, we will define a coordinated regime as one in which every government chooses its macroeconomic instruments in order to maximize a *global* objective function which, in turn, is an average of each country's welfare function. It is unlikely that macroeconomic policies have ever been set in a manner that satisfies this strict definition of coordination. But there have certainly been occasions when policies have been chosen with an eye to meeting mutually agreed objectives, in contrast to times when they have clearly been chosen independently, without regard for the objectives of other governments. Choosing policies in this coordinated manner can, in principle, enhance the ability of each government to attain its own goals. We shall explore how reaching coordinated agreements is affected by uncertainty concerning the effects of policies, and how monitoring and enforcement of agreements is affected by imperfect information concerning the relevant economic variables.

Coordination in Practice

In the Appendix to this book, we survey some of the ways in which governments have cooperated (or coordinated) in the area of macro-economic policies. In particular, we focus there and in the rest of the book on international monetary cooperation, mainly because it has been more extensive; fiscal policy has in general *not* been coordinated. Fiscal policy is subject to longer decision and implementation lags and also requires *domestic* coordination for decisions to be made, e.g. between the executive and legislative branches.

When discussing experience with policy coordination, it is useful to distinguish between *ad hoc* and institutionalized coordination (Artis and Ostry, 1986). In the former case, a particular policy action is taken only when agreement is reached, on a case by case basis. In the latter, a mechanism is created for centralized decision-making, by which decisions are made either collectively by member countries or by an institution acting on behalf of that membership. The coordinated response can be expected to vary depending on the extent of uncertainty and the expected persistence of the problem. If the problem is structural, then it may make sense to create a formal mechanism for dealing with it, while *ad hoc* coordination may be adequate when the need is expected to be short-term. Without an institutional framework in place, however, *ad hoc* coordination may take too long to negotiate and to implement, so that governments are not able to respond in a flexible and effective manner. For *ad hoc* coordination to be successful, some institutional forum for government interchanges must exist. Such a forum, moreover, may serve to make information available in a timely and credible fashion to the various national authorities.

Examples of both *ad hoc* and institutionalized coordination may be found in the postwar period. The Bretton Woods System of pegged exchange rates ruled out exchange rate parity changes except in cases of "fundamental disequilibrium," to be determined in consultation with the International Monetary Fund. More recently, G-7 summits and finance ministers' meetings have at time reached agreements on various aspects of economic policies: on a package of fiscal stimulus in Japan and Germany and energy policy changes in the United States (the 1978 Bonn Summit), on the need for exchange rate adjustments (the Plaza Agreement of September, 1985), and on the need for exchange stability (the Louvre Accord of February, 1987). In practice, no mechanism for the international monetary system is likely to operate complete automatically – not even the classical gold standard (see Eichengreen, 1985). Therefore, monetary relations between countries are likely to involve more than just agreements concerning the "rules of the game" but also elements of *ad hoc* coordination of policies.

Forms of Uncertainty

There are various forms of uncertainty that affect policymaking. Jeffrey Frankel (1988a), for instance, has enumerated various obstacles that policymakers face in deciding what to aim for, prior to attempting to reach agreement with other governments. These obstacles include uncertainty about the initial position of the economy, uncertainty about the proper weights to give objectives, and uncertainty about the relevant policy multipliers. All of these can have serious repercussions, and lead to the wrong policies being chosen.

The initial position is obviously important because whether the economy is in a recession or in a boom will influence (among other things) whether to aim at stimulative or contractionary policies. In fact, estimates of GNP growth are made available with a lag of several months and are also subject to substantial revisions later. Not only current variables, but their future values, are needed if policies are to be chosen correctly, given that there are lags both in the implementation of policies and in their ultimate effects on the economy. It is also not known with certainty what the *target values* should be: is the natural rate of unemployment 6 percent or 8 percent, and is zero inflation or 2 percent a better goal?

The appropriate weights to give to the objectives, for instance, to unemployment versus inflation, are also uncertain. In part, this reflects the fact that preferences across objectives are not well defined nor unchanging. Instead, they emerge from the political process and are the result of aggregating across different interest groups.

Finally, the values of policy multipliers are unknown. Different econometric models imply quite different things about the effects of policies. It is unrealistic to think that this form of uncertainty can be eliminated – especially since models are only rudimentary characterizations of a complex and changing economic reality.

In addition to the above, there are other manifestations of uncertainty that are specifically related to bargaining between governments. First, there is uncertainty about the true beliefs and preferences of other governments. Are their policymakers sincere when they express a desire to reach a GATT agreement? Do they really think that fiscal expansion will not be effective in lowering unemployment? Second, can foreign governments be trusted to deliver in good faith their side of the bargain? Here, the issue is how to monitor agreements in the face of unexpected occurrences that make achieving those commitments difficult. Finally, does the other policymaker exploit "private information" and misrepresent the situation in his or her own country in order to gain a bargaining advantage?

All of these aspects of uncertainty will be considered in the book. The next chapter (Chapter 2) shows that there is a useful distinction to be made between *strategic* and *technological* uncertainty, and within the latter, between *additive* and *multiplicative* uncertainty. These terms are defined there, and their implications for policy coordination are discussed in the remainder of the book.

Policy Coordination and Uncertainty about the Effects of Policies

One view about what uncertainty means for policy coordination is that it makes it very much less likely that agreements can be reached and, even if they are, that such agreements will in fact be beneficial. This view has been expressed perhaps most strongly by former Chairman of the U.S. Council of Economic Advisers, Martin Feldstein. In 1983, for example, he wrote:

Economists armed with econometric models of the major countries of the world can, under certain circumstances, identify co-ordinated policies that, quite apart from balance-of-payments constraints, are better than uncoordinated country choices. But in practice, the overwhelming uncertainty about the quantitative behavior of individual economies and their interaction, the great difficulty of articulating policy rules in a changing environment . . . all make such international fine tuning unworkable.   (Feldstein, 1983, p. 44)

We will argue below that this view of the effect of uncertainty on the gains from policy coordination is much too simplistic. Though it is true that any policy – coordinated or uncoordinated – may prove in retrospect to have been misguided because its effects were not correctly anticipated, there may in fact be circumstances in which greater uncertainty provides an additional incentive to coordinate policies.

One reason for coordinating policies in the face of uncertainty is that coordination internalizes a part of that uncertainty, in particular uncertainty related to foreign governments' actions. The transmission effects of policies onto other countries are not known with certainty, and joint decision-making can help reduce that part of uncertainty related to events abroad. Governments acting independently would not be able to minimize the effects of such *transmission uncertainty*. We show in Chapter 3 that gains from policy coordination may *increase* with increases in uncertainty related to transmission multipliers.

An example of the suboptimality of uncoordinated policies is the use of the exchange rate for beggar-thy-neighbor purposes: in the face of a global depression, countries may try to engage in a competitive devaluation, as was the case in the 1930s. More recently, in the aftermath of the 1979–80 oil price shock, several countries used exchange rate appreciation for anti-inflationary purposes. Even if each government has only one target (say inflation) and one instrument (monetary policy), it will still not be able to hit its target exactly because it cannot gauge exactly the effects of its policies, or those of foreign governments. Coordination can improve the effectiveness of monetary policy in achieving its objective.

Coordination may simply involve agreement that governments will not actively respond to various shocks. This suggests international rules of conduct to prohibit certain actions may be appropriate in some circumstances, when the symptoms can be precisely identified. Even though there may be uncertainty about whether the problem will actually occur, it may be possible, when it does, to infer from observations on macroeconomic variables whether policy choices of a particular government are appropriate or not. Because the effects of policies can, in this case, easily be monitored, it may be relatively straightforward to reach agreement simply to rule out such behavior.

For instance, the 1930s saw competitive devaluations among the industrial countries, as governments tried to reduce unemployment at home at the expense of employment in their trading partners. In the immediate post-war period, it was felt that eliminating this policy option was of prime importance. Clearly fixed exchange rates remove this distortion, and the exchange rate itself is a simple monitoring variable in this case.

Another instance is developed in Chapter 4. The stock market crash of October 1987 provides a clear example of the positive effects of uncertainty on incentives to coordinate policies. Shifts in portfolio preferences leading to sharp declines in stock markets worldwide provoked concern about the stability of the financial system in a number of countries. In circumstances of a generalized shift out of equities or bonds into safer assets, central banks may all want to increase liquidity to avoid bankruptcies of securities dealers that might threaten the stability of the banking system, but a constraint on their willingness to lower interest rates might be the desire to avoid exchange rate depreciation. Coordinated interest rate declines – as occurred following the 1987 crash – would avoid this problem. The response of the central banks in the major industrialized countries gives an interesting example of coordination that is partly *ad hoc* and partly institutionalized. Though a response to a unique, unexpected event, it was undertaken at a time when the G-7 coordination process had been recently strengthened by the experience of the Plaza Agreement and the Louvre Accord, so that an effective institutional framework was in place.

Empirical Estimates of Gains from Policy Coordination in the Presence of Model Uncertainty

While the case for policy coordination – even when we do not know the precise effects of policies – seems strong in principle, the crucial question is how large these gains actually are in practice, because, as is discussed below, there are costs to coordinating and difficulties in making agreements stick. An estimate of these gains is attempted in this book. We start by specifying in Chapter 5 four plausible alternative models, which are estimated on data for the United States and the aggregate of the rest of the world. These models are based on a standard open-economy paradigm, but differences in the models relate to whether inflation is sticky or not, to the form of money demand, and to whether potential output is a deterministic trend or a random walk. They all fit the data reasonably well. As a result, we have four models that have some claim to being adequate descriptions of the world economy, as well as representing schools of thought that have some influence today on the economics profession. We assume that one of these four models may be the correct one, but even if we knew the correct model, we would not know the exact parameter values, since the parameters have standard errors associated with them.

Using these estimated models, we then proceed in Chapter 6 to do stochastic simulations, in which governments, not knowing which is the correct model, attach probability values to each of the models being true. We see to what extent being "wrong," that is, putting a low weight on the model that is in fact a correct description of reality, affects gains from policy coordination. It turns out that, in some cases, being wrong not only produces losses from policy coordination, but in fact results in very large welfare losses, because a policy chosen on the basis of an incorrect model destabilizes the world economy. There are also cases, however, in which the optimal *uncoordinated* policies are destabilizing when chosen on the basis of the wrong model. Accordingly, simple, non-activist rules may be preferable. We compare optimal cooperative and noncooperative policies to the following simple rules: fixing the growth rate of the money supply and allowing the exchange rate to float freely; targeting nominal income; fixing the nominal exchange rate; fixing the real exchange rate; and a synthetic rule in which the money supply is adjusted as a decreasing function of output and producer prices and as an increasing function of the rate of interest.

It is hard to believe, though, that in the perverse cases in which activist policies are destabilizing and welfare losses unbounded, policymakers would not modify their views about the functioning of the economy in the light of manifestly incorrect predictions. We therefore go on to consider the possibility of learning the correct model, through Bayesian updating of the probabilities applied to each of the four models. In other words, governments are assumed to set policies on the basis of their assessments of the likelihood that each model is correct, but they also update those assessments each period. Observing macroeconomic outcomes, and assumed to know the distribution of shocks affecting the world economy, they recalculate the probabilities that each of the models could have generated those outcomes. These simulations no longer contain the destabilizing effects of policy coordination, even if the initial priors are very wrong. Moreover, these simulations do not assume that policymakers eventually learn the true model in the sense of knowing every parameter exactly; rather, policymakers endogenously learn the *basic* structure of the model, not its precise parameter values. This occurs at a sufficiently rapid rate that the gains from coordination materialize, relative to either uncoordinated optimal policies or simple rules.

A further interesting experiment consists in assuming that none of the four models is in fact correct. Instead, a completely atheoretical, time series model is fitted to the historical data and is used in the simulations to generate new observations. As before, policymakers attempt to learn from observed outcomes which of the four models is correct, even though none of them really is. This case presents a potential caveat to the relative optimism of coordination with learning: Though coordination does much better than uncoordinated optimization, fixed, non-activist rules now generally come out quite well.

Cooperation versus Coordination

Another aspect of cooperation is sharing information about policy actions, and it is sometimes argued that information sharing, not explicit coordination, is the major source of gains from cooperation among the major industrial countries (Canzoneri and Minford, 1988). We examine the case for this view in Chapter 7, and find, using a simple model, that information exchange alone may actually *lower* welfare. For instance, if the incentives for beggar-thy-neighbor policies exist (and have not been removed by an attempt at *coordination*), knowledge about the other governments' actions may lead to increased efforts to use domestic policy in a way which has further negative effects abroad. We do not view this as an argument against international cooperation (i.e. information exchange) but rather as an argument for recognizing the inherent limitations of forms of international cooperation which do not entail actual *coordination* of macroeconomic policies.

In practice, it may be difficult to separate coordination from simple information exchange. The latter typically results from active consultation and negotiation among governments that accompany the process of coordination. Keohane (1984) has argued that only by entering into agreements to carry out specific policies can governments actually reduce uncertainty through the provision of information: "Uncertainty pervades world politics. International regimes reduce this uncertainty by providing information, but they can only do this insofar as governments commit themselves to known rules and procedures and maintain these commitments even under pressure to renege" (p. 257). Sharing information without any policy commitment may be valueless, because the temptation would exist to mislead; hence information provided about future policies would not be credible.

Obstacles to Reaching and Sustaining Coordinated Policies

Chapter 8 pursues this issue by examining the problems of verifying that agreements are actually kept. A well-known example of a coordination problem is the "prisoner's dilemma" in which each of two prisoners has the incentive to accuse the other, though the first-best policy (for the prisoners!) is for each to remain silent. However, even if they agree to remain silent, it is impossible to enforce compliance. In this example, and also in real-world international economic policy coordination, there are incentives for the parties to agreements to renege on those agreements. While the temptation to cheat may be overwhelming if the agreement is considered in isolation, such behavior would of course lead other governments to refuse to cooperate in the future, so that cheating should be a rare event: governments, like individuals, care about their reputations.

Unfortunately, macroeconomic uncertainty makes it more difficult to observe cheating because it can always be claimed that outcomes were not attained because of events beyond the control of the policymaker. Putnam and Henning (1986) argue that recognition of this resulted in a switch at the 1977 London summit to framing macroeconomic policy agreements in terms of policies, not outcomes. Such a procedure does not, however, really solve the problem because the choice of actual instrument settings will generally depend upon *forecasts* of outcomes for macroeconomic variables. Germany, for example, may be urged to stimulate its economy (as it was in the late 1970s and again in the mid-1980s) but may counter that the economy is about to pick up, making stimulus inappropriate.

Such problems in verifying that governments are not misrepresenting their positions or the state of their economies may provide a rather strong argument for bringing into the process of coordination international organizations that can provide independent assessments. Because governments have *asymmetric* information, in the sense that they know more about their own economies than about foreign economies, there may be a suspicion that they are in some circumstances exploiting that information. Wendy Dobson (1991), for instance, has argued forcefully that the G-7 Finance Ministers should draw on the services of a secretariat. This proposal is not pursued here, but the problems of verifiability are considered in the abstract.

Finally, Chapter 9 discusses obstacles to reaching agreements. Just as there may be incentives to misrepresent private information, there may be strategic reasons for governments to misrepresent either their own preferences or their views about the effects of their policies in the face of model uncertainty. This may be another obstacle to policy coordination. For instance, the United States government may be urged to reduce its budget deficit, as it was in 1983–84, but respond that its budget deficits are not the cause of high interest rates or the soaring dollar, and thus reducing the deficit would not have the desired effects. America's trading partners, however, are likely to consider these arguments a disingenuous attempt to shift the gains from any coordinated agreement in her own favor. The problems of bargaining over the exact outcome of a coordinated agreement when there is asymmetric information about beliefs or preferences are in fact so severe that a coordinated regime may be unattainable. Again, it may be important – to enable coordinated policy agreements to be reached – for a respected, unbiased organization to confront various theories and evaluate the empirical evidence, thus narrowing the extent of differences in views.

A Note to the Reader

Evaluating the benefits of international policy coordination, particularly when there is macroeconomic uncertainty, is an inherently complex issue: simple intuitions are often misleading and sometimes outright incorrect. We have therefore taken an unashamedly analytic approach in this book, articulating our arguments fully and showing how they can be formally derived from our assumptions. Inevitably this leads to a somewhat mathematical treatment but we have tried to limit the mathematics to a minimum. At each point we have tried to explain the economic intuition involved and the more technical chapters start with an overview section which outlines the main arguments of that chapter in non-technical language. Even the most technical parts do not require mathematical knowledge beyond elementary calculus and statistics.

Notation

Equations are numbered consecutively within each section, references to equations outside the current section are prefixed by the section number, and, if necessary, the chapter number as well. Thus equation 1 of section 2 of Chapter 3 may be written (1), (2.1), or (3.2.1) depending upon where the reference is being made. Throughout, asterisks identify foreign country variables, Greek letters usually refer to parameters and Roman letters to variables (the main exception being π, which we use to denote inflation).

Note

1   Putnam and Henning (1989) in a careful analysis conclude that this was true of the agreement reached at the Bonn summit in 1978.

2

A Theoretical Framework for Modeling the Open Economy

1. Introduction

In this chapter we set the stage for both our theoretical discussion, and our empirical analysis, of the welfare benefits of coordination under macroeconomic uncertainty in subsequent chapters. We begin with a general overview of the different types of uncertainty which prevail in the context of international economic relations, and the various approaches to modeling such uncertainties.

Amongst the types of uncertainty considered, perhaps the most important is the uncertainty about the correct structure of the world economy, what we will call *model* uncertainty. In section 3 of this chapter, therefore, we examine the structure and properties of some of the major multi-country econometric models. Most, though not all, of these models are variants of the Mundell–Fleming structure, first developed in the early 1960s, which has become the workhorse of open economy macroeconomics. The modern form of this model, due to Dornbusch (1976), incorporates both a forward-looking exchange rate and the important assumption that asset markets clear more quickly than the goods or labor markets. The Dornbusch model provides a convenient framework for understanding the various means through which monetary policies operate between countries and is briefly reviewed in this chapter. The chapter closes with a survey of the substantial literature on international policy coordination.

2. Macroeconomic Uncertainty

Policymakers must contend with various forms of uncertainty when setting their macroeconomic instruments. Data on real economic activity – such as the quarterly growth in GDP – are often available only with a significant lag so that there is uncertainty about the initial position of the economy relative to the optimum. As Frankel (1988a) notes, moreover, subsequent revisions of such data are at times so large that they change the direction of the desired movement of the economy: rather than being in recession, for example, the economy may in fact be in danger of over-heating. Even if the initial position of the economy is known with a reasonable degree of confidence, the inherent delays in implementing macroeconomic policies – particularly when they involve international negotiation – often result in policies which, though appropriate when envisioned, are no longer appropriate at the time of implementation. Perhaps the most dramatic example of this occurred at the 1978 Bonn summit where Japan and Germany agreed to act as a "locomotive" for the world economy by pursuing stimulative policies, only to find that the 1979 oil crisis rendered their policies overly inflationary. Given implementation lags as well as lags in the effects of policies on such variables as output and inflation, those policies must be chosen on the basis of forecasts of key macroeconomic variables, which inevitably have substantial standard errors associated with them.

The desired target values themselves may be uncertain as well. In a democracy economic policies represent compromises between various competing interests. An individual's view of the optimal rate of inflation, for example, may depend very heavily on whether he is a net creditor or a net debtor. Likewise, the "natural" rate of unemployment shifts over time; given frictional unemployment it would be foolish to aim for zero unemployment but the choice between, say, 4 or 6 percent may be much less clear cut. More generally, policymakers will be uncertain about their constituents' preferred trade-off between unemployment and inflation. Indeed, such preferences are likely to shift over time and with the state of the economy.

Even if policymakers know both the initial position of the economy and the desired target values, there is no guarantee that they will be able to move the economy in the correct direction, let alone to the optimum point. In choosing their instrument settings policymakers must rely on econometric models which predict the influence of their policies on key macroeconomic variables. Yet different models suggest very different policy multipliers; this is particularly true of the effects of one country's policies on another. Different models may not even agree on the *sign* of such transmission multipliers.

A further difficulty in gauging what the effects of macroeconomic policies will be arises from what is known as the Lucas critique (Lucas, 1976). In essence Lucas' argument is that the use of reduced-form econometric models to set policies is potentially dangerous because the behavioral relationships assumed in the model will vary systematically with the policies themselves. Increasing the money supply may stimulate output by reducing real wages, but over time workers will learn the central bank's policies and will adjust their nominal wage demands accordingly. A model which embodies a stable output-inflation trade-off may then yield the incorrect prediction that a monetary expansion will stimulate output. Early large-scale econometric models often gave seriously misleading predictions about the effects of policy changes precisely because they failed to take account of this *endogenous* behavior of the private sector. In effect the model changes just when the policymaker tries to use it for setting policies. Lucas proposed a solution to this problem, namely to treat as constant only such "deep" structural parameters such as an individual's utility function and then evaluate different policies by solving endogenously for the agent's optimal behavior. In practice, it seems quite unrealistic to hope to estimate empirically these deep parameters as a basis for even a medium sized macroeconometric model of the world economy. A more viable alternative is to treat some relationships as structural, even when they clearly embody some endogenous behavior by the private sector, and to allow for endogenous private sector responses only in instances in which it is likely to be particularly important. Ultimately, the decision about which relationships to treat as structural and which to treat as endogenous must be a judgment call by the designers of the model. If no relationship is treated as structural, or invariant, then the model will of course be useless for policy purposes. Unfortunately, the *degree* to which the private sector reacts may be very difficult to predict. In some instances the private sector may learn about the intended policies, understand the structure of the economy (including the reactions of other individuals in the economy), and react accordingly. In other instances it may take a significant length of time before the private sector learns about new policies or incorporates this knowledge into its behavior.

In the context of international policy coordination another source of uncertainty arises from the strategic behavior of foreign governments. Is the information being supplied by the foreign government correct? Or is the government deliberately misrepresenting its preferences and beliefs with a view to improving its own bargaining position? Both the ability and the willingness of the foreign government to adhere to a cooperative agreement may also be in doubt. Indeed, as discussed in Chapter 8 below, each government has an incentive to deviate from the cooperative agreement as long as it believes that the other government is following the agreement. Therefore each government is likely to be suspicious about the other government's behavior whenever the outcome of a cooperative agreement is less favorable than expected.

In order to discuss the effects of uncertainty on the coordination process it is useful at the outset to define a taxonomy of the various forms of uncertainty. These are not rigid definitions – and there are certainly instances in which a particular form of uncertainty fits more than one category – but they are nonetheless useful for analytic purposes. At the most fundamental level, a distinction can be made between purely *technological* uncertainty – such as the standard error of the interest elasticity of aggregate demand, or the correct deflator in the money demand function – and *strategic* uncertainty; that is, uncertainty about the behavior of other governments. Strategic uncertainty arises because a government's preferences, honesty, and degree of commitment to an agreement are all likely to be largely unknown to other parties. Of course, the distinction is not completely clear cut. For example, uncertainty about the value of a shock to the foreign country may be reduced if the foreign government will share its own information about that shock. Yet the home government may be uncertain about the incentives of the foreign government to report the shock honestly, or at least not to exaggerate a little in the hope of improving its own welfare.

Technological uncertainty is perhaps the easiest to model formally and it is undoubtedly the form of uncertainty which has received the most attention in the literature. The simplest form of uncertainty may be termed *additive* uncertainty and it refers to shocks that affect macroeconomic targets but do not change the policy multipliers. An example would be an exogenous fall in aggregate demand which lowers output but does not change the effectiveness of monetary or fiscal policy in expanding output. In essence, we can think of additive uncertainty as referring to uncertainty about where the economy is relative to the bliss point. *Multiplier* uncertainty refers to possible changes in the economy which alter the effects of monetary and fiscal policies. For example, a change in the interest elasticity of money demand arising, perhaps, from financial innovation, will alter the impact of a monetary expansion on the level of output. As we shall see in Chapter 3, multiplier uncertainty has quite different implications from additive uncertainty for policy making.

Multiplier uncertainty itself can arise either from *parameter uncertainty* or from *model uncertainty*. The first occurs when the general structure of the model is known to be correct but exact parameter values are uncertain. The second refers to a situation in which we do not know the fundamental *structure* of the correct model. Should we use a Keynesian model or a New Classical model? Are prices sticky? Is there a long-run Phillips curve? With linear models, model uncertainty can nearly always be expressed as parameter uncertainty since one can trivially include or exclude variables from any equation by an appropriate choice of parameters.[1] But it is probably more useful to think of the existence of different economic paradigms as a manifestation of fundamental model uncertainty, than to try to incorporate philosophically different models into a giant nested model. In our empirical work in Chapter 6 we shall consider both parameter and model uncertainty as sources of multiplier uncertainty.

In a completely closed economy with a single policymaker, the government faces only technological uncertainty. Once we allow foreign policies to have an impact on the home economy, however, the home government will face uncertainty about the foreign government's actions. We call this *strategic* uncertainty because much of it arises from strategic behavior on the part of governments. Such uncertainty can take numerous forms. First, there are likely to be shocks, or developments in the foreign economy, which are more readily observed or forecast by the foreign government. Assuming the foreign government is honest in reporting such shocks, a simple intergovernmental exchange of information will suffice in such instances. Indeed, many commentators view the process of policy coordination as largely unnecessary as long as there is a credible and honest exchange of information between governments. This idea is critically reviewed in Chapter 7, where we will see that the welfare benefits of such information sharing depend crucially on how governments act upon that information. Second, there may be uncertainty about whether the foreign government will deliver on its promises in a coordinated regime or instead renege on its commitments. This could either reflect the *ability* of the government to stick to its commitments or its *willingness* to do so. In the United States, for example, the Treasury Department is generally involved in international negotiations but its ability to commit either monetary or fiscal policy depends upon the Federal Reserve and the Congress, both of whom guard their autonomy jealously. Thus there may be a genuine inability to stick to an international agreement. If the agreement is expressed in terms of target variables rather than instruments then, because of technological constraints of the form discussed above, the government may not be able to abide by the agreement. Moreover, even if the government is *able* to stick to the coordinated agreement it generally has the incentive to deviate from the agreement that is, to *cheat* on the agreement. For whatever reason, then, there will be uncertainty about whether the foreign government is actually following the coordinated policy. In Chapter 8 we examine the implications of such uncertainty for the sustainability of the coordinated regime. Third, there will be uncertainty about the *preferences* of the foreign government. Is the foreign government really as averse to a monetary expansion (or inflation) as it claims? Or is such a stance merely a device to improve its bargaining position?

Given these various forms of uncertainty, what is the appropriate way to evaluate the benefits of coordinated versus uncoordinated macroeconomic policies? The usual way to calculate welfare under uncertainty is by means of the *expected utility* approach which postulates that agents have a subjective probability distribution over the outcomes of events, and that they evaluate their welfare by taking the expected value of the utility under each outcome (Savage, 1954; von Neumann and Morgenstern, 1953). While the expected utility approach has a long tradition, and solid analytic underpinnings, it is worth considering the plausibility of its assumptions. Perhaps its most unrealistic assumption is that agents have well defined probability distributions over uncertain outcomes. To use the expected utility approach one must either believe that individuals know the objective probability distribution or one must be willing to evaluate their welfare using their own subjective probabilities even if the latter do not coincide with the objective probabilities. While this may be acceptable at the level of the individual, it is more troublesome to evaluate a country's welfare using its policymakers' subjective priors when the latter do not coincide with objective probabilities.[2]

More generally, individuals may have *no* prior distribution over uncertain events.[3] Keynes (1937), for example, distinguishes between events which are truly uncertain and those which are merely probable. "The game of roulette is not subject, in this sense, to uncertainty. . . . The sense in which I am using the terms is that . . . there is no scientific basis on which to form any calculable probability whatever. We simply do not know." But it is probably going too far to suggest that we have no idea of the range of possible outcomes, and the associated probabilities, of different monetary and fiscal policies.

Even when a well-defined probability distribution exists, it is not clear that the *ex ante* expected utility is the appropriate criterion. It is of little comfort to a politician who loses his office because of an unfavorable random drawing of the economic model to know that in an *ex ante* expected sense he had chosen the right policy. Here normative and positive implications diverge. If we are trying to predict the actions of a policymaker then indeed he may be more concerned about the actual outcomes which occur during his own tenure than the expected benefits of a policy. In fact, a policymaker may well act according to the *regret approach* which states that when faced by uncertainty individuals choose actions which minimize their possible regret. This tends to give a bias towards the status quo, which, if the status quo is taken to be uncoordinated macroeconomic policies, presumably makes coordination less likely.[4]

From a social, normative perspective, however, the *expected* benefits, rather than particular realizations may be the more relevant criterion precisely because macroeconomic policies will be repeated many times. Even then, we might be interested in more risk sensitive ways of evaluating macroeconomic policies, such as a minimax criterion. Essentially, such a criterion would rule out policies which have very bad outcomes, even if those outcomes are highly unlikely to occur.

Mainly for analytic convenience, however, we stick to the expected utility approach in both our theoretical and empirical work. In the theoretical chapters it is assumed that all individuals know the appropriate probability distribution functions and we use the *ex ante* expected utility as the welfare criterion. (Alternatively, we are assuming that subjective probability priors equal the objective distribution function.) At a *theoretical* level this seems to be the only sensible way to evaluate policies because, in the absence of specific alternative models one cannot otherwise rank different policies. *Empirically*, where one might have specific alternative models, an *ex post* welfare criterion may be useful in ranking different policies.

In our empirical work, we do allow for the possibility that agents do not have the correct probability distribution, and evaluate welfare in terms of the realized, *ex post*, level of utility under a variety of assumptions about the error being made by agents. Specifically, we assume that agents face both *model* uncertainty and *parameter* uncertainty; that is, there are a number of competing, but philosophically distinct models of the world (one is New Classical, another more Keynesian etc.). Within a model, agents are assumed to know the probability distribution function of the parameter values so that the *ex ante* expected welfare coincides with the *ex post* average utility. But agents are not assumed to know the correct probability distribution function *across* different models. Indeed, in the simulations reported in Chapter 6, one of the models (e.g. the New Classical model) is being used to generate history so that unless the probability priors are equal to unity for that model and are zero on the other models, agents necessarily have the wrong probability distribution. We then evaluate coordinated and uncoordinated policies conditional on each of the models in turn being correct.

3. Modeling the Open Economy

Crucial to gains from coordination are the transmission effects of domestic policies. The main linkages between economies take the form of trade flows and capital movements and depending upon the degree of capital mobility, the exchange rate reflects the forces of either the current account or the capital account, or perhaps a combination of the two. In this section we discuss theoretical models of these international transmission mechanisms,[5] and then survey their implementation in empirical multi-country models.

By the 1960s, capital movements were playing a more important role in both theory and practice. Fleming (1962) and Mundell (1962), (1963) examined the implications of high or perfect capital mobility. The results were startling: in the case of a small open economy, monetary policy was shown to be completely ineffective in controlling output under fixed exchange rates but quite the opposite under floating rates. With high capital mobility, a monetary expansion under fixed rates leads to an incipient fall in the domestic interest rate, a capital outflow, and a fall in reserves. The outflow of reserves, however, offsets the original increase in domestic credit in the absence of sterilization, thus reversing the decline in interest rates. With floating exchange rates, a monetary expansion depreciates the exchange rate, thereby improving the trade balance and raising the level of income. In the case of large economies with fixed nominal wages, the transmission effect of monetary policy (i.e. the impact of a domestic monetary expansion on foreign income) in the original Mundell–Fleming model is necessarily negative. A monetary expansion by the home country would depreciate its exchange rate and lower world interest rates. The former has an adverse effect on foreign income and the latter a beneficial effect. From the foreign country's money market equilibrium, however, one can show that as long as money balances are deflated by the producer price (which is fixed in the Mundell–Fleming model), the negative effect outweighs the benefit from the home country's expansion. If the foreign country's money supply has remained unchanged, the fall in world interest rates can only be consistent with money market equilibrium if there is a fall in foreign income. The same need not hold if money balances are deflated by the consumer price index: the appreciation of the foreign country's exchange rate will lower the consumer price index abroad, where real money balances rises. As a result, income need not decline to restore equilibrium following the fall in world interest rates (Branson and Buiter, 1983).

Fiscal policy, in contrast, is ineffective under floating rates. Expansionary fiscal policy appreciates a floating exchange rate, makes exports uncompetitive, and hence lowers the trade balance and reverses the stimulus to output. Yet in an open economy with fixed rates and high capital mobility, fiscal policy will be more powerful than in a closed economy. With fixed exchange rates, expansionary fiscal policy raises the domestic interest rate, which draws reserves from abroad. Unless this capital inflow is sterilized, the rise in reserves expands the money supply, thereby giving an additional boost to output.

With real rather than nominal wage rigidity, of course, the results for floating rates are reversed: monetary policy has no effect since the depreciation of the exchange rate will be offset by an increase in nominal wages. Expansionary fiscal policy, however, appreciates the exchange rate and improves the terms of trade, lowering the real wage in terms of producer prices (but not in terms of consumer prices) and bringing about an expansion of output (Sachs, 1980).

The Mundell–Fleming model: a theoretical exposition

The Mundell–Fleming model became, and remains, the workhorse of open economy macroeconomics. The most important addition to its basic structure was the incorporation of dynamics and, in particular, the assumption of a forward-looking exchange rate. Dornbusch's (1976) seminal contribution provided an explanation for the volatility of nominal exchange rates. Monetary shocks lead to exchange rate overshooting because asset markets clear more quickly than labor markets. Since a two-country version of the Dornbusch model underlies both our theoretical work and several of the empirical models estimated in Chapter 5 we provide a brief exposition here (see also Oudiz and Sachs, 1985, and especially Gavin, 1986).

We divide the world economy into two symmetric regions, which we call the home country and the foreign country. Variables with asterisks refer to the foreign country. Each country is specialized in the production of a good which is an imperfect substitute for the other country's good. The model exhibits typical Keynesian features, because both prices and wages are predetermined in the current period. All variables except the interest rate are expressed in logarithms and represent deviations from zero-disturbance equilibrium values. Stochastic shocks are assumed to be independently and identically distributed, with mean zero and constant variance. It is assumed that parameter values, but not necessarily the stochastic shocks, are the same for the two countries. Since our purpose here is to discuss the basic structure of the Mundell–Fleming model, we do not consider parameter uncertainty; thus all structural parameters will be assumed to be constant.

Output is demand-determined; it is assumed to be a decreasing function of the real interest rate and, via the trade balance, an increasing function of activity in the partner country and of the real exchange rate:

$$y = -\delta(p - e - p^*) + \gamma y^* - \sigma[i - (p_{+1} - p)] + u \qquad (1)$$

$$y^* = \delta(p - e - p^*) + \gamma y - \sigma[i^* - (p^*_{+1} - p^*)] + u^* \qquad (2)$$

where e is the home country's exchange rate (expressed as the price of foreign currency), y is output or income, i is the interest rate and p the producer price level. All structural parameters are written in Greek letters and are positive, and the notation $(_{+1})$ denotes the led value of a variable. The disturbances u and u^* represent shocks to aggregate demand, arising, for example, from fiscal policy or changes in desired investment. Money demand functions are written in inverted form as:

$$i = \xi y - \varepsilon(m - p) + v \tag{3}$$

$$i^* = \xi y^* - \varepsilon(m^* - p^*) + v^* \tag{4}$$

where v and v^* are transformed velocity shocks, ε is the reciprocal of the interest elasticity of money demand, and ξ the ratio of the income elasticity to the interest elasticity.

Wage-price dynamics are given by a modified Phillips curve in which domestic output prices are an increasing function of the level of output and the change in the real exchange rate. The latter effect, which follows Argy and Salop (1979) and Gavin (1986), is a proxy for the attempts of wage-setters to recoup real wage erosion resulting from an increase in consumer prices. The change in the consumer price index is assumed to be an increasing function of the change in the real exchange rate because of its effects on the cost of imported goods. At the cost of complicating the dynamics of the system, it would be possible to make the Phillips curve a function of the change in consumer prices themselves but little additional insight to the theoretical discussion is gained by making this assumption.[6] The output price in the current period is pre-determined, so the inflation shock affects only next period's price:[7]

$$p_{+1} - p = -\theta\Delta(p - e - p^*) + \psi y + w \tag{5}$$

$$p_{+1}^* - p^* = \theta\Delta(p - e - p^*) + \psi y^* + w^* \tag{6}$$

where Δ is the (backward) first difference operator.

Since an increase in output raises both nominal interest rates and the expected future price level, a higher level of output *could* be associated with a lower *real* interest rate. Such a model, however, would not exhibit static Walrasian stability in the goods market because the IS curve would be upward sloping in interest rate–income space; here we impose the restriction $\xi - \psi > 0$. As an empirical matter, this inequality is satisfied in most estimated models.

Finally, interest rates in each country are linked by an arbitrage condition which requires a positive interest differential to be offset by expected depreciation of the currency:

$$i = i^* + e_{+1}^e - e \tag{7}$$

Throughout we assume that expectations are rational so $e_{+1}^e = E(e_{+1})$, where $E(\cdot)$ is the expectations operator conditional on the contemporaneous information set, which includes the current realizations of the shocks u, u^*, v, v^*, w and w^*. Suppose that expected future policy setting for the money supply is equal to the disturbance-less baseline value of zero.[8] It can be shown, then, that the dynamics of the model imply that the expected real exchange rate, $p^*_{+1} + e^e_{+1} - p_{+1}$, is zero (see Gavin, 1986). We will use this fact to substitute out for e^e_{+1}. This implies that the interest arbitrage condition can also be written:

$$i = i^* + (p_{+1} - p^*_{+1}) - e \qquad (8)$$

In addition, since the current price level is pre-determined, it can be normalized to zero without loss of generality.

It is shown in the Appendix to this chapter that the reduced form for output is given by:

$$y = \alpha m + \beta m^* + q \qquad (9)$$

$$y^* = \alpha m^* + \beta m + q^* \qquad (10)$$

where $\alpha > 0, \beta \gtrless 0$ and $\alpha + \beta > 0$, and q and q^* are combinations of the shocks to the two economies. Notice that q and q^* are *additive shocks*; that is, they affect the level of output but leave the policy multipliers, α and β, unchanged. We call α a *domestic* multiplier because it determines the impact of an increase in the home country's monetary policy on the home country's level of output and the foreign country's policy on its own output. β is a termed a *transmission* multiplier since it gives the effect of an increase in the home country's policy on the foreign country and vice versa. The domestic multiplier is necessarily positive: $\alpha > 0$. The transmission multiplier may be either positive or negative; however, $\alpha + \beta > 0$. As discussed above, in the traditional Mundell–Fleming model monetary stimulus is negatively transmitted; in the model presented here there is a variety of transmission channels so the net transmission effect is ambiguous. The two crucial parameters which determine whether β is positive or negative are the real exchange elasticity of demand, δ, and the foreign income elasticity of demand, γ. It is readily shown that $\partial \beta / \partial \delta$ is negative since the greater the real exchange rate elasticity the larger the improvement in the home country's current account in response to a depreciation of its currency. Conversely, $\partial \beta / \partial \gamma$ is positive: the greater the foreign activity elasticity of demand the larger the positive impact on the foreign country of an expansion in home output.

Turning to the reduced forms for inflation, we obtain:

$$p_{+1} - p \equiv \pi = \phi m + \eta m^* + s \qquad (11)$$

$$p^*_{+1} - p^* \equiv \pi^* = \phi m^* + \eta m + s^* \tag{12}$$

where s and s^* are combinations of the shocks to the two countries. Again, the domestic effect of monetary expansion is to raise inflation, $\phi > 0$, while the transmission effect is potentially ambiguous, $\eta \gtrless 0$. A foreign monetary expansion appreciates the home country's exchange rate thus reducing inflation at home. If the foreign monetary expansion has a negative effect on home income, then it necessarily reduces home inflation. Only if the transmission effect of monetary policy on income is positive is the transmission effect on inflation ambiguous.

One important inequality, which we use below, concerns the "comparative advantage" of foreign monetary policy *vis-à-vis* domestic policy in affecting output and inflation. By manipulating the expressions for α, β, ϕ and η one can show:

$$\beta\phi - \alpha\eta > 0 \tag{13}$$

that is, an expansion in the foreign money supply has a larger expansionary effect – or smaller contractionary effect – on domestic output (relative to a domestic expansion) than it does on domestic inflation (again, relative to a domestic expansion).[9]

Multi-country empirical implementation of the Mundell–Fleming model

The basic Mundell–Fleming paradigm has served as the basis of large-scale multi-country models, which began to be constructed in the late 1960s and early 1970s. Generally, Keynesian demand-driven models were linked together using models of trade flows and capital flows (or exchange rates), with various degrees of capital mobility and different exchange rate regimes being either imposed or estimated from the data. Multi-country models also differ in the degree of consistency between the component national models, and in the extent they have been estimated jointly rather than separately. The early vintages of multi-country models assumed non-rational expectations, which make the transmission effects operating through a flexible exchange rate relatively unimportant. In particular, adaptive expectations tend to increase fiscal multipliers and reduce crowding out under floating, for two reasons: the exchange rate does not appreciate much (if at all), and long-term interest rates do not rise very much.

Project LINK, for instance, relied on a trade model to link national models that were specified and estimated independently by researchers working in different countries (Ball, ed., 1973). As in most other multi-country models, the trade framework was based on national equations for total imports; these imports were then allocated to other countries' exports using a trade share matrix that depended on relative export prices (Hickman and Lau, 1973). Exchange rates were assumed to be fixed, but nevertheless there was scope for independent national monetary policies; implicitly, the degree of capital mobility was low. Because country models were constructed by national specialists, they incorporated valuable institutional detail; however, the differing choices made by the national modelers concerning disaggregation, dynamic specification, and the like, made the interactions of these national models difficult to understand.

The OECD's INTERLINK model in its early versions used a quite different approach, in that national models had the same structure, but were parameterized differently, using the evidence of national studies (OECD, 1979). Because of the simple structure of the national models, which focused on real activity, simulation results were relatively simple to understand. As was the case for Project LINK, the main mechanism for linking national models consisted in a trade matrix that depended on relative export prices (Samuelson, 1973). Fixed exchange rates were imposed, and issues of monetary independence were ignored because of the focus on the real sector. A flexible exchange rate version of INTERLINK was introduced in the early 1980s (see Holtham, 1984); this international financial block exhibits quite high capital mobility, in that asset stocks have only a small effect on exchange rates. However, exchange rates themselves are not very flexible, because they are tied down by the assumption of adaptive, PPP-based expectations.

The Federal Reserve Board of Governors constructed a multi-country model, the MCM, which followed a different strategy in several respects from the preceding models (Stevens *et al.*, 1984). First, because of a smaller set of countries (five of the more important trading partners of the United States, plus some aggregate regions), it could use bilateral trade equations, rather than the trade matrix approach discussed above. Second, the originators of various versions of the model paid more attention to the endogeneity of the exchange rate, and experimented with alternatives (Hooper *et al.*, 1983). The first version of the model contained trade and capital flow equations, and solved for the exchange rate using the condition that the balance of payments must equal official intervention. This approach however led to instability in simulation, possibly because of a downward bias in the estimated degree of capital mobility, and it was subsequently abandoned in favor of explicit exchange rate equations; in these equations capital mobility was indirectly estimated to be high. Third, though national models were not formulated completely independently, they were also subject to some arbitrary specification choices by different researchers.

The Japanese Economic Planning Agency (EPA) global model is another example of a large-scale model in which trade matrices provide the main linkage, adaptive expectations are assumed, and the exchange rate is solved for using the balance of payments constraint (see for instance, EPA, 1986). Though the trade linkage submodel has been the result of thorough consideration of alternative specifications (see Amano, Kurihara, and Samuelson, 1980), some of the national models have strange properties that make simulation results difficult to interpret.

Other multi-country models that are mainly based on trade linkages, assume adaptive expectations, and have relatively differentiated national component models are the following: DRI (Brinner, 1985), EEC (Dramais, 1986), and Wharton (Green and Howe, 1987).

Later vintages of multi-country models based on the Mundell–Fleming paradigm have incorporated rational expectations (and, in essence, follow the structure outlined in the previous section), which tended to increase the importance given to international financial linkages, since exchange rates tended to fluctuate more in response to either monetary or fiscal policy changes. These models have also typically paid closer attention to asset stock dynamics and intertemporal budget constraints. Examples of recent versions of such models are the MSG model (McKibbin and Sachs, 1991), the Taylor model (Taylor, 1989) and MULTIMOD (Masson et al., 1990). Each of these models does not differentiate much in the specifications of the national models; differences derive from differences in estimated (or imposed) parameters or in such structural features as trade patterns or in the degree of openness of each economy. Such relative uniformity makes the interpretation of simulation results much simpler, since the differences in response to a common shock can usually be traced to a few key parameters.

In 1986, the Brookings Institution undertook a comprehensive survey of the properties of twelve multi-country models (listed in Table 2.1). Of these models, only the LIVERPOOL model and the VAR model deviate significantly from the basic Mundell–Fleming paradigm. The LIVER-POOL model is based on New Classical macroeconomics, in which wage-setting behavior is fully forward-looking, so that monetary policy has little effect on output (and a large impact effect on prices).

Table 2.1 (adapted from table 2-3 in Bryant et al., 1988) reports the various policy multipliers that resulted from the Brookings exercise. The table gives the effect of a monetary expansion, equal to a 1% increase in the money supply, in the United States and in an aggregate Rest of the World region. Figure 2.1 gives the average multipliers and their standard deviations across the models. A monetary expansion in the U.S. raises

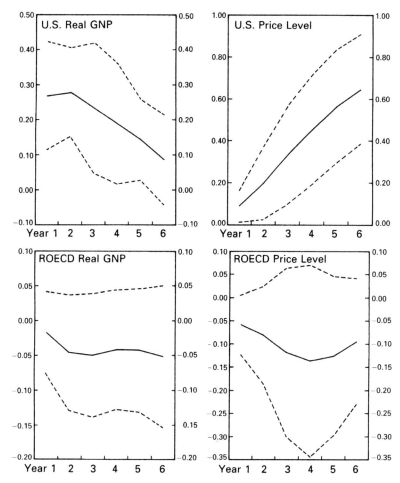

Figure 2.1 Averages and standard deviations across models for simulated effects of a U.S. monetary expansion[1]

[1]Increase of the money supply above baseline by one percent, maintained for the six years. Effects on the United States and the Rest of the OECD.

Source: Bryant, Helliwell, and Hooper (1989), table 2.

output in the U.S. under all of the models (although the effect is minimal under the LIVERPOOL model).[10] Such an expansion reduces foreign output in six of the twelve models. A monetary expansion in the Rest of the World region reduces U.S. income in only two of the twelve models. A potential explanation for this reversal of the negative transmission effect, mentioned above, is that the appreciation of the non-expanding country's currency increases real money balances, or lowers non-wage costs (such as imported inputs) or wages themselves (if the latter are at least partially indexed to the consumer price index). Frankel (1988b), however, has shown that this cannot be the explanation in the case of the models included in the Brookings survey, since an exogenous appreciation of non-U.S. currencies leads to a fall in output in those countries. Frankel offers an alternative explanation: in the case of the EEC, Wharton, and OECD models, a monetary expansion in the U.S., despite depreciating the dollar, deteriorates the U.S. current account position and, by improving the foreign current account, raises income abroad.[11]

Included in Table 2.1 is a measure of the extent of disagreement across the models.[12] The statistic ζ equals $\mu^2/(\mu^2 + \sigma^2)$ where μ is the mean of the multipliers across models, and σ^2 is the variance. Notice that this is a dimensionless statistic equal to unity when there is no disagreement across the models and tending towards zero as the variance rises relative to the mean. The highest ζ ratios (i.e. the lowest degree of disagreement) are for the effects of monetary policy on domestic output. Even here, though, ζ is only about 0.70. The transmission multipliers (U.S. on ROW and ROW on U.S.) tend to be much more uncertain: ζ is close to zero for the U.S. effect on ROW and less than 0.20 for the effect of an ROW expansion on the U.S.. Thus even with this rather limited selection of models, the extent of disagreement between them is considerable.

4. The Literature on Coordination

While both historians and economists have long studied the process of central bank cooperation – particularly under the gold standard – the formal literature on international policy coordination really started with work by Meade (1951), Mundell (1963), and Fleming (1962) who modeled the transmission effects of monetary and fiscal policies from one country to another.[13] As discussed above, these models emphasized the importance of the degree of international capital mobility in determining whether, for example, a monetary expansion in one country would raise or lower income abroad.

Cooper (1969) showed that if governments assigned their policy instruments to respond to both domestic and foreign targets then the world economy would return to equilibrium more quickly following a shock than if each government focused exclusively on its own targets. Niehans (1968) appears to have been the first to use concepts from industrial organization and game theory to model the choice of monetary and fiscal policies in interdependent economies. Hamada (1974), (1976), (1979) examined the need for coordination under fixed and flexible

Table 2.1 Policy multipliers of some global econometric models: effect in the second year of a 1 percent increase in the money supply

Model	U.S. on U.S. Output α	U.S. on U.S. Inflation ϕ	U.S. on ROW Inflation η	U.S. on ROW Output β	$(\beta\phi - \alpha\eta)$
DRI	0.45	0.10	−0.325	−0.15	0.131
EEC	0.25	0.20	−0.10	0.05	0.035
EPA	0.30	0.25	−0.125	−0.1	0.013
LINK	0.25	−0.1	−0.025	−0.025	0.008
LIVERPOOL	0.025	0.925	0.0	0.0	0.000
MCM	0.375	0.10	−0.15	−0.175	0.038
MINIMOD	0.250	0.20	−0.05	−0.05	0.003
MSG	0.075	0.375	−0.175	0.10	0.051
OECD	0.40	0.175	−0.025	0.075	0.023
TAYLOR	0.15	0.30	−0.05	−0.05	−0.008
VAR	0.75	0.10	0.025	0.10	−0.009
WHARTON	0.175	0.00	−0.025	0.10	0.004
mean μ	0.288	0.219	−0.085	−0.010	0.024
variance σ^2	0.034	0.060	0.009	0.009	
$\zeta = \mu^2/(\sigma^2 + \mu^2)$	0.71	0.44	0.45	0.012	

Model	ROW on ROW Output α	ROW on ROW Inflation ϕ	ROW on US Inflation η	ROW on US Output β	$(\beta\phi - \alpha\eta)$
DRI	N.A	N.A	N.A	N.A	N.A
EEC	0.20	0.25	0.025	0.025	0.0012
EPA	0.00	0.00	0.0	0.0	0.0
LINK	0.20	−0.15	0.0	0.025	−0.004
LIVERPOOL	0.10	0.70	−0.85	0.4	0.365
MCM	0.375	0.15	−0.05	0.0	0.019
MINIMOD	0.20	0.05	−0.125	−0.075	0.021
MSG	0.05	0.375	−0.15	0.075	0.035
OECD	0.20	0.075	−0.025	0.025	0.007
TAYLOR	0.20	0.175	−0.125	−0.025	0.020
VAR	0.175	−0.125	−0.175	0.30	−0.007
WHARTON	0.05	−0.025	0.0	0.0	0.0
mean μ	0.159	0.134	−0.134	0.068	0.042
variance σ^2	0.009	0.054	0.055	0.019	
$\zeta = \mu^2/(\sigma^2 + \mu^2)$	0.72	0.25	0.24	0.019	

Source: Frankel (1988b), table 2-3.

exchange rates. He established the basic definition of a coordinated regime as one in which both governments maximize a weighted sum of each country's welfare function. In the uncoordinated regime each government maximizes its own welfare, taking as given the policies of the other government. Under fixed exchange rates, uncoordinated policies would result in a deflationary bias if each central bank tried to accumulate reserves;[14] under floating rates, no such deflationary bias would exist, assuming central banks no longer targeted the level of reserves but only the level of output.[15] Canzoneri and Gray (1985) argued that uncoordinated policies did not have an inherent bias towards being overly-contractionary or deflationary: in their model the uncoordinated equilibrium can be too expansionary or too contractionary depending upon the sign of the transmission effect.[16]

Sachs (1983) and Oudiz and Sachs (1984) showed that, following an inflationary shock, if governments are not coordinating their monetary policies (that is, if they are maximizing their individual objective functions) they will pursue overly contractionary monetary policies in order to export inflation via a competitive appreciation of their exchange rate. In equilibrium, both countries cannot simultaneously appreciate their bilateral exchange rate, thus neither country is able to export the inflationary shock and both suffer from excessively contractionary monetary policies relative to a coordinated regime.[17] Oudiz and Sachs (1984) also provided the first empirical estimates of the gains from coordination. Their results were somewhat disappointing for proponents of coordination: for plausible assumptions about governments' utility functions, they found welfare gains for each country amounting to no more than one percent of its GDP.[18] Canzoneri and Minford (1988) have argued that the rather small welfare gains reported by Oudiz and Sachs may be attributable to their assumption of a single, one-time shock, rather than on-going conflicts between governments.[19]

During the mid-1980s there was a flurry of research on the intertemporal and dynamic aspects of international interdependence. An ingenious paper by Ken Rogoff (1985) showed how the time-inconsistency of optimal policies could lead to welfare deteriorating policy coordination. In this model, as in that by Barro and Gordon (1983), central banks have an incentive to inflate in order to lower unemployment. In the non-cooperative equilibrium the incentive to expand the money supply is restrained by the knowledge that the exchange rate will depreciate, which will lead to additional inflation. In the cooperative equilibrium, where all central banks expand the money supply simultaneously, the exchange rate is unaffected so that each central bank has a greater incentive to inflate than it would in the uncoordinated equilibrium. Given this larger incentive to inflate – which is foreseen by rational wage-setters – the equilibrium inflation rate will be higher but unemployment will be the same.

Rogoff's model was remarkable in that it showed that international coordination could actually lower welfare. This seemed to counter revealed preference arguments: since policymakers in a coordinated regime can always choose the same policies as they would under non-coordination, the fact that goverments coordinate is evidence in favor of gains from coordination. The fallacy in this argument lies in assuming that the structural model facing policymakers is invariant to the policy regime. As stressed by Lucas (1976) this need not be the case once there is a forward-looking private sector (the wage-setters in Rogoff's model). Once the private sector knows that monetary policies will be coordinated across countries its behavior changes, and the structural model facing policymakers is not the same in the coordinated and un-coordinated regimes.[20]

Other researchers have explored more fully the dynamic aspects of international coordination which were raised by the Rogoff example (Buiter and Marston, 1985).[21] Miller and Salmon (1985) gave a numerical example in which coordination again lowers welfare because of time-consistency problems. Subsequent work by Kehoe (1989), and van der Ploeg (1988), moreover, showed that these results could also arise in fully optimizing models.

But Oudiz and Sachs (1985) provided a counter-example in which coordination improves welfare despite the inability of central banks to pre-commit themselves to a particular path of the exchange rate. In their model, the forward-looking behavior comes from participants in the foreign exchange market. Under non-cooperation each central bank pursues overly-contractionary monetary policy in order to export inflation. Time inconsistency arises because the central bank has the incentive to promise tight policies in the future in order to appreciate the exchange rate today and thereby export inflation. Once the future arrives, of course, the central bank has less of an incentive to pursue tight monetary policy since some the benefits have already been obtained. Since both central banks try to export inflation simultaneously there is no net effect on the exchange rate. In equilibrium, the uncoordinated equilibrium simply results in overly-contractionary monetary policies. In the coordinated regime, governments recognize the futility of trying to achieve a competitive appreciation of the exchange rate and therefore do not pursue overly contractionary monetary policy. Coordination removes the time consistency problem here because governments are no longer trying to manipulate the exchange rate in order to export inflation. Comparing the Rogoff result to the findings of Oudiz and Sachs (1985) shows that there is little hope for general conclusions about the desirability of international coordination when there is a forward-looking private sector. Levine and Currie (1987) and Currie, Levine and Vidalis (1987) conclude that, unless the government can follow time inconsistent policies, there is no guarantee that coordination will be welfare improving. Conversely, unless policies are coordinated, it is not certain that the ability to credibly set time inconsistent policies will be beneficial.[22]

Given the political and technical difficulties of reaching coordinated agreements, an important research goal is to see whether simple policy rules can emulate full coordination reasonably well. At the very least, one would like to know whether uncoordinated discretionary policies are superior to fixed rules; otherwise, constraining autonomy, as in a fixed exchange rate regime, may be a worthwhile goal if full coordination is not possible. Currie, Levine and Vidalis (1987), Hughes Hallett, Holtham and Hutson (1989), Taylor (1989), McKibbin and Sachs (1989), Frenkel, Goldstein and Masson (1989), Currie and Wren Lewis (1989), and McKibbin and Sachs (1991) consider the performance of such rules and in some cases compare them to full coordination. Typically, the rules considered include some form of fixed exchange rate regime, possibly with global monetary targeting (McKinnon, 1984, 1988); real exchange rate targeting rules (Williamson and Miller, 1987; and Boughton, 1988); nominal income targeting rules (Frankel, 1991); and floating exchange rates with money targeting in each country. Not surprisingly, perhaps, the performance of each rule depends upon the specific shocks being considered. In general, however, the usual intuition that floating exchange rates are preferable under real shocks and fixed exchange rates under nominal shocks continues to hold.

A second line of research consisted in explicitly incorporating the effects of macroeconomic uncertainty in the gains from coordination. Ghosh (1986) studied the effects of introducing model uncertainty, in the vein of Brainard (1967), into the Oudiz and Sachs (1985) model.[23] Sufficiently high degrees of uncertainty about policy multipliers were shown to eliminate the welfare benefits from coordination. Ghosh (1987), Ghosh and Ghosh (1986), (1991), extended this result (and partly reversed it) by deriving conditions under which uncertainty could actually raise welfare. In previous work (Ghosh and Masson, 1988) we tried to add some empirical content to the literature on coordination under uncertainty by analyzing the welfare benefits of coordination in the MINIMOD model, whose parameters were assumed to be uncertain for this exercise.[24] We found that model uncertainty could roughly double the gains from coordination.

All of these papers assumed that policymakers take explicit account of the prevailing uncertainty when choosing their policies. More precisely, the subjective probability priors over the possible models used by policymakers in setting their policies are assumed to coincide with the objective probability of the model being true. Frankel and Rockett (1988), instead, assumed that policymakers ignore the problem of uncertainty when choosing their optimal policies.[25] It is not surprising, therefore, that they find instances in which coordination reduces welfare, relative to non-coordination, when policymakers are using the wrong model of the world economy. In Ghosh and Masson (1991), however, we argued that even in the framework envisioned by Frankel and Rockett, the result that model uncertainty will lead to welfare deteriorating coordination is unlikely to hold once policymakers are assumed to learn about the true model using Bayesian updating.[26] Moreover, Holtham and Hughes Hallett (1987) showed that if cases in which either policymaker (given his beliefs about the true model) perceives a loss from coordination are ruled out, the proportion of cases in which there can be welfare deteriorating coordination falls substantially.[27]

Ultimately, the issue of whether coordination will raise welfare is an empirical one. Yet, in order to understand how uncertainty affects gains from coordination, we first need to develop the theory of macroeconomic policy coordination under uncertainty in a more systematic manner than has been done hitherto. This is the subject of Chapter 3.

Appendix

In this appendix we solve the theoretical model developed in section 2. Substitute the money demand functions (3) and (4) and the Phillips curve equations (5) and (6) into the aggregate demand functions (1) and (2). Adding the resulting aggregate demand functions yields:

$$y + y^* = \frac{(u + u^*) + \sigma((w - v) + (w^* - v^*)) + \sigma\varepsilon(m + m^*)}{1 - \gamma + \sigma(\xi - \psi)} \tag{A1}$$

Adding the two Phillips curves gives world inflation:

$$\pi + \pi^* = \psi(y + y^*) + w + w^* \tag{A2}$$

where $\pi \equiv p_{+1} - p$ is the rate of producer price inflation. Subtracting (2) from (1) and using (8):

$$y - y^* = \frac{(2\delta + \sigma)e + (u - u^*)}{(1 + \gamma)} \tag{A3}$$

The difference between the two countries' levels of income thus depends only on the exchange rate and the demand shocks. Substituting the two Phillips curves into (8) yields an expression for the current exchange rate in terms of the difference between each country's income, the difference of their money supplies, and the difference of their velocity shocks and inflation shocks. Substituting this expression into (A3), and solving for $y - y^*$ gives:

$$y - y^* = \frac{(2\delta + \sigma)[\varepsilon(m - m^*) + (v^* - v) + (w - w^*)] + (1 - 2\theta)(u - u^*)}{(1 + \gamma)(1 - 2\theta) + (2\delta + \sigma)(\xi - \psi)}$$

(A4)

Once $y - y^*$ has been obtained it is readily shown that the exchange rate equals:

$$e = \frac{(1 + \gamma)[(m - m^*) + (v - v^*) + (w - w^*)] - (\xi - \psi)(u - u^*)}{(1 + \gamma)(1 - 2\theta) + (2\delta + \sigma)(\xi - \psi)}$$

Adding and subtracting (A1) and (A4) gives: (A5)

$$y = \alpha m + \beta m^* + q$$

(A6)

$$y^* = \alpha m^* + \beta m + q^*$$

(A7)

where α and β are given by:

$$\alpha = \frac{1}{2}\left\{\frac{\sigma\varepsilon}{1 - \gamma + \sigma(\xi - \psi)} + \frac{(2\delta + \sigma\theta)}{(1 - 2\theta)(1 + \gamma) + (2\delta + \sigma)(\xi - \psi)}\right\}$$

(A8)

$$\beta = \frac{1}{2}\left\{\frac{\sigma\varepsilon}{1 - \gamma + \sigma(\xi - \psi)} - \frac{(2\delta + \sigma\theta)}{(1 - 2\theta)(1 + \gamma) + (2\delta + \sigma)(\xi - \psi)}\right\}$$

(A9)

$$q = \frac{1}{2}\left\{\frac{(u + u^*) + \sigma((w - v) + (w^* - v^*))}{1 - \gamma + \sigma(\xi - \psi)}\right.$$

(A10)

$$\left. + \frac{(2\delta + \sigma)[(v^* - v) + (w - w^*)] + (1 - 2\theta)(u - u^*)}{(1 + \gamma)(1 - 2\theta) + (2\delta + \sigma)(\xi - \psi)}\right\}$$

Turning to inflation, we can subtract the two Phillips curves to obtain:

$$\pi - \pi^* = 2\theta e + \psi(y - y^*) + (w - w^*)$$

(A11)

Then adding and subtracting (A2) and (A11) gives the reduced forms for inflation:

$$\pi = \phi m + \eta m^* + s$$

(A12)

$$\pi^* = \phi m^* + \eta m + s$$

(A13)

where ϕ, η, and s are given by:

$$\phi = \psi a + \frac{\theta(1+\gamma)}{(1+\gamma)(1-2\theta)+(2\delta+\sigma)(\xi-\psi)} \tag{A14}$$

$$\eta = \psi b - \frac{\theta(1+\gamma)}{(1+\gamma)(1-2\theta)+(2\delta+\sigma)(\xi-\psi)} \tag{A15}$$

$$s = \psi q + \theta\frac{(1+\gamma)[(v-v^*)+(w-w^*)]-(\xi-\psi)(u-u^*)}{(1+\gamma)(1-2\theta)+(2\delta+\sigma)(\xi-\psi)} + \frac{(w+w^*)}{2} \tag{A16}$$

Notes

1   For example, if money balances should be deflated by the consumer price index in one model and by the producer price index in another model then one could embody this by writing (in logs) a nested equation in the form $m - \alpha p - (1-\alpha)p^c$ and set $\alpha = 1$ or $\alpha = 0$ to capture the two models.
2   There are ways around the assumption that individuals know the probability distribution; one is the state-preference approach of Arrow (1953), Debreu (1959) and Hirshleifer (1966) (see Machina, 1987).
3   See Davidson (1991) for an excellent discussion of this issue; Knight (1921) termed this situation as one of *uncertainty* as opposed to *risk*.
4   In the regret approach, the same final outcome can yield different levels of utility since it is both the action and the outcome which determine welfare. For example, losing money by gambling is worse than losing money in a bank failure because in the former case one *regrets* the irresponsible act.
5   Chapter 5 below considers more generally various alternative frameworks for macroeconomic modeling.
6   Our empirical work below, however, uses the more realistic formulation of the Phillips curve which writes the output price as a function of the change in the consumer price index.
7   Since the share of imported goods in the consumer price index is quite low (generally no more than 20%) we assume that $\theta < (1/2)$.
8   This is correct in the monetary policy games considered in Chapter 3.
9   Although the structural parameters $\{\alpha,\beta,\phi,\eta\}$ embody the private sector's expectations, they are independent of the monetary policy settings. (This only holds when the conditional expectation of all future shocks, and therefore of the monetary policies, is zero. This condition is fulfilled in the policy games we analyze below). Therefore, the structural model facing policymakers is independent of the regime under consideration, and results such as those obtained by Rogoff (1985) are not possible here. This has the practical benefit that we can use revealed preference arguments about instrument settings to rank

different regimes: When the coordinated and uncoordinated policy-settings differ, the former must yield a higher level of welfare.

10   It should be noted that more recent versions of some of these models no longer give effects of the same sign.

11   The original static Mundell–Fleming model becomes unstable unless the Marshall–Lerner condition is satisfied, but with real dynamics and properly modeled expectations, instability does not necessarily occur. Frankel discusses how a monetary expansion could lead to a capital inflow (which is required to match the current account deficit) when speculators expect the currency to appreciate again in the future (which will be a rational expectation in Dornbusch type overshooting models).

12   Also shown in Table 2.1 is the statistic $(\beta\phi - \alpha\eta)$ which is related to the comparative advantage condition discussed above and to which we will refer below.

13   On central bank cooperation see Bloomfield (1959) who argues that central banks would routinely vitiate the adjustment process under the classical gold standard (1880–1914).

14   A similar conclusion is reached by Eichengreen (1985) in his study of the classical gold standard.

15   Johansen (1982) qualified the need for coordination under fixed exchange rates by noting that coordination would only raise welfare if economies were not already at full employment. Kenen (1991) also discusses conditions under which fixed exchange rates obviate the need for policy coordination.

16   In their book, Canzoneri and Henderson (1991) explore the bias of the non-cooperative equilibrium under different types of shocks.

17   Sachs (1983) also showed that the extreme assumptions of a Nash equilibrium are not necessary to make the uncoordinated regime inefficient relative to the coordinated regime. Similar inefficiencies exist if governments are in a "consistent conjectural variations" (CCV) equilibrium in the non-cooperative regime. See Turnovsky *et al.* (1988) and Brandsma and Hughes Hallett (1984).

18   This "GDP-equivalent" welfare gain has become a standard measure of welfare gains. A GDP-equivalent utility gain of 3 per cent, for example, means that the country would be indifferent between the choice of moving from the coordinated to the uncoordinated regime and the choice of losing 3 percent of its GDP. In Oudiz and Sachs's paper, the gain was less than 1 percent of GDP for each country, in each year, that coordination was undertaken. See also Hughes Hallett (1986).

19   See Ghosh (1991) for a model of fiscal coordination in which there is a permanent conflict between the objectives of different governments. This model also provides an example in which the need for coordination increases as each country becomes atomistic.

20   Carraro and Giavazzi (1991) and Lennblad (1991) criticize Rogoff's model on game-theoretic grounds. As Canzoneri and Henderson (1991) point out, what drives the Rogoff result is that not all players in the game are coordinating their actions (governments in each country coordinate their policies but play non-cooperatively *vis-à-vis* the private sector). With only a subset of the players

coordinating, there is no guarantee that welfare will increase for any of the players.

21   Other related papers, not presented at this conference, include Taylor (1985) and Carlozzi and Taylor (1985).

22   Canzoneri and Henderson (1991) discuss these issues in greater detail. Miller, Salmon, and Sutherland (1991) show that the higher is the rate of discounting by governments, the greater is the likelihood that coordination will lower welfare relative to non-coordination.

23   Other early work on the effects of uncertainty on the incentive to coordinate includes Hughes Hallett (1986a) who argues that coordinated policies are more robust to model mis-specification and that the degree of "extra" robustness increases the more uncertainty there is.

24   MINIMOD is a two-country model whose parameters are derived from the Federal Reserve Board's Multi-Country Model (see Haas and Masson, 1986).

25   In one part of their paper, Frankel and Rockett allow policy makers to take account of model uncertainty but the subjective priors used by the policymakers do not coincide with the objective probability distribution. This issue is discussed further in Chapter 6, below.

26   Cripps (1991) looks at the effects of endogenous learning about the preference parameters of a leader country by follower countries.

27   They also find that basing policies on a synthetic model whose multipliers are an average across models results in very poor outcomes.

3

The Theory of Policy Coordination under Uncertainty

1. Introduction

This chapter sets out the basic analytic framework that we use for examining the effects of uncertainty on the incentives of governments to coordinate their macroeconomic policies. The main conclusion of this chapter is perhaps surprising. We show that macroeconomic uncertainty, far from reducing the incentive to coordinate policies, can increase the benefits from international coordination. Since much of the discussion is quite technical, section 2 gives an overview of the main arguments of the chapter; subsequent sections develop these arguments in more detail.

Section 3 begins with a review of the theory of policy coordination in a deterministic setting; conditions under which coordination would be beneficial are identified. We show that there will be welfare gains from policy coordination so long as each government has more macroeconomic targets than it has policy instruments. Assuming this condition is met, moreover, the move from the non-coordinated regime to the coordinated regime will yield welfare gains akin to those associated with the shift from autarky to free trade in, for example, the Ricardian model of international trade.

In order to isolate the effects of uncertainty on the gains from coordination from any other argument for coordination, we first adopt a framework in which each government has exactly as many policy instruments as it has targets. We then introduce uncertainty of the simplest form: in section 4, macroeconomic targets are assumed to be subject to additive shocks whose magnitude is independent of the policy instrument settings. Although this changes the average level of welfare attained under both the coordinated and the uncoordinated regimes, it has no effect on the gains from coordination.

In sharp contrast, section 5 shows how uncertainty about the structure of the model – and therefore about the effects of policy instruments on the target variables – provides an incentive for macroeconomic coordination which is distinct from the usual arguments in favor of coordination. This is apparent since, by our assumption that each government has as many instruments as it has targets, there are no gains from coordination in the absence of the uncertainty.

Section 6 returns to the case in which governments have more targets than instruments and examines how introducing multiplier uncertainty alters the gains from coordination which already exist in the deterministic model. Here we show that the effects of uncertainty depend upon whether the uncertainty surrounds the effects of domestic multipliers or transmission multipliers. In either case, however, plausible assumptions about the magnitudes of the various multipliers, and the uncertainty surrounding them, suggest that uncertainty will increase the gains from coordination. Section 7 summarizes the discussion.

2. An Overview

Issues of uncertainty aside, the argument for the superiority of coordinated macroeconomic policies over uncoordinated ones is quite robust.[1] The argument rests on the inefficiencies which arise from ignoring the externalities of the policies of one country on macroeconomic targets of other countries. Indeed, one way to think about the benefits from policy coordination is in terms of public goods and public bads. If a monetary expansion in one country raises income abroad as well as at home but the country is concerned about the inflationary effects of such an expansion – which may be exacerbated by a depreciation of the exchange rate – then from a global social perspective it will "under-supply" the monetary expansion. Thus when the world economy is suffering from an unemployment problem due to inadequate demand uncoordinated monetary policies may be insufficiently expansionary. In a microeconomic context, problems of a public good nature are solved by the government imposing taxes or providing subsidies which align private costs and benefits to the social costs and benefits. Alternatively, the government may provide the supposedly optimal level of public goods itself directly. In the arena of international macroeconomic policy no such central authority exists. Nonetheless, it is possible to achieve socially optimal outcomes by countries *jointly* pursuing policies which alter the trade-offs faced by an individual country in such a way that each country is led to choose the socially optimal policies. To continue the above example, if both countries agreed to a joint expansion then part of the inflationary effect may be abated since neither country's exchange rate will depreciate (*vis-à-vis* the other).

Since a monetary expansion is not as inflationary as before, each country is more willing to expand, thus raising output and income.

Several points about this example are worth emphasizing. First, nothing rests upon our assumption that exchange rates float. Under fixed exchange rates, each government would be concerned about the reserve outflow and again reluctant to expand on its own; there are also benefits from coordination in this case. Second, the argument for coordination does not depend upon the presence of *positive* externalities; the existence of *negative* externalities provides an equally strong incentive to coordinate. The assumed symmetry of shocks to the two countries, or regions, though analytically very convenient, is likewise innocuous.[2] Third, coordination does not eliminate the trade-offs between the various targets of the government but it does alter those trade-offs so that the maximum possible level of welfare may be attained. Fourth, both countries benefit from coordination, relative to non-coordination; though, as in the standard gains from international trade, theory has relatively little to say on how those potential gains are divided.

The need for coordinated policies is equally important when the world economy has suffered an inflationary shock. Indeed, this is a case which is frequently cited in the literature and in our discussions below. When choosing its monetary policy each government must trade off the benefits of lower inflation against the costs of higher unemployment. If policies are not coordinated then, by definition, neither government takes account of the spill-overs of its policies onto the other country. In this instance, there is likely to be a *negative* externality since a monetary contraction by one country will appreciate its own exchange rate thus depreciating the other country's exchange rate and, by increasing the price of imported goods, raise the other country's inflation rate. Monetary policies will therefore be overly-contractionary in the uncoordinated equilibrium. In the coordinated regime, each government pursues less contractionary monetary policy and both governments attain a higher level of welfare.

In the uncoordinated regime neither government takes account of the welfare repercussions of its own policies on the other government. As a result, each is also effectively ignoring the induced policy reactions of the other government (in formal game theoretic terms the uncoordinated regime is a *Nash equilibrium*). If, for instance, the home government pursues a very tight monetary policy because it does not care about the higher inflation abroad then the foreign government is likely to retaliate by pursuing a very tight monetary policy as well. But the home government chooses its policy as though it believed that the foreign government would not retaliate. Note, though, that there is no uncertainty here; all players within the model know each other's utility functions and the nature of the equilibrium. This suggests an element of irrationality or myopia on the part of governments when they are not coordinating their policies. But that is not necessarily true. Rather, one can interpret the uncoordinated regime – that is, a Nash equilibrium in monetary policies – as a sovereign nation's inability to precommit itself to particular policies. For if the foreign government were to promise to take into account the home country's welfare when choosing its own policy, and the home government believed this promise and chose its own policy to maximize both countries' welfare functions then the foreign government would have the incentive to renege and choose policies which maximized only its own welfare. Likewise, the home government has the incentive to renege on the coordinated agreement if the foreign government is sticking to it. The (inefficient) game theoretic outcome is that both governments set their policies in an uncoordinated fashion because they were unable to precommit themselves to coordination. In general, one would need an external mechanism to enforce the coordinated regime. In a dynamic context, it may be possible to achieve the coordinated outcome without such a mechanism because governments will recognize that reneging on the coordinated equilibrium in the current period will be punished by subsequent periods of uncoordinated policies. This possibility is discussed in some detail in Chapter 8.

Notice that one cannot, without specifying the nature of the shock (and, indeed, the structure of the world economy), characterize the uncoordinated equilibrium as involving too much or too little policy activism relative to the coordinated regime. In the first example, governments which are not coordinating their policies are not sufficiently expansionary in face of a global fall in demand. In the second example, uncoordinated policies lead governments to pursue excessively contractionary monetary policies as they try to counter the inflationary shock. Trade theory provides a good analogy: although we cannot predict the direction of trade without knowing a great deal about the structure of technology and preferences, we do know that there will be gains from international trade as long as autarky prices differ. It turns out that a similar comparative advantage condition determines whether there are gains from coordination. Suppose we take output and inflation to be the two policy targets, and monetary policy to be the single policy instrument. In this case the comparative advantage requirement is that the effect of a foreign monetary expansion on domestic output, relative to the effect of a domestic expansion, be different from the effect of a foreign monetary expansion on domestic inflation (again, relative to the effect of a domestic expansion). Put differently, the relative price of an increase in output in terms of inflation associated with a domestic expansion must differ from the relative price of output for inflation associated with a foreign monetary expansion. As soon as these relative prices differ, there are gains from policy coordination (just as there are gains from trade when autarky relative prices differ).

This comparative advantage interpretation of the gains from international policy coordination immediately implies the well-known result that there are no gains from coordination when each government has as many instruments as it does targets. For in that case, there is no "relative price" because there is no trade-off between targets. If, for example, the government has two targets – inflation and output – and two instruments – monetary and fiscal policy – then it can direct its monetary policy at targetting inflation while using fiscal policy to target output. There need be no trade-off between the two targets and no "relative price" of output for inflation (or vice versa).

What then, are the effects of macroeconomic uncertainty on these gains from coordination? In this chapter we shall be concerned exclusively with what we called *technological* uncertainty in Chapter 2; that is, uncertainty about the structure of the world economy or about the shocks impinging upon countries. Throughout this chapter, moreover, we shall use the concept of *ex ante* expected utility as our measure of welfare. As argued in Chapter 2, this is probably the only sensible criterion when we do not have specific alternative models in mind. The effects of uncertainty are actually quite complicated since they operate through a variety of channels. In particular, uncertainty must lower the level of welfare attained in the coordinated regime since governments can obviously achieve a higher level of welfare when they face less uncertainty. In the uncoordinated regime, however, uncertainty may either raise or lower welfare depending upon the nature of the inefficiency of the uncoordinated equilibrium. As is well known from the theory of international trade, when the initial equilibrium is not Pareto optimal, adding a "distortion" (in this case, uncertainty) can have ambiguous effects on welfare (Bhagwati, 1983). Since we are interested in the effects of uncertainty on the welfare *gains* from coordination, all depends upon whether the rate at which welfare is lowered in the coordinated regime is higher or lower than the rate at which welfare is lowered in the uncoordinated regime (if at all) as uncertainty increases.

To understand the effects of uncertainty it is simplest to start with a case in which there are no gains from coordination in the absence of uncertainty. This is quite common in other instances of welfare economics; in analyzing the effects of a tariff, for example, it is customary to evaluate those effects around a zero initial tariff distortion. To construct a situation in which there are no pre-existing gains from coordination we assume that each government as has many instruments as it has targets. We then analyze the effects of introducing uncertainty. This gives a particularly dramatic demonstration of the effects of uncertainty because if we do find any gains from coordination they can only be the result of the uncertainty itself.

We first show that additive shocks, that is shocks which affect the target variables directly while leaving policy multipliers unchanged, do not give rise to welfare gains from coordination: welfare under the coordinated and the uncoordinated regimes falls by an equal amount so that there are no benefits to coordination. This result, moreover, does not rely on any specific assumptions about the form of the model or the policymakers' welfare functions.[3]

Next we examine the effects of multiplier uncertainty; that is, uncertainty about the effects of policy instruments on target variables. As discussed in Chapter 2, such uncertainty may reflect stochastically shifting structural parameters within a given model, or more fundamental uncertainties about the correct model of the world economy. Once we introduce multiplier uncertainty we find that there are welfare gains from policy coordination where no such gains existed in the absence of the uncertainty. Thus (multiplier) uncertainty itself gives rise to an incentive to coordinate macroeconomic policies. Again, the result is completely robust to different assumptions about the structure of the world economy, the nature of the shock (and, in particular, whether shocks are correlated across countries), and the exact form of the utility function (assuming that policymakers are not risk-neutral).

There are at least two ways of understanding the intuition behind this result. The simpler, though perhaps less interesting, way is to note that once we introduce uncertainty policymakers effectively have more targets than before. To see why, suppose that policymakers have a quadratic preference function; that is, they try to minimize $E\{y^2\}$ where y is the target variable, and $E\{\cdot\}$ denotes the expected value (the argument does not depend upon quadratic utility but is simplified by the assumption). Notice that the utility function can be rewritten as $E\{y^2\} = \mu_y^2 + \sigma_y^2$ so that as long as $\sigma_y^2 > 0$, policymakers have two targets – the average value of the target and the variability around the average – with which to contend.[4] Since we start with a case in which policymakers have exactly the same number of policy instruments as targets, uncertainty implies that they now have more macroeconomic targets than instruments. And, as argued above, this is sufficient for there to be welfare benefits from coordination. Under *additive* uncertainty both the mean and the variability of the target also matter but since, as discussed below, the variance of the target variable is independent of policy, the effective number of targets (i.e. ones which the policymaker can influence) remains the same. With multiplier uncertainty, in contrast, the variance of the target is influenced by policy so that the effective number of targets increases.

A second way to understand the intuition is in terms of the mean-variance analysis of policy pioneered by Brainard (1967). Brainard showed (in a domestic context) that when faced by multiplier uncertainty, policies must be set so that the marginal rate of substitution (MRS) between setting the average value of a target variable to its prescribed level and minimizing the variability around the optimal level must be equated to the policy instrument's marginal rate of transformation (MRT) between these two quantities. As discussed above, the uncoordinated regime is characterized by each government setting its policies as though the other government is not going to respond. In consequence, governments do not correctly set the MRS to the MRT in the uncoordinated regime. Suppose, for example, there is a great deal of uncertainty associated with the transmission effect of monetary policy. Now in choosing its monetary policy the home government considers an incremental change in the money supply, dm. Such a change would bring the average value of the target closer to its optimal value but would also increase the variance of the target. According to Brainard's analysis, in a closed economy the government would simply trade-off these effects until it is just indifferent between the disutility of increased variance and the utility of getting the average value closer to the optimal level. But in the international context that is not the end of the story. For the perturbation in the home country's money supply, dm, will induce the foreign country to respond since, in equilibrium, $\partial m^*/\partial m \neq 0$. And the perturbation in the foreign country's policy, dm^*, will affect both the mean and the variance of the home country's target. If the degree of transmission uncertainty is large (as is likely to be the case) then there will be a large increase in the variance of the home country's target variable. Thus the marginal rate of transformation used by the home government when choosing its policy in the uncoordinated equilibrium is not the correct marginal rate of transformation, where the latter includes the induced effects of the foreign government's policies. As before, the results are robust to different assumptions about the type of shock, and the structure of the world economy.

Once we start from a situation in which there are pre-existing welfare gains from coordination we are comparing two "second best" equilibria and, as in trade theory, the analysis becomes more difficult and less unambiguous. In general, the greater the degree of transmission multiplier uncertainty the greater the gains from coordination. This is not surprising since in the uncoordinated equilibrium governments are failing to internalize the transmission effects of their policies. The result is not completely robust, however, since, depending upon the nature of the initial inefficiency of the uncoordinated equilibrium (i.e. the inefficiency in the absence of uncertainty), it is conceivable that an increase in transmission uncertainty could lower the gains from coordination.[5] As the degree of transmission uncertainty increases, however, it is necessarily true that (eventually) the welfare gains from coordination are an *increasing* function of the transmission uncertainty. Greater uncertainty about the domestic multipliers, in contrast, will (at least eventually) lower the gains from coordination. The reason for the latter result is straightforward: with sufficiently large domestic multiplier uncertainty governments do not pursue any activist policy at all. At that point, it clearly makes no difference whether policies are coordinated or uncoordinated. Since there is generally more uncertainty about transmission effects than about domestic multipliers, it is probable that taking account of multiplier uncertainty will raise our estimates of the gains from coordination. Ultimately, though, that is an empirical issue, which we address in Chapter 6.

3. Conflict and Coordination in a Deterministic Setting

Before considering the implications of different types of uncertainty, we first establish some results about coordinating policies internationally in the deterministic case. We assume that policymakers try to achieve a zero rate of inflation while maintaining output at its full employment level. We assume, moreover, that the policymaker's instantaneous loss function may be written in terms of the inflation rate squared and the output deviation squared, which implies that the disutility from inflation or unemployment rises at an increasing rate. In a dynamic model, in which actions taken today affect output or inflation in the future, the policymaker's objective function should be the discounted sum of the single period loss functions. Since we shall use a static model in this chapter, however, we simply assume that policymakers target output and inflation, period by period.

The objective functions are therefore written:

$$V = \text{Max} - \left(\tfrac{1}{2}\right)\{y^2 + \omega\pi^2\} \tag{1}$$

$$V^* = \text{Max} - \left(\tfrac{1}{2}\right)\{y^{*2} + \omega\pi^{*2}\} \tag{2}$$

We assume that output and inflation are given by the following reduced-form equations:

$$y = \alpha m + \beta m^* \tag{3}$$

$$y^* = \alpha m^* + \beta m \tag{4}$$

$$\pi = \phi m + \eta m^* + s \tag{5}$$

$$\pi^* = \phi m^* + \eta m + s \tag{6}$$

where s is an inflationary shock. Such a reduced form could of course arise from the model developed in Chapter 2, or indeed from any generic Mundell–Fleming model. We assume that the domestic multipliers, α and ϕ, are both positive. The transmission multipliers, β and η, can be either positive or negative but in either case are assumed to be smaller in magnitude than the corresponding domestic multipliers (α and ϕ). For simplicity, we will frequently assume that both transmission multipliers are negative when explaining the intuition about the results, but it bears emphasizing that the assumption of negative transmission multipliers is not generally necessary for the results themselves.

In addition, to avoid a tedious taxonomy of cases, we assume that the following "comparative advantage" condition holds:

$$\beta\phi - \alpha\eta > 0 \Rightarrow (\beta/\alpha) > (\eta/\phi)$$

which requires that an expansion in the foreign money supply has a larger expansionary effect – or smaller contractionary effect – on domestic output (relative to a domestic expansion) than it does on domestic inflation (again, relative to a domestic expansion). If both transmission multipliers are negative, then this condition states that a foreign monetary expansion has a comparative advantage in lowering the home country's inflation, relative to its contractionary effect on the home country's level of output (where both effects are measured relative to the corresponding domestic multipliers). This condition is satisfied by the theoretical model developed above, and virtually all of the empirical models surveyed in the Brookings study – the exceptions being the LINK and VAR models (see Table 2.1).

In the absence of any shocks, policymakers would not face an output-inflation trade-off. As long as $s \neq 0$, however, each policymaker faces a conflict between achieving its target of zero inflation and full employment. Figure 3.1 shows the family of indifference curves, which are generally ellipses centered at zero. (When deviations from full employment and inflation are weighted equally in the objective function, moreover, ω equals one, and the indifference curves are circles.) Moving away from the origin indicates a lower level of welfare.

Suppose, first, that each central bank leaves the money supply unchanged in face of the inflationary shock. The outcome would be a point such as A, where output is at its full employment level but there is a positive rate of inflation; the government's welfare level is $\mathcal{V}_A$. Given the

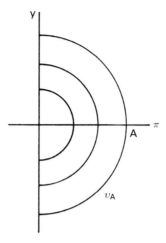

Figure 3.1 Welfare under an inflationary shock

money supply of the other country, each policymaker can make its nation better off by contracting the money supply. A reduction of the money supply leads to a large welfare gain from lowering inflation against a small welfare loss from reducing output.

But that is not the end of the story. In its attempt to improve its own welfare, each country reduces the welfare of the other. Should the home country contract its money supply, for example, this will appreciate the home country's exchange rate and raise the inflation rate further in the foreign country.[6]

Since the actions of each government affect the welfare of the other, their actions can be characterized by a policy game between them. The outcome of this game will depend upon the policy regime. We consider two such regimes: coordinated and uncoordinated.

In the uncoordinated, or Nash, regime each country seeks to maximize its own welfare, taking the actions of the other government as given. More specifically, neither government internalizes the welfare spillovers of its actions on the other country when choosing its optimal policy. Thus the home government chooses its own monetary policy setting, m, in order to maximize its own objective function, $\mathcal{V}$, taking m^* as given. Mathematically, the condition for optimality when choosing policies independently may be written:

$$\partial \mathcal{V}/\partial m = \partial(y^2 + \omega\pi^2)/\partial m = 0 \qquad (7)$$

That is, for any given m^*, the home government should choose its monetary policy in such a way that no perturbation of its policy could raise its welfare. Substituting the reduced-form expressions (3) and (5) into (7) gives the home government's optimal policy, as a function of the foreign government's monetary policy (this is called the "reaction function"):

$$m^N = \frac{-\{(\alpha\beta + \omega\phi\eta)m^{N*} + \omega\phi s\}}{\alpha^2 + \omega\phi^2} \tag{8}$$

where the N superscript stands for the Nash, or uncoordinated, equilibrium. The foreign country's reaction function may be found by maximizing V^*, with respect to m^*, and taking as given m. The resulting reaction function is analogous to (8):

$$m^{N*} = \frac{-\{(\alpha\beta + \omega\phi\eta)m^N + \omega\phi s\}}{\alpha^2 + \omega\phi^2} \tag{9}$$

The uncoordinated equilibrium is given by the intersection of the two reaction functions and is depicted in Figure 3.2. Algebraically, it may be found by solving (8) and (9) simultaneously to yield:

$$m^N = m^{N*} = \frac{-\omega\phi s}{\alpha(\alpha + \beta) + \omega\phi(\phi + \eta)} \tag{10}$$

The symmetry of the model, coupled with the assumption of symmetric shocks to the two countries, implies that the home country's monetary policy setting will be equal to that of the foreign country. Accordingly, whichever regime we consider, the equilibrium will lie along the 45° line. The Nash equilibrium has the property that neither country can unilaterally improve its welfare: therefore, the home country's indifference curve (in m–m^* space) must be vertical at that point, and that of the foreign country must be horizontal. Starting at the Nash equilibrium point neither country can *unilaterally* raise its welfare but it is possible to improve one or both country's welfare by a *joint* change in monetary policies. We can see this in Figure 3.2, where the two countries' indifference curves form a lens-shaped area which defines the Pareto-improving set of monetary policies.

To prove that such an area exists, we must show that there exist perturbations in the home and foreign country's policies, from their uncoordinated equilibrium settings, which improve the welfare of at least one country, while leaving the other country indifferent. Suppose we start at the uncoordinated equilibrium, and perturb the home country's monetary policy. What is the welfare effect on the foreign country? We find this by calculating the derivative of the foreign country's welfare function with respect to the home country's policy instrument, and evaluating this derivative at the uncoordinated equilibrium:

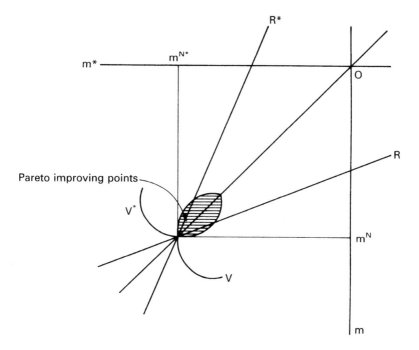

Figure 3.2 Nash Equilibrium under an inflationary shock

$$\partial \mathcal{V}^* / \partial m = -\{\beta(\alpha m^N + \beta m^{N*}) + \omega \eta(\phi m^N + \eta m^{N*} + s)\}$$
$$= -(\alpha m^N + \beta m^{N*})(\beta \phi - \alpha \eta)/\phi \tag{11}$$

Since $m^N = m^{N*} < 0$, this derivative will be non-zero (except in the very special case that $\beta \phi = \alpha \eta$). Therefore, a change in the home country's policy setting can improve the foreign country's welfare.

What about the effect on the home country? It turns out that a small perturbation of the home country's policy setting around the uncoordinated equilibrium has *no* first-order effect on its own welfare (otherwise the original policy could not have been optimal from the home country's perspective):[7]

$$\partial \mathcal{V} / \partial m = -\{\alpha(\alpha m^N + \beta m^{N*}) + \omega \phi(\phi m^N + \eta m^{N*} + s)\} = 0 \tag{12}$$

where the second equality comes from substituting for m^N and m^{N*} from (10). While there is no first-order effect, the home country will suffer a second-order loss.[8] Therefore, the home country cannot unilaterally achieve a Pareto improvement. If the foreign country undertakes a symmetric perturbation of its own instrument, however, it can achieve a first-order gain for the home country which outweighs this second-order loss. Therefore, acting jointly, both countries can improve world welfare as long as $\partial \mathcal{V}^*/\partial m$ and $\partial \mathcal{V}/\partial m^*$ are non-zero.

Will this move involve tighter or looser monetary policy? Recall the "comparative advantage" inequality which assumed that $(\beta\phi - \alpha\eta) > 0$. Using this fact, we see from (11) that $\partial \mathcal{V}^*/\partial m > 0$, thus an expansion of the home country's money supply will benefit the foreign country. (Given the symmetry of the model, of course, an expansion by the foreign country benefits the home country.) It follows that the uncoordinated equilibrium has a contractionary bias in the face of a positive inflation shock.

To understand why this contractionary bias exists, recall that, at the Nash equilibrium, each country sets its monetary policy in order to equate the ratio of the marginal disutilities of inflation and unemployment to the technological rate of transformation between output and inflation achievable using domestic monetary policy. The foreign country, for example, chooses its monetary policy to set:

$$\frac{\partial \mathcal{V}^*/\partial \pi^*}{\partial \mathcal{V}^*/\partial y^*} = -\frac{\alpha}{\phi} \tag{13}$$

In other words, at the uncoordinated equilibrium, the foreign policy-maker would be indifferent between a 1 percent decrease in output and an (α/ϕ) percent increase in inflation. In Figure 3.3, we denote by B_1 the values of output and inflation at the uncoordinated equilibrium. As α increases, or ϕ decreases, the policymaker chooses a higher rate of

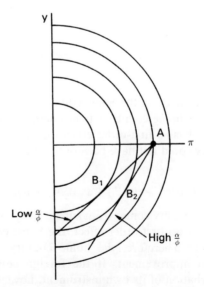

Figure 3.3   Optimal unemployment/inflation trade-off for different (α/ϕ)

inflation and a smaller loss in output, B_2. This is because the cost of lowering inflation, in terms of lost output, becomes greater with higher values of α, and lower values of ϕ.

Now suppose that the home country expands its money supply. This lowers both output and inflation in the foreign country, but the trade-off between the two is given by β/η. The change in the foreign country's welfare is therefore:

$$\partial V^*/\partial m = \beta \partial V^*/\partial y + \eta \partial V^*/\partial \pi \tag{14}$$

Substituting for $(\partial V^*/\partial y)$ from (13) gives:

$$\partial V^*/\partial m = -(\phi/\alpha)\beta \partial V^*/\partial \pi + \eta \partial V^*/\partial \pi = [\partial V^*/\partial \pi](\alpha \eta - \beta \phi)/\alpha \tag{15}$$

Since $\partial V^*/\partial \pi < 0$ at the uncoordinated equilibrium (because the country already has too high an inflation rate), $\partial V^*/\partial m$ will be positive as long as the comparative advantage condition, assumed above, holds. In essence, this comparative advantage condition ensures that the benefit of lowering inflation exceeds the cost of lost output, in terms of the foreign country's marginal valuation. An increase in the home country's money supply therefore raises the foreign country's welfare. Again, by symmetry, an expansion of the foreign country's monetary policy (which has no first-order effect on itself) will improve the home country's welfare. Since both countries can be made better off, the uncoordinated equilibrium cannot be Pareto efficient.

This joint move from the uncoordinated regime can be interpreted in terms of the classical (Ricardian) model of international trade. First note that when $(\beta/\alpha) = (\eta/\phi)$ the foreign country has no "comparative advantage" in terms of affecting the home country's output or inflation, relative to the home country. Not surprisingly, therefore, there are no gains from coordination.[9] Suppose each government agrees to expand its money supply. When $(\beta/\alpha) > (\eta/\phi)$, the fall in home output from the foreign monetary expansion will be low, relative to the gain in terms of lower inflation. In other words, the foreign country has a comparative advantage in "producing" low inflation for the home country. Likewise, the home government has a comparative advantage in "producing" low inflation for the foreign country. Thus there is scope for mutually beneficial trade.

If governments internalize the welfare spillovers arising from their choice of monetary policy, then this scope for beneficial trade will be fully exploited. We can think of a coordinated regime as one in which there is a single global social planner who chooses both countries' monetary policies in order to maximize a weighted average of both countries' objective functions. Thus the global social planner's objective function may be written:

$$\mathcal{V}^G = \chi\mathcal{V} + (1 - \chi)\mathcal{V}^* \quad 0 \leq \chi \leq 1 \tag{16}$$

Since the two countries are entirely symmetric, it is natural to assume that the global social planner assigns equal weight to each country so that the objective function becomes:

$$\mathcal{V}^G = \text{Max} - \left(\tfrac{1}{4}\right)\left\{y^2 + \omega(\pi^2) + y^{*2} + \omega(\pi^{*2})\right\} \tag{17}$$

The cooperative planner's first order conditions, with respect to the two policy instruments, are given by:

$$\partial\mathcal{V}^G/\partial m = \chi\partial\mathcal{V}/\partial m + (1 - \chi)\partial\mathcal{V}^*/\partial m = 0 \tag{18}$$

$$\partial\mathcal{V}^G/\partial m^* = \chi\partial\mathcal{V}/\partial m^* + (1 - \chi)\partial\mathcal{V}^*/\partial m^* = 0 \tag{19}$$

Substituting the structural model (3)–(6) into (18) and (19) and assigning equal weight to each country, gives:

$$\begin{aligned}
\partial\mathcal{V}^G/\partial m = \left(\tfrac{1}{2}\right)&\left\{\alpha(\alpha m + \beta m^*) + \omega\phi(\phi m + \eta m^* + s)\right. \\
&\left. + \beta(\alpha m^* + \beta m) + \omega\eta(\phi m^* + \eta m + s)\right\} = 0
\end{aligned} \tag{20}$$

$$\begin{aligned}
\partial\mathcal{V}^G/\partial m^* = \left(\tfrac{1}{2}\right)&\left\{\beta(\alpha m + \beta m^*) + \omega\eta(\phi m + \eta m^* + s)\right. \\
&\left. + \alpha(\alpha m^* + \beta m) + \omega\phi(\phi m^* + \eta m + s)\right\} = 0
\end{aligned} \tag{21}$$

Solving these two equations simultaneously gives the coordinated policy setting:

$$m^C = m^{C*} = \frac{-\omega(\phi + \eta)s}{(\alpha + \beta)^2 + \omega(\phi + \eta)^2} \tag{22}$$

Comparing (10) and (22) shows that the uncoordinated policy is overly contractionary in the face of a positive shock $(s > 0)$ as long as $(\beta\phi - \alpha\eta) > 0$:

$$m^N - m^C = \frac{\omega s}{[(\alpha + \beta)^2/(\phi + \eta)] + \omega(\phi + \eta)} - \frac{\omega s}{(\alpha/\phi)(\alpha + \beta) + \omega(\phi + \eta)} \tag{23}$$

Thus $m^N - m^C < 0$ if $[(\alpha + \beta)^2/(\phi + \eta)] > [(\alpha/\phi)(\alpha + \beta)]$ or $\beta\phi > \alpha\eta$, which is, of course, consistent with our conclusion above that a Pareto improving move from the uncoordinated equilibrium requires that both countries expand their money supplies.[10]

It is easy to show that the coordinated equilibrium is Pareto efficient. The welfare levels attained by the home country and the foreign country may be written as functions of the two monetary policies: $\mathcal{V} = \mathcal{V}(m, m^*), \mathcal{V}^* = \mathcal{V}^*(m, m^*)$. Suppose, starting at the coordinated equilibrium, we perturb the two monetary instruments in a manner which raises the home country's welfare. A change in the home country's welfare, $d\mathcal{V}$, can be written:

$$d\mathcal{V} = \partial \mathcal{V}(\cdot)/\partial m + \partial \mathcal{V}(\cdot)/\partial m^*$$

Substituting (18) and (19), gives:

$$d\mathcal{V} = \partial \mathcal{V}(\cdot)/\partial m + \partial \mathcal{V}(\cdot)/\partial m^*$$
$$= \frac{-(1-\chi)}{\chi}\{\partial \mathcal{V}^*(\cdot)/\partial m + \partial \mathcal{V}^*(\cdot)/\partial m^*\} = \frac{-(1-\chi)}{\chi} d\mathcal{V}^* \quad (24)$$

At the coordinated equilibrium, therefore, there exists no change in the policy settings which can raise the home country's welfare without simultaneously lowering the foreign country's welfare (or vice versa). One final point to note about the coordinated solution is that there is no need to assume the existence of a global social planner simultaneously choosing the monetary policies in each country. If, instead, we simply endow both governments with the objective function $\mathcal{V}^G$ and allow them to play a Nash strategy (i.e. each chooses its own policy and takes as given the actions of the other), the two reaction functions will be identical to (20) and (21). This equivalence holds so long as the information available to each government is the same (or they credibly share their information) and so long as the strategic game has a unique equilibrium. In the examples we consider in this chapter, both conditions are satisfied.

Another way to understand the inefficiency of the uncoordinated equilibrium is in terms of each government's conjectural variation at the Nash equilibrium. The term "conjectural variation" – which comes from classic models of duopoly – refers to the beliefs of one player about the response of the other player to his own actions (see Kreps, 1990, Chapter 10). A typical example from the industrial organization literature would be the beliefs of one firm about whether the other firm in a duopoly would lower its price in response to a price decrease by the first firm. In our application, each government must hold some belief about whether a change in its monetary policy will elicit a corresponding response by the other government. In the Nash equilibrium, each government has a conjectural variation of zero, i.e. each government assumes that the other will not respond to a change in its own monetary policy. (This conjecture is correct only at the equilibrium point.) The coordinated equilibrium can be described as a situation in which both governments correctly anticipate that the other government will respond (symmetrically in this case, since objective functions and behavioral equations are the same) to its own actions. The home government, for example, will not be tempted to competitively appreciate the exchange rate if it knows that its actions will be vitiated by the foreign government acting symmetrically. In the uncoordinated regime, by contrast, each government takes as given the actions of the other government, and therefore both try to export inflation by an exchange rate appreciation. It is clear, however, that given symmetric shocks (and therefore symmetric monetary policies), it is not possible to affect the value of the exchange rate. In consequence, governments playing non-cooperatively choose monetary policies with a deflationary bias, resulting in a high level of unemployment.

We can see the role of the conjectural variation from the home country's first-order condition, written in its most general form:

$$\partial V/\partial m = - \{[\alpha + \beta(\partial m^*/\partial m)](\alpha m + \beta m^*) + \omega[\phi + \eta(\partial m^*/\partial m)](\phi m + \eta m^* + s)\} = 0 \qquad (25)$$

If one substitutes the Nash conjectural variation, $(\partial m^*/\partial m) = 0$, one obtains the first-order condition characterizing the uncoordinated equilibrium. If one substitutes the (symmetric) coordinated conjectural variation $(\partial m^*/\partial m) = 1$, on the other hand, one obtains the coordinated first-order condition (16). Therefore, the inefficiency of the uncoordinated regime can be characterized in terms of the conjectural variation instead of the welfare spillovers. The existing literature on coordination has used both characterizations: McKibbin and Sachs (1991), for example, use the conjectural variations approach, while Canzoneri and Henderson (1991) focus on the welfare spillovers of the uncoordinated regime. We will use both characterizations, depending upon which is more intuitive and more convenient to the discussion at hand.

There is one special case in which the coordinated and uncoordinated equilibria coincide. Suppose that governments care about only one of the macroeconomic targets, say inflation; the objective functions then become:

$$V = \text{Max} - \left(\tfrac{1}{2}\right)\{\pi^2\} \qquad (26)$$

$$V^* = \text{Max} - \left(\tfrac{1}{2}\right)\{\pi^{*2}\} \qquad (27)$$

The uncoordinated outcome is given by the intersection of the reaction functions:

$$\partial V/\partial m = 0 \Rightarrow m^N = \frac{-\{\eta m^{N*} + s\}}{\phi} \qquad (28)$$

$$\partial V^*/\partial m^* = 0 \Rightarrow m^{N*} = \frac{-\{\eta m^N + s\}}{\phi} \qquad (29)$$

Solving (28) and (29) simultaneously yields:

$$m^N = m^{N*} = \frac{-s}{(\phi + \eta)} \tag{30}$$

If each government (or a global social planner) maximizes $V^G = \left(\frac{1}{2}\right)\{V + V^*\}$, then the coordinated home country reaction function is:

$$m^C = \frac{-\{2\phi\eta m^{C*} + (\eta + \phi)s\}}{\phi^2 + \eta^2} \tag{31}$$

with a symmetric reaction function for the foreign country. The resulting equilibrium is given by:

$$m^C = m^{C*} = \frac{-s}{(\phi + \eta)} \tag{32}$$

Since the coordinated and uncoordinated policies are identical there are clearly no welfare gains to coordination. Substituting the policies under cooperation and non-cooperation into the utility functions shows:

$$V^C = V^{C*} = V^N = V^{N*} = 0 \tag{33}$$

So both countries achieve their bliss point under either regime. This is a very useful benchmark case which we use below when we consider the effects of uncertainty. If there are gains to coordination when uncertainty is introduced into this framework (in which each government has only one target and one instrument) it can only be the result of that uncertainty since we have shown that there is no incentive to coordinate in the certainty case.

We can see why there are no benefits to coordination here by calculating the welfare effect on the foreign country of a change in the home country's policy setting at the Nash equilibrium. This is found by partially differentiating the foreign country's objective function with respect to the home instrument and evaluating the derivative at the Nash equilibrium:

$$\partial V^* / \partial m = \eta\{\phi m^{N*} + \eta m^N + s\} \tag{34}$$

Rearranging the first-order condition (28), however, shows that the term $\{\phi m^{N*} + \eta m^N + s\}$ equals zero. Therefore, $\partial V^*/\partial m$ is zero as well. Simply put, the foreign country is indifferent to the policy setting of the home country. Armed with one instrument, and facing only one macroeconomic target, it can achieve its objective perfectly regardless of the actions of the home country. If the home country were to contract its money supply, for example, this would raise inflation abroad. But the foreign country could simply offset this imported inflation by contracting its money supply. Doing so would entail no welfare costs because (by assumption) the government does not care about the effect on output. More generally, if each government had n targets and n instruments, then the Nash equilibrium would be as efficient as a coordinated regime.

4. Additive Uncertainty and the Gains from Coordination

The discussion thus far has assumed that policymakers face no uncertainty in choosing their optimal (coordinated or uncoordinated) monetary policies. In reality, however, there are likely to be several sources of uncertainty: exogenous shocks, lags in the collection of data or in the implementation of policies, imperfect control of policy instruments, and, perhaps most importantly, imperfect knowledge about the structure of the world economy.

Analytically, these various sources of uncertainty may be divided into two categories. *Additive* uncertainty refers to shocks which affect the level of output or inflation but do not change the policy multipliers. *Multiplier* or *model* uncertainty refers to shocks which change the reduced-form multipliers. In terms of the structural model of Chapter 2, additive shocks are the disturbances u, v, and w, while multiplier uncertainty arises from imprecise estimation, or changes in the structural parameters (or, of course, imperfect knowledge of the theoretical structure of the economy), and refers to uncertainty about α, β, ϕ, or η. This section examines how making the additive disturbances uncertain affects the welfare gains from coordination, and the next section analyzes the case of multiplier uncertainty.

Above, we assumed that policymakers observed the shock, s, before choosing their optimal policies. Suppose, instead, that the shock s is composed of two components, s^O and s^U, where $s^O(s^U)$ is observed before (after) the current period's monetary policy is chosen. The shock s^U has zero mean and variance σ_s^2. For analytic simplicity we maintain the assumption made at the end of the previous section that each policymaker has as many instruments as macroeconomic targets. The objective functions are thus given by:

$$V = Max - \left(\tfrac{1}{2}\right)E\{\pi^2\} \tag{1}$$

$$V^* = Max - \left(\tfrac{1}{2}\right)E\{\pi^{*2}\} \tag{2}$$

where $E\{\cdot\}$ is the expectations operator and where the expectation is taken over the stochastic shock, s^U. Since both governments have the same information set (they both observe s^O, and both know that the other is setting its policies on the basis of this information), there is no uncertainty about what the other government will do: the home (foreign) country observes $m^*(m)$.

The home country's first-order condition in the uncoordinated equilibrium is given by:

$$\partial V/\partial m = 0 \Rightarrow E\{\phi(\phi m + \eta m^* + s)\} = 0 \tag{3}$$

with a symmetric condition for the foreign country. Evaluating the expectations operator in (3), and noting that the multipliers ϕ and η are non-stochastic, yields:

$$m^N = m^{N*} = \frac{-s^O}{(\phi + \eta)} \tag{4}$$

with the associated welfare level:

$$V^N = V^{N*} = -\tfrac{1}{2}\sigma_s^2 \tag{5}$$

Comparing the monetary policy settings under uncertainty (4) to those without uncertainty (3.30) shows that additive uncertainty affects the optimal policies in a very simple way. The known stochastic shock, s, is just replaced by its expectation, s^O. This characteristic of the optimal program is known as *certainty equivalence* (see Simon, 1956) and obtains when the objective function is quadratic in the target variables and the targets are linear in the policy instruments.

Solving for the coordinated equilibrium in a similar fashion shows that the coordinated monetary policies may be written:

$$m^C = m^{C*} = \frac{-s^O}{(\phi + \eta)} \tag{6}$$

and the welfare level attained under coordination is:

$$V^C = V^{C*} = -\tfrac{1}{2}\sigma_s^2 \tag{7}$$

Comparing (5) and (7) to their no uncertainty counterparts (3.33) shows that purely additive uncertainty lowers the utility attained under both coordinated and uncoordinated regimes but has no effect on the *gains* from coordination (which are zero). One might suspect that this invariance is unique to the linear-quadratic framework. It turns out, however, that while certainty equivalence no longer holds when one assumes a more general functional form for either the utility function or the structural model, uncertainty which leaves policy multipliers unchanged does not alter the gains from coordination. Although the assumption of a quadratic penalty function and a linear model is ubiquitous in macroeconomics, examining the case of more general functional forms helps us understand why additive uncertainty has so little effect on the gains from coordination.

Accordingly, we now assume that the policymakers' objective functions are given by:

$$\mathcal{V} = \text{Max} - E\{\mathcal{U}(\pi)\} \tag{8}$$

$$\mathcal{V}^* = \text{Max} - E\{\mathcal{U}(\pi^*)\} \tag{9}$$

and the reduced form for the home country's inflation rate is:

$$\pi = \Phi(m, m^*) + s \tag{10}$$

At the uncoordinated equilibrium, the home government sets the partial derivative of its objective function with respect to its own instrument to zero:

$$\partial \mathcal{V}/\partial m = E\{(\partial \Phi/\partial m)\,\mathcal{U}'(\Phi(m, m^*) + s)\} = 0 \tag{11}$$

Unless $\mathcal{U}'(\cdot)$ is linear (i.e. $\mathcal{U}(\cdot)$ is quadratic) we cannot simply take the expectations operator "through" the equation. Indeed, except for certain special cases, it is not possible to obtain analytic solutions for the equilibrium monetary policies. Since the multiplier $(\partial \Phi/\partial m)$ is non-stochastic, however, it is possible to take this term outside the expectations operator to obtain:

$$\partial \mathcal{V}/\partial m = (\partial \Phi/\partial m)E\{\mathcal{U}'(\Phi(m, m^*) + s)\} = 0 \tag{12}$$

Next consider the effect on the home country of an expansion in the foreign country's money supply:

$$
\begin{aligned}
\partial \mathcal{V}/\partial m^* &= E\{(\partial \Phi/\partial m^*)\,\mathcal{U}'(\Phi(m, m^*) + s)\} \\
&= (\partial \Phi/\partial m^*)E\{\mathcal{U}'(\Phi(m, m^*) + s)\}
\end{aligned}
\tag{13}
$$

From (12), however, the term in curly brackets equals zero so that $\partial \mathcal{V}/\partial m^*$ is zero as well. Additive uncertainty has little effect on the gains from coordination because it does not change the nature of the policy spillovers from one country to the other.

5. Coordination Under Multiplier Uncertainty

Since structural parameters of a model cannot be estimated with complete precision – indeed they may change over time – any uncertainty about these parameters will be reflected in uncertainty in the policy multipliers. Moreover, there may be competing theoretical models of the economy, implying different domestic and transmission multipliers. Keynesian, Monetarist, and New Classical models, for example, predict very different impacts of monetary policy on both prices and output. Accordingly, it seems natural to assume that the policy multipliers $\{\alpha, \beta, \phi, \eta\}$ are not known constants but rather are random variables with means $\{\mu_\alpha, \mu_\beta, \mu_\phi, \mu_\eta\}$ and variances $\{\sigma_\alpha^2, \sigma_\beta^2, \sigma_\phi^2, \sigma_\eta^2\}$. If uncertainty about the reduced-form multipliers arises because there are competing models of the world economy (model uncertainty), each of which has some claim to being correct, then the mean and variance of any multiplier m is given by:

$$\mu_m = \sum_{i=1}^{k} \rho_i m_i \quad \sigma_m^2 = \sum_{i=1}^{k} \rho_i (m_i - \mu_m)^2 \quad m = \alpha, \beta, \phi, \eta \tag{1}$$

where it is assumed that there are k possible models of the world economy and where ρ_i is the probability that model i is the true model. If the multiplier uncertainty arises from individual structural parameters being uncertain, then the standard error of reduced-form multiplier becomes:

$$\sigma_m^2 = (\nabla m)' \Sigma (\nabla m) \tag{2}$$

where Σ is the variance-covariance matrix of the structural parameters and (∇m) is the gradient of the reduced-form multiplier with respect to the structural parameters.

In general the values of transmission multipliers and domestic multipliers will be correlated (particularly if the uncertainty stems from variations of the same structural parameters within a model). In fact, though, the assumption of uncorrelated multipliers is not grossly at odds with the data if one uses the twelve models surveyed in the Brookings (Bryant *et al.*, 1988) study as the sample. Correlations between the domestic and transmission multipliers for both inflation and output are generally very low. The only statistically significant correlation is between the domestic and transmission multipliers of the rest-of-the-world monetary policy on inflation. This correlation, moreover, stems from a single observation: the Liverpool model (see Minford,1984), which is an outlier in predicting that a very high proportion of a monetary expansion will be reflected in prices rather than in income. If this observation is dropped, the correlation across remaining models is close to zero and statistically insignificant. In any case, for expositional clarity, we assume that realizations of the domestic policy multipliers, α and ϕ, are independent of the transmission multipliers, β and η.

We begin with the case in which each government cares exclusively about inflation. (The appendix to this chapter treats the more general framework in which each government has n targets and n instruments.) The relevant objective functions are therefore:

$$V = \text{Max} - \left(\tfrac{1}{2}\right) E\{\pi^2\} \tag{3}$$

$$\mathcal{V}^* = \text{Max} - \left(\tfrac{1}{2}\right)E\{\pi^{*2}\} \tag{4}$$

but the expectation is now over the random variables ϕ and η (we go back to the assumption that the shock, s, is observed before policies must be chosen). Note that we are implicitly assuming that both governments hold the same expectation (both governments, for example, are assumed to have the subjective priors ρ across the competing models). Generalizing the analysis to different subjective expectations is straightforward, and does not alter the conclusions so long as each government's expected welfare is calculated using its own subjective probabilities.[11]

The first-order conditions of the uncoordinated equilibrium are given by:

$$\partial\mathcal{V}/\partial m = E\{\phi(\phi m + \eta m^* + s)\} = 0 \tag{5}$$

$$\partial\mathcal{V}^*/\partial m^* = E\{\phi(\phi m^* + \eta m + s)\} = 0 \tag{6}$$

Using the definition of the variance of a random variable, the reaction functions may be expressed as:

$$m^N = \frac{-\{(\mu_\phi\mu_\eta)m^{N*} + \mu_\phi s\}}{\sigma_\phi^2 + \mu_\phi^2} \tag{7}$$

$$m^{N*} = \frac{-\{(\mu_\phi\mu_\eta)m^N + \mu_\phi s\}}{\sigma_\phi^2 + \mu_\phi^2} \tag{8}$$

So the uncoordinated equilibrium is given by:

$$m^N = m^{N*} = \frac{-\mu_\phi s}{\sigma_\phi^2 + \mu_\phi^2 + \mu_\phi\mu_\eta} \tag{9}$$

As long as $\sigma_\phi^2 > 0$, monetary policy does not offset the inflationary shock fully because the more active the use of monetary policy, the greater the risk of increasing the variance of inflation.

At the coordinated equilibrium, each government maximizes the global social welfare function, yielding the following monetary policy settings:

$$m^C = m^{C*} = \frac{-(\mu_\phi + \mu_\eta)s}{\sigma_\phi^2 + \sigma_\eta^2 + (\mu_\phi + \mu_\eta)^2} \tag{10}$$

How do the coordinated and uncoordinated solutions compare? The first point to note is that as long as either $\sigma_\phi^2 > 0$ or $\sigma_\eta^2 > 0$ the coordinated and uncoordinated solutions differ. Since the coordinated equilibrium is the unique symmetric Pareto efficient outcome it must be welfare superior to the uncoordinated equilibrium. Thus there are gains to policy coordination. This is in sharp contrast to the deterministic case (3.33) where there is no incentive to coordinate policies as long as each government has as many policy instruments as it has targets. *Multiplier uncertainty itself, therefore, gives rise to welfare benefits from coordination.*

It is straightforward to calculate the circumstances under which the uncoordinated policy setting is overly contractionary. Begin by expressing the objective function as:

$$\mathcal{V} = -\tfrac{1}{2}\{(E(\pi))^2 + \sigma_\pi^2\} = -\tfrac{1}{2}\{(\mu_\phi m + \mu_\eta m^* + s)^2 + \sigma_\phi^2 m^2 + \sigma_\eta^2 m^{*2}\}$$
(11)

(an analogous decomposition exists for $\mathcal{V}^*$ of course). Using this decomposition of the objective function, it is easily shown that the home country's first-order condition at the Nash equilibrium implies:

$$\mu_\phi m + \mu_\eta m^* + s = -m\sigma_\phi^2/\mu_\phi$$
(12)

Consider, next, the spillover to the home country of a foreign monetary expansion:

$$\partial \mathcal{V}/\partial m^* = -\{\mu_\eta(\mu_\phi m + \mu_\eta m^* + s) + \sigma_\eta^2 m^*\}$$
(13)

Substituting the home country's first-order condition (12) into (13) gives:

$$\partial \mathcal{V}/\partial m^* = \frac{\{\mu_\eta \sigma_\phi^2 - \mu_\phi \sigma_\eta^2\}m^N}{\mu_\phi}$$
(14)

The uncoordinated equilibrium is overly contractionary if:

$$\partial \mathcal{V}/\partial m^* > 0 \text{ i.e. } \mu_\eta/\sigma_\eta^2 < \mu_\phi/\sigma_\phi^2$$
(15)

If monetary policy is negatively transmitted, then the Nash equilibrium is unambiguously overly contractionary in response to a positive inflation shock: an increase in the foreign country's money supply would lower both the level and the variance of inflation at home. If monetary policy is positively transmitted, however, then a foreign monetary expansion only benefits the country when condition (15) is fulfilled.

This condition is reminiscent of the the "comparative advantage" condition (3.11); the intuition here is similar. Suppose that the ratio μ_ϕ/σ_ϕ^2 is low; in that case, it is very costly – in terms of induced increase in the variance of inflation – to reduce the mean level of inflation. Therefore, at the uncoordinated equilibrium each country will have a high average inflation rate, and a high marginal disutility of inflation. A monetary expansion abroad raises the level of home inflation but lowers its variance.[12] When μ_ϕ/σ_ϕ^2 is low, however, the marginal disutility of a higher average inflation rate is very high so that the monetary expansion abroad lowers the home country's welfare.

Conversely, when μ_ϕ/σ_ϕ^2 is high, condition (15) is likely to be fulfilled: the low marginal disutility of the mean level of inflation at the uncoordinated equilibrium, implies that a foreign monetary expansion will raise the home country's welfare. Figure 3.4 illustrates the coordinated and uncoordinated reaction functions when there is model uncertainty and a negative mean transmission effect.

A slightly different way to understand this intuition is in terms of the mean-variance diagram developed by Brainard (1967), and the "conjectural variations" of the coordinated and uncoordinated equilibria.[13] Recall that, in the Nash equilibrium, each government believes that the other government will not respond to changes in its own monetary policy. In the (symmetric) coordinated equilibrium, in contrast, each government knows that any action on its own part will elicit an equal action by the other government.

From (11), the objective function can be written in terms of the mean level of inflation, μ_π, and its variance, σ_π^2. As depicted in Figure 3.5, the indifference curves – which are given by $\mu_\pi^2 + \sigma_\pi^2 = $ constant – are concentric circles, centered at (0,0). If monetary policy were not used to offset the inflationary shock, then the economy would be at the point (0,S) – with the mean inflation rate above the bliss point of zero. The

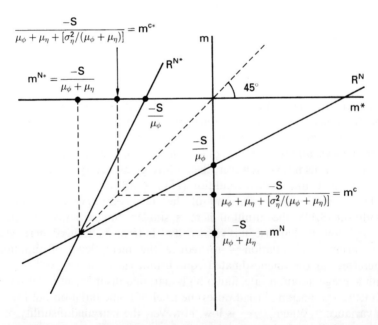

Figure 3.4 Coordinated and uncoordinated equilibrium (transmission uncertainty)

slope along any indifference curve can be found by setting its total derivative equal to zero:

$$dV = 0 \Rightarrow 2\mu_\pi d(\mu_\pi) = -2\sigma_\pi d(\sigma_\pi)$$

Therefore, the marginal rate of substitution between the mean level of inflation and its variance is given by:

$$MRS = \frac{d(\mu_\pi)}{d(\sigma_\pi)} = \frac{-\sigma_\pi}{\mu_\pi} \tag{16}$$

where

$$\mu_\pi = \mu_\phi m + \mu_\eta m^* + s \text{ and } \sigma_\pi = \sqrt{\sigma_\phi^2 m^2 + \sigma_\eta^2 m^{*2}} \tag{17}$$

Next we need to find the marginal rate of transformation between the level and the variance of inflation, MRT. To solve for the marginal rate of transformation we simply consider the effect on the ratio of μ_π/σ_π of a perturbation in the monetary instrument, dm. At the coordinated equilibrium, where the home government conjectures an equal response by the foreign government, we have:

$$d(\mu_\pi) = \mu_\phi dm^C + \mu_\eta (\partial m^{C*}/\partial m^C) dm^C = (\mu_\phi + \mu_\eta) dm^C \tag{18}$$

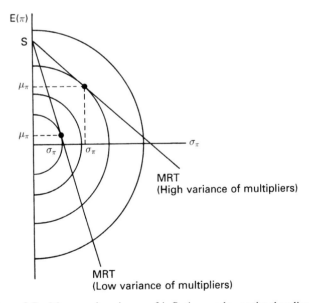

Figure 3.5 Mean and variance of inflation under optimal policy

where the second equality uses the fact $(\partial m^{C*}/\partial m^{C}) = 1$ at the coordinated equilibrium. Similarly,

$$d(\sigma_\pi) = \frac{\{\sigma_\phi^2 m^C dm^C + \sigma_\eta^2 m^{C*}(\partial m^{C*}/\partial m^C)dm^C\}}{\sqrt{\sigma_\phi^2 m^2 + \sigma_\eta^2 m^{*2}}} = \sqrt{\sigma_\phi^2 + \sigma_\eta^2}\,dm^C$$

The ratio, $MRT = d(\mu_\pi)/d(\sigma_\pi)$, is therefore: $\qquad\qquad$ (19)

$$MRT^C = \frac{(\mu_\phi + \mu_\eta)}{\sqrt{\sigma_\phi^2 + \sigma_\eta^2}} \qquad\qquad (20)$$

At an optimum, the marginal rates of substitution and transformation must be equated, as illustrated in Figure 3.5. As the variance of the policy multipliers decreases the MRT curve becomes more steep and the optimal policy involves bringing the the mean level of inflation closer to the bliss point of zero. In the limiting case in which there is no uncertainty, the MRT schedule becomes vertical, and the policymaker attains a zero inflation rate with no variance.

Consider, next, the Nash equilibrium. Policymakers again equate the MRS to the MRT but now, in calculating their optimal policies, each government ignores the feedback from the other country. The marginal rate of substitution is again:

$$MRS = \frac{d(\mu_\pi)}{d(\sigma_\pi)} = \frac{-\sigma_\pi}{\mu_\pi} \qquad\qquad (21)$$

where

$$\mu_\pi = \mu_\phi m + \mu_\eta m^* + s \text{ and } \sigma_\pi = \sqrt{\sigma_\phi^2 m^2 + \sigma_\eta^2 m^{*2}} \qquad (22)$$

The marginal rate of transformation at the uncoordinated equilibrium, however, differs from that at the coordinated equilibrium. Specifically, the expressions for $d(\mu_\pi)$ and $d(\sigma_\pi)$ now become:

$$d(\mu_\pi) = \mu_\phi dm^N + \mu_\eta(\partial m^{N*}/\partial m^N)dm^N = \mu_\phi dm^N \qquad (23)$$

$$d(\sigma_\pi) = \frac{\{\sigma_\phi^2 m^N dm^N + \sigma_\eta^2 m^{N*}(\partial m^{N*}/\partial m^N)dm^N\}}{\sqrt{\sigma_\phi^2 m^2 + \sigma_\eta^2 m^{*2}}} = \frac{\sigma_\phi^2 dm^N}{\sqrt{\sigma_\phi^2 + \sigma_\eta^2}} \qquad (24)$$

where use has been made of the Nash conjectural variation $(\partial m^{N*}/\partial m^N) = 0$. Thus the marginal rate of transformation, at the Nash equilibrium, is:

$$MRT^N = \frac{\mu_\phi}{\sigma_\phi^2}\sqrt{\sigma_\phi^2 + \sigma_\eta^2} \qquad\qquad (25)$$

Let us consider some special cases. Suppose that there is no uncertainty about the domestic multiplier so that σ_ϕ^2 is zero but that transmission effects are uncertain. From (15) we know that, in this case, the uncoordinated equilibrium is overly-contractionary. To understand why, observe from (25) that when there is no domestic multiplier uncertainty the MRT^N schedule becomes vertical, i.e. the government sets its monetary policy as though there were no multiplier uncertainty at all. This would be correct if there was no response by the foreign government to a contraction in the home country's money supply. In equilibrium, however, a monetary contraction by the home country will induce an equal contraction by the foreign country. Since transmission effects are uncertain this implies a higher variance in the home country's inflation rate. Because each government ignores the equilibrium feedback from the other government in choosing its uncoordinated policy, both governments offset the inflationary shock too actively; that is, the policy setting is too contractionary. Under coordination, each government takes account of the feedback from the other country. The home government, for example, knows that a monetary contraction will elicit an equal contraction by the foreign government. Since transmission effects are uncertain this, in turn, will raise the variance of the home country's inflation rate. Accordingly the MRT^C schedule is less steep than the MRT^N schedule and less use of monetary policy is made in bringing the mean value of inflation to the zero bliss point. As depicted in Figure 3.6, the points chosen in the coordinated and uncoordinated regimes are A^C and A^N respectively. The *equilibrium* outcome in the uncoordinated regime is not zero inflation with a zero variance but is given by the point $(\sigma_\pi^N, 0)$ where the mean level of inflation is zero but the variance is higher than it would be under cooperation. Note, of course, that the level of welfare attained at this point, V^N, is lower than under coordination, V^C.

Suppose, in contrast, there is no uncertainty about transmission effects so that σ_η^2 is zero but that the domestic multiplier is uncertain, $\sigma_\phi^2 > 0$. In this case, the relative steepness of the MRT^C and the MRT^N curves depends upon whether the transmission effect is positive or negative. Let us consider the case of a positive transmission multiplier. If the home government contracts its monetary policy to reduce inflation it knows that it will raise its variance. Under positive transmission, monetary contraction by the home country will be reinforced by the resulting contraction of the foreign country since both lower the mean level of inflation. By ignoring the foreign country's response, the home country would, at the uncoordinated equilibrium, believe that its policy had a smaller effect on the mean level of inflation than in fact it had. As a result, the uncoordinated regime involves too little use of policy in offsetting the inflationary shock and thus it has an expansionary bias in the

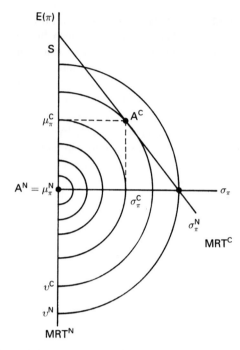

Figure 3.6   Uncertainty about transmission multipliers

face of positive inflation shocks. Diagrammatically, the MRT^N schedule is less steep than the MRT^C schedule so that governments acting non-cooperatively try to offset less of the inflation shock (see Figure 3.7).

Next consider the case of a negative transmission multiplier. Monetary contraction by the home country is partially offset by the foreign country's contraction. This implies that the MRT^N line is more steep than the MRT^C line. Therefore, the uncoordinated equilibrium, which ignores this response, involves too great a use of policy in reducing inflation, i.e. the uncoordinated equilibrium has a contractionary bias.

The important distinction between additive uncertainty, considered above, and multiplier uncertainty is that the latter alters the nature of the spillovers between the two countries. It is for this reason that multiplicative uncertainty alters the gains from international policy coordination. Unlike additive uncertainty, multiplier uncertainty gives an incentive to coordinate macroeconomic policies even where such an incentive did not otherwise exist. It bears emphasizing that the results of this section are quite robust. In particular, they hold for more general functional forms for the utility functions (although some risk aversion is, of course, required) and the assumed structure of the world economy (see

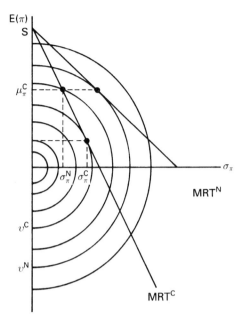

Figure 3.7 Uncertainty about domestic multipliers (positive transmission effect)

the appendix to this chapter). Likewise, the assumption that a common inflationary shock afflicts both countries is made purely for analytic convenience: all of the basic results continue to apply with asymmetric shocks.[14]

6. Multiplier Uncertainty and the Gains from Coordination

We have seen how the introduction of multiplier uncertainty may provide an incentive to coordinate macroeconomic policies even when such an incentive did not exist in the absence of that uncertainty. Next we ask a somewhat different question: Suppose that there exist welfare gains from coordination, does the introduction of multiplier uncertainty raise those gains or lower them? To answer this question we consider the more general case in which each government has one policy instrument, but targets for both inflation and output. The objective functions are therefore:

$$\mathcal{V} = Max - \left(\tfrac{1}{2}\right)E\{y^2 + \omega\pi^2\} \tag{1}$$

$$\mathcal{V}^* = Max - \left(\tfrac{1}{2}\right)E\{y^{*2} + \omega\pi^{*2}\} \tag{2}$$

and the reduced form of the model is:

$$y = \alpha m + \beta m^* \tag{3}$$

$$y^* = \alpha m^* + \beta m \tag{4}$$

$$\pi = \phi m + \eta m^* + s \tag{5}$$

$$\pi^* = \phi m^* + \eta m + s \tag{6}$$

The shock, s, is assumed to be observed before policies are chosen, and the expectations in (1) and (2) are taken over the random variables $\{\alpha, \beta, \phi, \eta\}$. As described above, at the uncoordinated equilibrium the home country maximizes $\mathcal{V}$ taking as given m^*. This leads to the following first-order condition:

$$\partial \mathcal{V}/\partial m = -\tfrac{1}{2} E\{\alpha(\alpha m + \beta m^*) + \omega\phi(\phi m + \eta m^* + s)\} = 0 \tag{7}$$

Evaluating the expectations operator in (7) yields the reaction function for the home country:

$$m^N = -\frac{\{(\mu_\alpha\mu_\beta + \omega\mu_\phi\mu_\eta)m^N + \omega\mu_\phi s\}}{\{\mu_\alpha^2 + \sigma_\alpha^2 + \omega(\mu_\phi^2 + \sigma_\phi^2)\}} \tag{8}$$

and analogously for the foreign country.

Solving the two reaction functions simultaneously gives the uncoordinated monetary policies:

$$m^N = m^{N*} = \frac{-\omega\mu_\phi s}{\mu_\alpha^2 + \sigma_\alpha^2 + \mu_\alpha\mu_\beta + \omega(\mu_\phi^2 + \sigma_\phi^2) + \omega(\mu_\phi\mu_\eta)} \tag{9}$$

In the coordinated equilibrium each government maximizes $\mathcal{V}^G$, which yields the following monetary policies:

$$m^C = m^{C*} = \frac{-\omega(\mu_\phi + \mu_\eta)s}{(\mu_\alpha + \mu_\beta)^2 + \omega(\mu_\phi + \mu_\eta)^2 + \sigma_\alpha^2 + \sigma_\beta^2 + \omega(\sigma_\phi^2 + \sigma_\eta^2)} \tag{10}$$

Uncertainty about the model's parameters necessarily reduces welfare in the coordinated regime. Since the uncoordinated regime is already a "second best" equilibrium, however, increased uncertainty could actually raise welfare.[15] In that case, model uncertainty would reduce the gains from coordination. (More precisely, uncertainty will decrease the welfare gains from coordination if it lowers welfare in the coordinated regime at a higher rate than it lowers welfare in the non-coordinated regime.)

To calculate the effects of model uncertainty we could substitute (9) and (10) into the utility functions and then calculate the derivative with respect to σ_α^2, σ_β^2, σ_ϕ^2 and σ_η^2. It is much simpler, however, to calculate the effect of model uncertainty on the gains from coordination by determining the effects of uncertainty on the inefficiency of the uncoordinated equilibrium. Consider the effect on the foreign country's welfare of a perturbation in the home country's policy setting, at the uncoordinated equilibrium. Again, it is useful to re-write the objective functions in terms of the means and variances of inflation and output:

$$\mathcal{V} = -\tfrac{1}{2}\{\mu_y^2 + \sigma_y^2 + \omega(\mu_\pi^2 + \sigma_\pi^2)\} \tag{11}$$

Substituting the structural model (3) – (6) gives:

$$\mathcal{V} = -\tfrac{1}{2}\{(\mu_\alpha m + \mu_\beta m^*)^2 + \sigma_\alpha^2 m^2 + \sigma_\beta^2 m^{*2} \\ + \omega[(\mu_\phi m + \mu_\eta m^* + s)^2 + \sigma_\phi^2 m^2 + \sigma_\eta^2 m^{*2}]\} \tag{12}$$

The home country's first-order condition implies:

$$\mu_\alpha(\mu_\alpha m + \mu_\beta m^*) + \sigma_\alpha^2 m + \omega\mu_\phi(\mu_\phi m + \mu_\eta m^* + s) + \omega\sigma_\phi^2 m = 0 \tag{13}$$

An expansion of the foreign money supply, at the uncoordinated equilibrium, has the following effect on the home country:

$$\partial\mathcal{V}/\partial m^* = -\{\mu_\beta(\mu_\alpha m + \mu_\beta m^*) + \sigma_\beta^2 m^* \\ + \omega\mu_\eta(\mu_\phi m + \mu_\eta m^* + s) + \omega\sigma_\eta^2 m^*\} \tag{14}$$

Substituting (13) into (14), gives:

$$\partial\mathcal{V}/\partial m^* = -\{(\mu_\phi\mu_\beta - \mu_\alpha\mu_\eta)(\mu_\alpha m + \mu_\beta m^*)/\mu_\phi \\ + (\sigma_\beta^2 + \omega\sigma_\eta^2)m^* - \mu_\eta(\sigma_\alpha^2 + \omega\sigma_\phi^2)m/\mu_\phi\} \tag{15}$$

Let $\Xi^N \equiv \partial\mathcal{V}/\partial m^*$ then we are interested in whether $\mathrm{sgn}(\partial\Xi^N/\partial\sigma_m^2) = \mathrm{sgn}(\Xi^N)$; $m = \alpha, \beta, \phi, \eta$. If $\Xi^N > 0$ then a monetary expansion by the foreign country would benefit the home country; if $(\partial\Xi^N/\partial\sigma_m^2) > 0$ as well, then an increase in multiplier uncertainty raises the benefit of this monetary expansion and therefore raises the gains from coordination. Conversely, if $\Xi^N < 0$, a monetary contraction benefits the home country and if $(\partial\Xi^N/\partial\sigma_m^2) < 0$, the benefit of the contraction is larger. Thus multiplier uncertainty increases the gains from coordination if $\mathrm{sgn}(\partial\Xi^N/\partial\sigma_m^2) = \mathrm{sgn}(\Xi^N)$.

First note that evaluated around a point of no uncertainty, Ξ^N is given by:

$$\Xi^N \equiv \partial\mathcal{V}/\partial m^* = -\{\mu_\beta(\mu_\alpha m + \mu_\beta m^*) + \omega\mu_\eta(\mu_\phi m + \mu_\eta m^* + s)\}$$

Substituting for the uncoordinated monetary policies:

$$\Xi^N \equiv d\mathcal{V}/\partial m^* = \frac{\omega(\mu_\beta\mu_\phi - \mu_\alpha\mu_\eta)(\mu_\alpha + \mu_\beta)s}{\mu_\alpha(\mu_\alpha + \mu_\beta) + \omega\mu_\phi(\mu_\phi + \mu_\eta)} \tag{16}$$

therefore $\text{sgn}(\Xi^N) = \text{sgn}(s)$.

Consider, first, an increase in domestic multiplier uncertainty: $d\sigma_\alpha^2 > 0$ (or $d\sigma_\phi^2 > 0$):

$$\partial\Xi^N/\partial\sigma_\alpha^2 = \frac{-\omega s\{\mu_\phi[\mu_\beta(\mu_\alpha + \mu_\beta) + \omega\mu_\eta(\mu_\phi + \mu_\eta)]\}}{\{\mu_\alpha(\mu_\alpha + \mu_\beta) + \omega\mu_\phi(\mu_\phi + \mu_\eta)\}^2} \tag{17}$$

Thus $\text{sgn}(\partial\Xi^N/\partial\sigma_\alpha^2) = \text{sgn}(\Xi^N)$ if and only if $[\mu_\beta(\mu_\alpha + \mu_\beta) + \omega\mu_\eta(\mu_\phi + \mu_\eta)] < 0$; negative transmission multipliers are sufficient, though not necessary for this condition to hold.

An increase in transmission uncertainty, $d\sigma_\beta^2 > 0$ or $d\sigma_\eta^2 > 0$ unambiguously increases the gains from coordination since:

$$\partial\Xi^N/\partial\sigma_\beta^2 = \frac{\omega\mu_\phi s}{\mu_\alpha(\mu_\alpha + \mu_\beta) + \omega\mu_\phi(\mu_\phi + \mu_\eta)} \tag{18}$$

so $\text{sgn}(\partial\Xi^N/\partial\sigma_\beta^2) = \text{sgn}(\Xi^N)$.

It is important to note, though, that these results only hold for a marginal increase in uncertainty, starting from no uncertainty. As the degree of uncertainty rises, the welfare gains from coordination may either increase or decrease, depending upon whether the uncertainty is about the domestic multipliers or the transmission multipliers. An increase in uncertainty about the transmission multipliers necessarily raises the benefits from coordination. This can be seen by comparing (9) and (10). We know that the uncoordinated policy setting tries to offset too much of the inflationary shock. As the degree of transmission uncertainty rises (σ_η^2 or σ_β^2 increases) the coordinated policy offsets even less of the inflationary shock. Therefore, the divergence between the coordinated and uncoordinated policies increases. Since the structural model facing policymakers in each regime is the same, a greater divergence between the coordinated and uncoordinated policies implies larger gains from coordination.[16]

In contrast, increases in uncertainty about the domestic multipliers (σ_ϕ^2 or σ_α^2) will eventually begin to reduce the gains from coordination. In the limit, as σ_ϕ^2 or σ_α^2 tends to infinity, the gains from coordination are completely eliminated.[17] Again, this can be seen from (9) and (10), as σ_ϕ^2 or $\sigma_\alpha^2 \Rightarrow \infty, m^C = m^N \Rightarrow 0$. With the coordinated and uncoordinated policies the same, there can be no welfare gains from coordination.[18] Quite simply, as the degree of domestic multiplier uncertainty becomes arbitrarily large it is optimal not to undertake any activist policies at all.

In that case, it clearly makes no difference whether policies are coordinated or not.

7. Summary

We examined here the theoretical case for international policy coordination. We showed that so long as governments have more targets than policy instruments there will be an incentive to coordinate macroeconomic policies. These gains from coordination, moreover, are similar to the gains from international trade in the Ricardian model.

We then considered the effects of various types of uncertainty. Additive uncertainty was shown to have no effect on the gains from coordination, since the uncertainty itself does not alter the nature of the welfare spillovers between countries. Multiplier, or model, uncertainty does substantially alter the gains from coordination. This was first shown by introducing model uncertainty under the assumption that each policymaker has as many instruments as targets. Under this assumption, there are no benefits to coordination in the absence of model uncertainty. Thus it is the uncertainty alone which can account for the welfare gains from coordination. Next, we considered the more general case in which targets outnumbered instruments. We were able to show that model uncertainty is likely to increase the gains from coordination. As the degree of model uncertainty increases, however, the effect on the gains from coordination depends upon whether the uncertainty is about domestic or transmission multipliers. A sufficiently high degree of uncertainty about domestic multipliers reduces the gains from coordination while increased transmission multiplier uncertainty raises the welfare gains. It is worth noting, in this context, that the multi-country multipliers reported in Chapter 2, and the theoretical ambiguities of the Mundell–Fleming model suggest that uncertainty about transmission effects is likely to dominate the uncertainty surrounding domestic multipliers.

Appendix

In the text, we show that when each country has one macroeconomic target and one policy instrument there are no gains from coordination. Introducing multiplier uncertainty into this framework, moreover, results in an incentive to coordinate macroeconomic policies. In this appendix we extend the argument to consider the case of multiple targets and an equal number of policy instruments. Consider a symmetric, two-country, model:

$$Y = \alpha M + \beta M^* \tag{A1}$$

where Y is a $(N \times 1)$ vector of target variables, M is a $(K \times 1)$ vector of domestic instruments, M^* is a $(K \times 1)$ vector of foreign instruments, α is a $(N \times K)$ matrix of domestic multipliers, and β is a $(N \times K)$ matrix of transmission multipliers. (Throughout we shall adopt the perspective of the home country and appeal to the symmetry assumptions to assert that identical effects and incentives exist for the foreign country.) Policy-makers have a utility function defined over the elements of Y:

$$V = Max \, \mathcal{U}(y_1, ..., y_N) \tag{A2}$$

In the uncoordinated equilibrium, the home country sets $\partial \mathcal{U}/\partial M = 0$:

$$\begin{pmatrix} \alpha_{11} & \cdots\cdots & \alpha_{1N} \\ \cdot & & \cdot \\ \cdot & & \cdot \\ \alpha_{K1} & \cdots\cdots & \alpha_{KN} \end{pmatrix} \begin{pmatrix} \mathcal{U}_1 \\ \cdot \\ \cdot \\ \mathcal{U}_N \end{pmatrix} = \begin{pmatrix} 0 \\ \cdot \\ \cdot \\ 0 \end{pmatrix} \tag{A3}$$

Or,

$$\partial \mathcal{U}/\partial M = \mathcal{A}\mathcal{U}_y(\cdot) = 0 \tag{A4}$$

where $\mathcal{U}_i \equiv d\mathcal{U}/\partial y_i, i = 1, ..., n$. Suppose that the home country has as many instruments as it has targets: $N = K$, then $\mathcal{A}$ is of full rank so that (A3) implies $\mathcal{U}_y(\cdot) = 0$ (an $N \times 1$ zero vector). The effect on the home country of a perturbation in the foreign country's instrument setting is given by:

$$\partial \mathcal{U}/\partial M^* = \begin{pmatrix} \beta_{11} & \cdots\cdots & \beta_{1N} \\ \cdot & & \cdot \\ \cdot & & \cdot \\ \beta_{K1} & \cdots\cdots & \beta_{KN} \end{pmatrix} \begin{pmatrix} \mathcal{U}_1 \\ \cdot \\ \cdot \\ \mathcal{U}_N \end{pmatrix} \tag{A5}$$

Or,

$$\partial \mathcal{U}/\partial M^* = \mathcal{B}\mathcal{U}_y(\cdot) \tag{A6}$$

From (A4), however, $\mathcal{U}_y(\cdot) = 0$ at the Nash equilibrium so that $\partial \mathcal{U}/\partial M^* = 0$ as well. Accordingly, the home country is indifferent to the policy settings of the foreign country at the Nash equilibrium. Hence there can be no gains from coordination.

Next suppose that there is multiplier uncertainty. Specifically, let there be J possible models:

$$Y^j = \alpha^j M + \beta^j M^* \qquad j = 1, ...J \tag{A7}$$

where the notation Y^j reads "the value of Y implied by model j." Policymakers are assumed to maximize expected utility, given by:

$$\mathcal{V} = Max \sum_{j=1}^{J} \rho^j \, \mathcal{U}(y_1^j, ..., y_N^j) \tag{A8}$$

The first-order conditions from the home country's optimization problem imply:

$$\begin{pmatrix} \rho^1\alpha_{11}^1 & \rho^2\alpha_{11}^2 & \cdots & \rho^J\alpha_{11}^J & \cdots & \rho^1\alpha_{1N}^1 & \rho^2\alpha_{1N}^2 & \cdots & \rho^J\alpha_{1N}^J \\ \cdot & \cdot & \cdots & \cdot & & \cdot & \cdot & \cdots & \cdot \\ \cdot & \cdot & \cdots & \cdot & & \cdot & \cdot & \cdots & \cdot \\ \rho^1\alpha_{k1}^1 & \rho^2\alpha_{k1}^2 & \cdots & \rho^J\alpha_{k1}^J & \cdots & \rho^1\alpha_{KN}^1 & \rho^2\alpha_{KN}^2 & \cdots & \rho^J\alpha_{KN}^J \end{pmatrix} \begin{pmatrix} \mathcal{U}_1(Y^1) \\ \cdot \\ \mathcal{U}_1(Y^J) \\ \cdot \\ \mathcal{U}_N(Y^1) \\ \cdot \\ \mathcal{U}_N(Y^J) \end{pmatrix} = \begin{pmatrix} 0 \\ \cdot \\ \cdot \\ 0 \end{pmatrix}$$

$$\tag{A9}$$

Under the assumption that the government has as many instruments as targets ($N = K$) and $J > 1$ (existence of multiplier uncertainty), the vector $\mathcal{U}_y(\cdot) \neq 0$. Hence the effect of the foreign country's instruments on the home country, at the Nash equilibrium, does not equal zero:

$$\partial \mathcal{U}/\partial M^* = \begin{pmatrix} \rho^1\beta_{11}^1 & \rho^2\beta_{11}^2 & \cdots & \rho^J\beta_{11}^J & \cdots & \rho^1\beta_{1N}^1 & \rho^2\beta_{1N}^2 & \cdots & \rho^J\beta_{1N}^J \\ \cdot & \cdot & \cdots & \cdot & & \cdot & \cdot & \cdots & \cdot \\ \cdot & \cdot & \cdots & \cdot & & \cdot & \cdot & \cdots & \cdot \\ \rho^1\beta_{k1}^1 & \rho^2\beta_{k1}^2 & \cdots & \rho^J\beta_{k1}^J & \cdots & \rho^1\beta_{KN}^1 & \rho^2\beta_{KN}^2 & \cdots & \rho^J\beta_{KN}^J \end{pmatrix} \begin{pmatrix} \mathcal{U}_1(Y^1) \\ \cdot \\ \mathcal{U}_1(Y^J) \\ \cdot \\ \mathcal{U}_N(Y^1) \\ \cdot \\ \mathcal{U}_N(Y^J) \end{pmatrix} \neq 0$$

$$\tag{A10}$$

Applying the envelope theorem, there exists a perturbation of the foreign country's instruments from their Nash equilibrium settings which raises the home country's welfare without any (first-order) effect on the foreign country. By symmetry, there exists a perturbation of the home country's instruments which raises the foreign country's welfare. A coordinated move from the Nash equilibrium will therefore raise both countries' welfare.

Notes

1   The main exception being the type of situation analyzed by Rogoff (1985) in which coordination can actually lower welfare.
2   That is not to say that the gains from coordination are not a function of the covariance between the shocks to each country but that, in general, there are gains from coordination regardless of whether both countries receive the same shock.
3   In particular, this result does not depend upon the "certainty equivalence" property of linear models combined with quadratic preferences.
4   Recall that by definition the variance of a stochastic variable is given by $\sigma_y^2 = E\{y - \mu_y\}^2 = E\{y^2 - 2y\mu_y + \mu_y^2\} = E\{y^2\} - \mu_y^2$ so $E\{y^2\} = \mu_y^2 + \sigma_y^2$. If preferences are not quadratic (and y is not normally distributed) then higher order moments will be important as well so that policymakers have even more targets.
5   This would occur if, in the absence of uncertainty, the coordinated strategy is more activist than the uncoordinated strategy. As shown below, increasing transmission uncertainty would make the coordinated policy setting less activist while leaving the uncoordinated policy unchanged. For small increases in transmission uncertainty, therefore, the coordinated and uncoordinated strategies become closer so the gains from coordination fall. Eventually, however, as the degree of transmission uncertainty increases, the coordinated policy will be less activist than the uncoordinated policy and the gains from coordination will be an increasing function of the degree of uncertainty.
6   Admittedly, the monetary contraction of the home country will raise output abroad. Since the foreign country has suffered an inflationary shock, however, the marginal cost of higher inflation outweighs the marginal benefit of higher output, so the home country's monetary contraction imposes a net welfare loss on the foreign country.
7   This is a result of the home country having optimally chosen m^N in order to maximize V. The result, known as the envelope theorem, is completely independent of the particular application at hand and holds for all optimization problems.
8   The second-order condition for an optimum ensures that the second-order effect will reduce welfare.
9   Likewise, in the Ricardian trade model, there will be no gains from trade if neither country has a comparative advantage relative to the other country. Hughes Hallett (1986b) and Martinez Oliva (1991) derive similar results.
10   In the face of a negative inflationary shock, the uncoordinated equilibrium is overly expansionary but is equally inefficient relative to the coordinated regime. One way to characterize the uncoordinated equilibrium, in this example, is that it is overly activist in response to inflationary shocks.
11   In the cooperative equilibrium, the global social planner would maximize:

$$V = \chi E(V) + (1 - \chi)E^*(V^*)$$

where $E(\cdot)$ is the expectation using the home country's priors and $E^*(\cdot)$ the expectation using the foreign country's priors.

12   Recall that the effect of foreign monetary policy on the variance of inflation is given by $\sigma_\eta^2 m^{*2}$. Since $m^{*N} < 0$, a foreign monetary expansion lowers $(m^{*N})^2$.

13   The discussion here draws on Ghosh and Ghosh (1991).

14   In fact, we do not even need the uncoordinated regime to be a Nash equilibrium; even if players are in a consistent conjectural variation (CCV) equilibrium similar results obtain.

15   As in trade theory, once we start from a Pareto inefficient equilibrium, the welfare effects of additional "distortions" are not unambiguous. See Bhagwati (1983).

16   If the uncoordinated policy offsets too little of the shock, relative to the coordinated policy, then an increase in transmission uncertainty would initially bring the coordinated policy closer to the uncoordinated policy, thus reducing the gains from coordination. Since the degree of activism of the uncoordinated equilibrium is unaffected by transmission uncertainty, while the activism of the coordinated policy is reduced by transmission uncertainty, eventually the coordinated policy must become less activist than the uncoordinated policy. At that point, a further increase in transmission uncertainty will raise the gains from coordination.

17   This is the case examined by Ghosh (1986) who concluded that model uncertainty can reduce the gains from coordination.

18   From (15) it would appear that increases in σ_α^2 or σ_ϕ^2 will continue to raise $\partial V/\partial m^*$ and will therefore raise the gains from coordination. While $\partial V/\partial m^*$ continues to be positive as $\sigma_\alpha^2 \Rightarrow \infty$ or $\sigma_\phi^2 \Rightarrow \infty$, eventually the second-order loss for the foreign country of a monetary expansion at the Nash equilibrium begins to dominate the first-order gain to the home country. Consider what happens as $\sigma_\phi^2 \Rightarrow \infty$. The welfare effect on each country of a symmetric monetary expansion at the Nash equilibrium is given by:

$$dV = \frac{\partial V}{\partial m} dm + \frac{\partial V}{\partial m^*} dm^* + \frac{\partial^2 V}{\partial m^2}(dm)^2 + \frac{\partial^2 V}{\partial m^{*2}}(dm^*)^2$$

These terms are given by:

$$\frac{\partial V}{\partial m} = 0; \quad \frac{\partial V}{\partial m^*} = \frac{\omega\{(\mu_\phi\mu_\beta - \mu_\alpha\mu_\eta)(\mu_\alpha + \mu_\beta) + \mu_\phi(\sigma_\beta^2 + \omega\sigma_\eta^2)\}s}{\{\mu_\alpha^2 + \sigma_\alpha^2 + \mu_\alpha\mu_\beta + \omega(\mu_\phi^2 + \sigma_\phi^2)\}}$$

$$\frac{\partial^2 V}{\partial m^2} = -\{\mu_\alpha^2 + \sigma_\alpha^2 + \omega(\mu_\phi^2 + \sigma_\phi^2)\} \quad \frac{\partial^2 V}{\partial m^{*2}} = -\{(\mu_\beta^2 + \omega\mu_\eta^2 + \sigma_\beta^2 + \omega\sigma_\eta^2)\}$$

Substituting these terms shows that a symmetric perturbation, $dm = dm^*$, around the non-cooperative equilibrium results in $dV \Rightarrow +\infty$ as $\sigma_\beta^2 \Rightarrow \infty$ or $\sigma_\eta^2 \Rightarrow \infty$ (with $dm > 0$) while $dV \Rightarrow -\infty$ as $\sigma_\alpha^2 \Rightarrow$ or $\sigma_\phi^2 \Rightarrow \infty$ (whether dm is positive or negative). Therefore, the benefits of coordination disappear with sufficiently large domestic multiplier uncertainty but increase with transmission multiplier uncertainty.

4

An Example: the Stock Market Crash of October 1987

1. Introduction[1]

In Chapter 3 we developed the theory of international policy coordination under uncertainty. In this chapter we elaborate on this theoretical framework by examining, in some detail, a specific episode of international policy coordination in which uncertainty appears to have played an important role. This episode is the response of the central banks of the major industrialized countries to the sudden drop of world equity prices in October 1987. During that month the fall in world stock prices ranged from 12 percent in Japan to more than 50 percent in Australia and Hong Kong; stock market prices in the U.S. and the U.K. plunged by more than 20 percent. We analyze the reactions of the central banks in terms of a model in which policymakers must take account of uncertainty concerning the preferences of investors across portfolio shares. These portfolio shares play the same role as model parameters, and they are assumed to be stochastic in the model presented here.

This view of investment decisions – that they contain a random component – is consistent with observed behavior in financial markets. Fluctuations in asset prices are not explainable solely by news concerning fundamentals, but are plausibly also the result of shifts in asset preferences. This is one interpretation that can be given to the evidence of variance bound tests, which suggests that the volatility of asset prices exceeds that of fundamentals.[2]

A recent example of sudden portfolio shifts is associated with the generalized crash of all major stock markets in October 1987, during which many investors dumped their shares on the market in an attempt to shift out of stocks into other assets at virtually any price.

Moreover, shifts in portfolio preferences that lead to sudden declines in stock prices are often associated with increased uncertainty, as evidenced by increased volatility of stock prices. This was the experience in the days following 19 October, 1987, and also in the August 1990 sell-off. From a macroeconomic policy perspective, the central concern in such an environment is that the real economy will be affected, due to declines in real wealth and increases in the cost of capital to firms. However, the effects of monetary and fiscal policies on ultimate target variables are also increasingly uncertain, since these policies operate through financial markets. The effects of uncertainty in domestic financial markets are compounded by uncertainty in foreign exchange markets: a sharp depreciation will have unfavorable effects on inflation, for instance, and may exacerbate loss of confidence.

Greater uncertainty in financial markets may increase the need for policy coordination because of a dilemma facing a central bank when responding to shocks. For instance, if the central bank responded to a stock market crash by loosening monetary policy, it might bring about a collapse in the value of the currency. Fear of such a possibility might well lead to an inappropriately timid monetary policy, in which monetary expansion was kept too low. In contrast, a coordinated reduction in interest rates by central banks would diminish the risk of sharp exchange rate movements, while neutralizing the unfavorable effects of a generalized shift out of equities. Consistent with this, the October 1987 crash led to coordination among central banks, or at least some consultation among them about the need to increase liquidity, and interest rates were lowered simultaneously in all major industrial countries.

More generally, variation over time in the amount of financial market uncertainty may explain why coordination tends to be episodic, rather than institutionalized.[3] In times of crisis, the outlook is very uncertain, as are the effects of policies; coordination of policies may decrease the danger of very bad outcomes. The incentives to pull together may be strengthened in such circumstances. It may be that in normal times gains from macroeconomic policy coordination are relatively small, consistent with estimates calculated using macroeconomic models.[4] However, great uncertainty about the effects of policies may make the gains from coordination larger, for instance when financial markets are turbulent and there is a danger that portfolio shifts may lead to large movements in asset prices and spillovers onto the real economy. Macroeconomic policy coordination may thus take on the character of "regime-preserving coordination" (Kenen, 1988) rather than a continuous attempt to maximize joint welfare, however defined.

The present chapter illustrates the effect of portfolio uncertainty on coordination with a simple model. The next section discusses both the events surrounding the October 1987 crash and the policies taken to avert a major economic crisis. Section 3 then presents a two-country, two-good model in which the portfolio preferences of investors between domestic money and an international equity are random variables,[5] goods prices are sticky, and the value of financial wealth affects real output. It is shown in section 4 that expected gains from policy coordination depend crucially on the perceived variances and covariances of the portfolio shifts. Section 5 concludes.

2. The Stock Market Crash of October 1987

February 1987 had seen the signing of the Louvre Accord at which the central banks of the G-7 had reaffirmed their desire for stable exchange rates. Yet by the middle of that summer, markets were beginning to doubt the degree of commitment of policymakers either to the objective of exchange rate stability or indeed to the coordination process itself. A continued deterioration of the U.S. trade balance was accompanied by downward pressure on the dollar. The U.S. trade balance figures released on 14 October 1987 were significantly worse than the market had expected and this triggered an immediate reaction in the stock market as investors feared that the Fed would raise interest rates to stave off the inflationary consequences of a sudden fall in the dollar. Momentum built up over the weekend and on Monday, 19 October, the Dow lost more than 500 points in a single day. But that was not the whole story since stockmarkets throughout the industrialized world, and not just in the U.S., reacted adversely. The worldwide nature of the stock price declines reflected deep rooted concerns of investors of the overall stability of the financial system in light of the apparent lack of coordination by the major players. Thus while the proximate cause of the stock market crash may have been the poor U.S. trade figures, the more fundamental cause of this generalized collapse seems to have been increased uncertainty. Destler and Henning (1989, p. 63) describe the context as follows:

> [O]pen verbal warfare among the G-7 apparently undermined the markets' confidence in finance ministers' and central bankers' ability to manage economic relations. These remarks came at a time, moreover, when the markets were already anxious about inflation, fearful that exchange rate stabilization would mean greater interest rate volatility, conscious of continuing poor monthly trade statistics, and shaken by the drop of several hundred points in the Dow Jones Industrial Average from its August peak of 2700. In combination with these factors, Baker's comments contributed to the worldwide stock market crash of 19 October 1987, which brought the Dow down 508 points in one day, to 1738.

In local currency terms, stock market indices declined in the period 30 September – 31 October by 21.5 percent in the United States, 26.1 percent in the United Kingdom, 22.9 percent in Germany, and 12.6 percent in Japan (see Figure 4.1 for a visual impression of the co-movements of major market indices). Other declines were even more dramatic: 58.3 percent in Australia and 56.3 percent in Hong Kong (FRBNY, 1988, p. 18). To a large extent, therefore, at least during this period world equity markets seemed globally integrated though the reasons for the

Figure 4.1   Stock market prices, January 1985 to September 1990
(*indices, 1985 = 100*)

common movement of prices are subject to dispute. To some extent, this may be the result of the gradual increase in interlisting of shares on different exchanges; however, correlations between the main trading zones increased by a factor of three from their levels in the previous nine months (Bertero and Mayer, 1989). Common movements in October 1987 did not seem to result from significant international investment flows, since cross-border selling was relatively small (FRBNY, 1988, p. 34). More fundamentally, then, increased economic integration and the globalization of information led to a common reassessment of equity prices in all major stock markets at the time of the stock market crash.

The question of whether equity prices move together (because they are good substitutes, for instance as a result of being claims to similar income streams) is logically separate from whether portfolio preferences for equities shift in the same way in different countries. Confirming a generalized shift out of equities, as opposed to a shift in investor sentiment in some countries but not in others, the sharp decline in equity values was associated with relatively small exchange rate movements (Figure 4.2). In the October 1987 crash, exchange rate movements do not seem to have been a consideration in the setting of monetary policies.[6]

What does seem to have been a major concern influencing policy was that the 1987 stock crash might be a replay of the 1929 one, which was followed by the Great Depression (Schwartz, 1988). In this regard, a high degree of uncertainty attached to the linkage between the stock market and the real economy – that is, the spending propensities of consumers, whose wealth had declined, and businesses, whose investment plans might be scaled back reflecting increased caution. Also subject to increased uncertainty was the stability of the financial system: whether the inability of individuals to cover margin calls, or of financial institutions to transact in financial markets, would lead to bankruptcies, and whether anticipation of such problems would cause the clearing and settlements system to collapse (Bernanke, 1990). It is hard to quantify the increase in uncertainty; however, one measure, the expected volatility implied by a comparison of equity and options prices, showed a dramatic increase in the United States in October 1987 (Figure 4.3).

Fear of financial collapse led governments and central banks to intervene by providing liquidity; moreover, they did so through closely coordinated actions. Of course, given the importance of the United States in world financial markets, the actions of the U.S. authorities were of paramount importance. The Federal Reserve reversed its tight monetary stance, flooding the system with liquidity; persuaded the banks to lend freely to securities firms; and monitored closely the situation, taking direct action where necessary (Bernanke, 1990). However, it did not act in isolation: ". . . we closely monitored the international ramifications of

Figure 4.2 U.S. Dollar exchange rates, January 1985 to December 1990 (*indices,*
1985 = 100)

the stock market crash . . . We communicated with officials of foreign
central banks . . ." (Greenspan, 1988, p. 92). In describing the role of G-7
policy coordination in this period, Dobson says:

> The risk in 1987 was that, in the absence of close G-7 cooperation, the
> financial crisis could have turned into an economic crisis. Had the
> authorities turned their backs and refused to cooperate among themselves,
> it is very likely that the crisis would have deepened. (Dobson, 1991, p. 128)

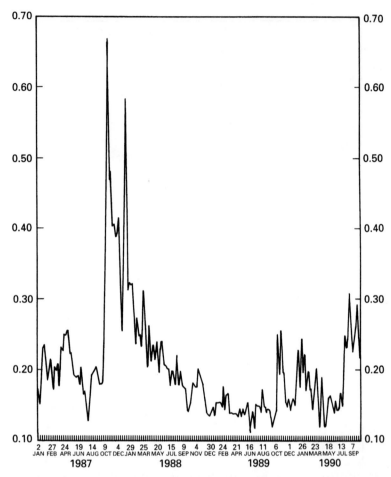

Figure 4.3   Implied volatility of S&P 500, 1 January 1987 to 12 October 1990

Source: Salomon Brothers. Calculated using the Black-Scholes option price formula, adjusted for dividend payments, and using the price of a put option on the Standard and Poor's 500 Stock Index and the interest rate on U.S. Treasury Bills.

What occurred was a generalized decline in short-term interest rates as all central banks expanded liquidity (Figure 4.4). To some extent, a decline in interest rates on government paper (though not on private claims) might be expected from a "flight to quality," but clearly central banks favored a fall in rates:

By helping to reduce irrational liquidity demands, and accommodating the remainder, the Federal Reserve avoided a tightening in overall pressures on reserve positions and an increase in short-term rates. In fact, we went even

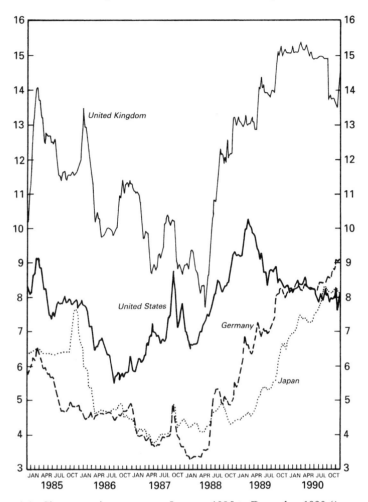

Figure 4.4   Short-term interest rates, January 1985 to December 1990 (*in percent per annum*)

further and eased policy moderately following the stock market collapse in light of the greater risk to continued economic expansion. (Greenspan, 1988, p. 90)

In sum, therefore, the October 1987 stock market crash is an example where there seems to be a direct link between increased uncertainty and increased policy coordination. In describing the risks to the clearing and settlement system posed by the October 1987 crash and other events, the Governor of the Bank of Canada stated:

These disturbances, and others since, were effectively contained through cooperation among major market participants . . . [T]he temporary injection of liquidity by central banks . . . helped to prevent the October 1987 financial problems from degenerating into solvency problems. In retrospect, it is clear that the global community has come altogether too close to situations where market difficulties could have been severe enough to inflict lasting damage on financial markets and even on national economies. (Crow, 1990, p. 2)

The model developed below suggests that the need for policy coordination might have been even greater if the portfolio shifts had been less symmetric, for instance if the fall in equity prices had been associated with severe weakness of the U.S. dollar. In this case, the Federal Reserve might have been much less willing to expand liquidity, for fear of adding to a run on the dollar. In cases such as these, a coordinated decline in interest rates in all countries would diminish the risk of disruptive exchange rate movements while minimizing the dangers of financial collapse.

3. A Macroeconomic Model with Money/Equity Substitution

In order to highlight the interaction between portfolio preferences, asset prices, and real activity, a simple, short-run model of two countries is specified. Portfolio preferences are stochastic, and can differ in the two countries. Longer-run questions such as wage adjustment and capital accumulation are ignored. Moreover, in this stylized model, there are only three assets: domestic money, foreign money, and a single equity, which is a claim to a composite consumption good (i.e. the equity pays a real return, which is assumed exogenous).[7] A feature of this model is that there is a single world equity price; this assumption reflects in extreme form the reality that co-movements of equity prices across countries have been very high in recent years – and especially so at the time of the October 1987 crash.

Each of the two countries is specialized in the production of a single good but consumes both. Utility is assumed to be Cobb-Douglas so that consumption shares are constant; in the home country, expenditure falls in proportion α on home goods and $(1 - \alpha)$ on foreign goods. Consumption is assumed to be proportional to the real value of financial wealth (W, to be defined later), so that

$$C = \lambda W / P \tag{1}$$

The consumption deflator P is a geometric average of the two goods prices, where p is the price of the home good, $p*$ the price of the foreign good, and s is the price of foreign currency:

$$P = p^\alpha (sp^*)^{(1-\alpha)} \tag{2}$$

Consistent with Cobb-Douglas utility, consumption is divided between the home good (C_1) and the foreign good (C_2) on the basis of fixed spending shares:

$$C_1 = \alpha(P/p)C \tag{3}$$

$$C_2 = (1 - \alpha)(P/sp^*)C \tag{4}$$

In what follows we will assume that for both the home and foreign countries, spending falls equally on the two goods so that $\alpha = 1/2$. Therefore, equations (2) and (3) can be written as follows:

$$P = \sqrt{(p)(sp^*)} \tag{5}$$

$$C_1 = 0.5(P/p)C \tag{6}$$

$$C_2 = 0.5(P/sp^*)C \tag{7}$$

Wealth is held in the form of money M, which is non-traded, and in international equities E, which are a promise to pay a given amount of the composite consumption good (which is the same in the two countries since $\alpha = \alpha^* = 1/2$), and for which there is a single world market. Money and equities are held in proportions m and $(1 - m)$; these proportions are random variables. The price of a real equity claim is q:

$$M = mW \tag{8}$$

$$qPE = (1 - m)W \tag{9}$$

Uncertainty in portfolio preferences is reflected in the variance of m. Shifts in domestic portfolio preferences may or may not be correlated with shifts in the preferences of foreign investors; the degree of correlation is shown below to be crucial to gains from coordination.

A symmetric foreign country has a similar structure, indicated by starred variables. Parameters are assumed identical, except the random portfolio share parameter, m^*, which may not be equal to m (in the next section the *distributions* describing m and $m*$ are, however, assumed to be the same). There is a single world equity price (i.e. $q* = q$) since both home and foreign equities pay returns in the same consumption basket. The counterparts of equations (1) and (5)–(9) are:

$$C^* = \lambda W^*/P^* \tag{1'}$$

$$P^* = \sqrt{(p^*)(p/s)} \tag{5'}$$

$$C_1^* = 0.5(sP^*/p)C^* \tag{6'}$$

$$C_2^* = 0.5(P^*/p^*)C^* \tag{7'}$$

$$M^* = m^*W^* \tag{8'}$$

$$qP^*E^* = (1 - m^*)W^* \tag{9'}$$

It is assumed that output prices are sticky, and that p and p^* are fixed in the short run; output is determined by demand:

$$y = C_1 + C_1^* \tag{10}$$

$$y^* = C_2 + C_2^* \tag{10'}$$

However, consumer prices can vary since the exchange rate s is flexible. Similarly, the price of equities q moves to equate the demand for equities and the outstanding stock of equity shares $K + K^*$, where K and K^* are the initial endowments of equities at home and abroad:

$$K + K^* = E + E^* \tag{11}$$

The exchange rate is determined by an equilibrium condition that the current account surplus equal the capital account outflow, which is equivalent to the condition that the distribution of equities between the two countries satisfies portfolio preferences. The net capital outflow CAP from the home country (i.e. net purchases of equities) is equal to

$$CAP = qP(E - K) \tag{12}$$

(which is of course equal, from (11), to $-qP(E^* - K^*)$, the inflow to the foreign country, which corresponds to net sales of equities). The current account surplus CUR is the excess of domestic output over domestic absorption (i.e. saving), or exports minus imports:

$$CUR = (y - C_1)p - s(y^* - C_2^*)p^*, \tag{13}$$

and the balance of payments condition is

$$CAP = CUR \tag{14}$$

4. Optimal Government Policy

In the context of this model, monetary policy has a role in cushioning portfolio preference shifts, which have real effects because prices are sticky and consumption depends on wealth. We will consider the optimal monetary policy of a government, or central bank, that desires to minimize deviations from target output – presumably its full employment level – and price stability, which implies that the price level equals its initial equilibrium value. As in Chapter 3 we postulate for reasons of tractability a quadratic objective function of deviations from bliss levels. We consider the optimal response of the money supply to a shock to the mean value of investors' portfolio preferences, in the face of uncertainty about these preferences. Thus, we consider a situation in which an initial portfolio shift is observed (as was the shift leading to the fall in equity prices on 19 October 1987), but there is uncertainty about *subsequent* shifts. Suppose that the home government's objective function is

$$V = Max - (1/2)E\{(y/\bar{y} - 1)^2 + \omega(P/\bar{P} - 1)^2\} \tag{15}$$

and similarly for the foreign government

$$V^* = Max - (1/2)E\{(y^*/\bar{y}^* - 1)^2 + \omega(P^*/\bar{P}^* - 1)^2\} \tag{15'}$$

We will assume that in initial equilibrium, money supplies and asset proportions are equal, so that $M = M^* = \bar{M}$ and $1/m = 1/m^* = \bar{n}$, and so $s = 1$, and $p = p^* = 1$. Consider a shift out of equities at home and abroad, so that now

$$E(1/m) \equiv E(n) = E(n^*) = \theta\bar{n}, \tag{16}$$

with $\theta < 1$. How does the optimal setting for monetary policy in the two countries, if each takes the other's policy as given, compare to the case of joint maximization of an equally-weighted global objective function V^G, where $V^G = 0.5(V + V^*)$? In the absence of uncertainty, it can be shown that the optimal response to such a shock will – not surprisingly – be to accommodate fully the increase in liquidity preference.[8] In this case, the appendix to this chapter shows that coordinated and uncoordinated policy settings are the same; they both involve an increase in the money supply equal to the increase in money demand, so $M = M^* = \bar{M}/\theta$. If there is no uncertainty, then in this model monetary policy can completely neutralize the negative output effects of the portfolio preference shock, and the uncoordinated and coordinated policies are the same. This is true because each government has as many targets as instruments; in this case, despite possible spillovers through the exchange rate, gains from policy coordination are zero.

However, if there exists uncertainty about portfolio preferences, then only in the case where the portfolio shifts in the two countries are expected to be perfectly correlated will the two policies be the same. It can be shown (see appendix to this chapter) that in general – unless the weight on inflation in the objective function is zero – the optimal uncoordinated policy will be too contractionary, relative to the optimal, coordinated solution. The reason for this bias is the externality associated with the exchange rate (Sachs, 1985): appreciation helps in moderating domestic prices, but exports inflation to the foreign country, and the latter effects are ignored in the absence of coordination. The difference between the uncoordinated and coordinated policies (derived in the appendix), and hence the gains from policy coordination, depend on both the common variance σ^2 of portfolio preferences and the correlation ρ between the two countries' portfolio preference shifts – directly in the first case, and inversely in the second:

$$\partial M^C / \partial \sigma^2 - \partial M^N / \partial \sigma^2 \propto (1 - \rho) \geq 0 \qquad (17)$$

and there are no gains from coordination when $\sigma^2 = 0$. Notice that the difference between the two policies increases monotonically as the correlation declines, and is maximized when their correlation is minus unity, i.e. they are perfectly negatively correlated. In this case, governments set policy with the risk that a monetary expansion may lead to a large exchange rate depreciation because portfolio preferences of domestic and foreign residents between money and equities are expected to shift in ways that reinforce their effects on the exchange rate. The depreciation is undesirable because of its price level effects.

This example provides an additional reason why policy coordination may be beneficial, compared to the traditional literature in which the effects of policies are assumed to be known. In Sachs (1985), for instance, uncoordinated monetary policies are too contractionary in response to an inflation shock because exchange rate appreciation improves the output/ inflation trade-off, and there are two targets and only one instrument. In the present example, the effects of policies are uncertain because of possible portfolio preference shifts, so that even if each government has as many instruments as targets it still has an incentive to coordinate. The fact that portfolio preferences are uncertain and that they contribute to the variance of the exchange rate makes uncoordinated policies over-contractionary in the face of an increase in liquidity preference.

5. Conclusions

The simple model presented above illustrates the link between uncertain portfolio preferences of private investors and the difference between coordinated and uncoordinated policies. Greater uncertainty makes coordination more desirable in this example where portfolio shifts generate variations in output and exchange rates. The analysis suggests that if the perceived degree of uncertainty varies over time – perhaps as described in recent articles, for instance by Flood, Bhandari and Horne

(1988) – then the incentives to coordinate policies will also vary. In particular, in situations of great uncertainty, where the prevailing international monetary system is threatened, policies are more likely to be influenced by shared goals.

In the particular source of uncertainty that is considered here – uncertainty on the part of policymakers about the portfolio preferences of private investors – the degree of correlation across countries of portfolio shifts between equities and money is crucial in determining the gains from policy coordination. That conclusion is likely to remain in more general models with a wider menu of traded assets, in which portfolio shifts may also occur between different countries' equities and bonds. Paradoxically, if portfolio shifts are expected to be correlated across countries – as was the case out of equities at the time of the October 1987 crash – they may not require policy coordination to the extent that less symmetric portfolio preference shifts would. Of course, what is important is policymakers' anticipations of the degree of correlation of portfolio shifts; these anticipations are unlikely to involve perfect correlation. Thus, uncertainty about the investors' preferences is at times likely to provide a powerful incentive to coordinate policies internationally.

Appendix: Solution of the Model

The solution for the variables that are of interest to us – we assume that policymakers have targets for domestic output and consumer prices – can be obtained as follows. Domestic output prices (but not consumer prices) are fixed in the current period. From (5) and (5′) in the text,

$$P^* = P/s \qquad (A1)$$

As a result, from (1), (8), and (A1)

$$C = \lambda(M/m)/P \qquad (A2)$$

$$C^* = s\lambda(M^*/m^*)/P \qquad (A2')$$

From the conditions for goods market equilibrium, (10) and (10′),

$$y = .5[\lambda M/m + s\lambda M^*/m^*]/p \qquad (A3)$$

$$y^* = .5[\lambda(M/m)/s + \lambda M^*/m^*]/p^* \qquad (A3')$$

Turning to equilibrium in financial markets, substituting (9), (9′) into (11) yields

$$qP = [(1 - m)M/m + (1 - m^*)sM^*/m^*]/(K + K^*) \qquad (A4)$$

Now the balance of payments equilibrium can also be expressed in terms of s and q; from (12)–(14):

$$qP(E - K) = .5\lambda(sM^*/m^* - M/m) \tag{A5}$$

Substitution of (9) and (A4) into (A5) yields an expression for s in terms of money supplies, portfolio preferences, and initial endowments of equities:

$$s = \{(1 - m)[K^*/(K + K^*)]M/m + .5\lambda M/m\}/$$

$$\{(1 - m*)[K/(K + K^*)]M^*/m^* + .5\lambda M^*/m^*\} \tag{A6}$$

In keeping with our assumption of symmetry, we further posit that initial endowments of the international equity are equal, so that $K/(K + K^*) = 0.5$. Therefore, the exchange rate can be written as

$$s = [(M/m)(1 - m + \lambda)]/[(M^*/m^*)(1 - m^* + \lambda)] \tag{A7}$$

Thus, for given portfolio preferences, the exchange rate is determined by relative money supplies; a shift out of equities into money (an increase in m) will tend to appreciate the currency (lower s). Using the expression for s, we can derive reduced-form expressions for domestic and foreign outputs. From (A3),

$$y = \lambda(M/m)\{[1 - .5(m + m^*) + \lambda]/(1 - m^* + \lambda)\}/p \tag{A8}$$

and from (A3′),

$$y^* = \lambda(M^*/m^*)\{[1 - .5(m + m^*) + \lambda]/(1 - m + \lambda)\}/p^* \tag{A8′}$$

We will assume that it is not possible to go short in equities, so that $1 - m > 0$ and $1 - m^* > 0$. Therefore, the terms in curly brackets in (A8) and (A8′) are positive, implying that an increase in the money supply in the home country increases output:

$$\partial y/\partial M > 0 \quad \text{and} \quad \partial y^*/\partial M^* > 0$$

while an increase in the desire to hold domestic money decreases it:

$$\partial y/\partial m < 0 \quad \text{and} \quad \partial y^*/\partial m^* < 0$$

In contrast, portfolio shifts abroad have the opposite effect (i.e. they are negatively transmitted); it can be shown that

$$\partial y/\partial m^* > 0 \quad \text{and} \quad \partial y^*/\partial m > 0$$

The first-order condition for optimal policy setting in the home country can be derived in the following way. Let $n \equiv 1/m$, $n^* \equiv 1/m^*$, and $F(n, n^*) \equiv [(\lambda + 1)n - 1]/[(\lambda + 1)n^* - 1]$, and note that both numerator and denominator of F are positive, from the assumption made above that portfolio shares must be positive. From equations (A7) and (A8) above,

$$\partial V/\partial M = -(1/2)E\{0.5M[n + n^*F(n, n^*)]^2/\bar{M}^2\bar{n}^2 - [n + n^*F(n, n^*)]/$$
$$\bar{M}\bar{n} + \omega[F(n, n^*)/M^*] - \omega[F(n, n^*)/M^*M]^{(1/2)}\} = 0$$

$$(A9)$$

Given the assumptions of symmetry, implying that $F(n^*, n) = 1/F(n, n^*)$, the foreign country's first-order condition is similar, and is not presented here. Consider an equal change in portfolio preferences in the two countries, such that the desired wealth proportion held in the form of money rises equally, i.e., n and n^* fall by the same amount. It is clear that, starting from the same position, the optimal policy response to the same portfolio shock will be the same in the two countries, so that $M = M^*$. Replacing M^* and M by M^N, the common uncoordinated policy setting, we obtain from (A9)

$$M^N = 2[\bar{M}\bar{n}]\frac{E[n + n^*F(n, n^*)]}{E[n + n^*F(n, n^*)]^2}$$

$$-(2\omega/M^N)\frac{\{EF(n, n^*) - E[F(n, n^*)]^{(1/2)}\}\bar{M}^2\bar{n}^2}{E[n + n^*F(n, n^*)]^2}$$

$$(A10)$$

If the two governments instead coordinate and minimize a joint objective function V^G that gives equal weights to V and V^*, then the first-order condition for the use of the home country's money supply instrument is:

$$\partial V^G/\partial M = E\left\{\frac{M[n + n^*F(n, n^*)]^2}{2(\bar{M}^2\bar{n}^2)} - \frac{[n + n^*F(n, n^*)]}{\bar{M}\bar{n}} + \frac{\omega F(n, n^*)}{M^*}\right.$$

$$\left. -\frac{\omega\sqrt{F(n, n^*)}}{\sqrt{MM^*}} - \frac{\omega F(n^*, n)}{(M^*/M^2)} + \frac{\omega\sqrt{(MM^*)F(n^*, n)}}{M}\right\} = 0 \qquad (A11)$$

Not surprisingly, the first-order condition for M^* is symmetrical, and therefore it will not be presented. Solving (A11) for the common coordinated money supply setting M^C,

$$M^C = \frac{(2\bar{M}\bar{n})E[n + n^*F(n, n^*)]}{E[n + n^*F(n, n^*)]^2}$$

$$-\frac{[\bar{M}^2\bar{n}^2\omega]}{M^C}\left\{E[F(n, n^*)] - \sqrt{E[F(n, n^*)]} - E[F(n^*, n)] + \sqrt{E[F(n^*, n)]}\right\}$$

$$(A12)$$

Equation (A12) simplifies further in the case (assumed here) where the distributions describing portfolio preference parameters are the same in the two countries, though not necessarily their realizations. In this case, $EF(n, n^*) = EF(n^*, n)$ and $EF(n, n^*)^2 = EF(n^*, n)^2$. Therefore, the term of (A12) between curly brackets is zero and the coordinated monetary policy is given by

$$M^C = \frac{2\bar{M}\bar{n}E[n + n^*F(n, n^*)]}{E[n + n^*F(n, n^*)]^2} \tag{A13}$$

In this case, though each country's objective includes inflation, and hence, indirectly, the exchange rate (and both countries' inflation targets are included symmetrically in V^G), the exchange rate plays no role in the coordinated monetary policy: the latter, given by (A13), is independent of the value of ω. What is the effect of increased liquidity preference in the two countries, under each policy regime? First assume absence of uncertainty. In this case, since $n = n^* = \theta\bar{n} < \bar{n}$

$$EF(n, n^*) = EF(n^*, n) = \sqrt{E[F(n, n^*)]} = \sqrt{E[F(n^*, n)]} = 1$$

and

$$E[n + n^*F(n, n^*)] = 2\theta n.$$

It can be verified from (A10) and (A13) that

$$M^N = M^C = \bar{M}/\theta \tag{A14}$$

so that both policy regimes fully accommodate the shift in liquidity preference. In the absence of uncertainty, no negative exchange rate repercussions are to be feared from a symmetric portfolio shift.

Next, consider the effect of an increase in uncertainty in the two policy regimes, starting from the initial position with a common monetary policy stance $M = M^* = \bar{M}$, and letting $E(n) = E(n^*) = \bar{n}$. The only element of uncertainty will relate to the common variance of n, i.e.

$$E(n - \bar{n})^2 = E(n^* - \bar{n})^2 = \sigma^2.$$

In order to evaluate expressions on the right hand sides of (A10) and (A13), first take a second-order Taylor series expansion of $F(n, n^*)$ and $\sqrt{F(n, n^*)}$ around $E(n) = \bar{n}$, and $E(n^*) = \bar{n}$, and take expectations (letting $\text{var}(n) = \text{var}(n^*) = \sigma^2$, $\text{cov}(n, n^*) = \rho\sigma^2$, and $\beta = [(\lambda + 1)\bar{n} - 1]^{-2}$):

$$EF(n, n^*) \cong 1 + (\lambda + 1)^2\beta(1 - \rho)\sigma^2 \tag{A15}$$

$$E\sqrt{F(n, n^*)} \cong 1 + (\lambda + 1)^2\beta(1 - \rho)\sigma^2/4 \tag{A16}$$

From approximations (A15) and (A16) it can be shown that

$$EF(n, n^*) - E\sqrt{F(n, n^*)} \cong 3(\lambda + 1)^2 \beta(1 - \rho)\sigma^2/4 \geq 0 \qquad \text{(A17)}$$

$$E[n + n^* F(n, n^*)] \cong 2\bar{n} + (\lambda + 1)\beta\sigma^2(1 - \rho) \qquad \text{(A18)}$$

$$E[n + n^* F(n, n^*)]^2 \cong 4\bar{n}^2 + 4\sigma^2 + 2[4(\lambda + 1)\bar{n} - 1]\beta\sigma^2(1 - \rho) \qquad \text{(A19)}$$

From (A10), (A13), and (A15)–(A19), it can be shown that increased uncertainty (a larger σ^2) makes both uncoordinated and coordinated policies more contractionary, but it increases the gap between them (unless $\rho = 1$): evaluated at $\sigma^2 = 0$,

$$
\partial M^C/\partial\sigma^2 - \partial M^N/\partial\sigma^2 = \frac{(\omega/2)\bar{M}}{(1 + \omega/2)}[(3/4)(\lambda + 1)
$$
$$
+ 1/2\bar{n}](\lambda + 1)\beta(1 - \rho) \geq 0 \qquad \text{(A20)}
$$

Thus, a moderate amount of uncertainty will imply gains from coordination. The general case is however ambiguous; starting from a position where $\sigma^2 > 0$, the effect of additional uncertainty cannot be signed.

Notes

1 This chapter draws heavily on Masson (1992).
2 For such evidence, see Shiller (1981). Whether variance bounds tests actually demonstrate the existence of excess volatility has been questioned, however; see, for instance, Flavin (1983) and Flood and Hodrick (1986).
3 The terminology is due to Artis and Ostry (1986).
4 For instance, Oudiz and Sachs (1984).
5 A number of articles have included equity markets in macroeconomic models, for instance Diamond (1967) and Helpman and Razin (1978). In the present chapter, there is no attempt to model capital accumulation, or to relate the riskiness of equities to technological uncertainty. Instead, it is the risk related to shifts in portfolio preferences that is at issue here.
6 They are not mentioned, for instance, in Alan Greenspan's testimony at hearings on "Black Monday" held by the U.S. Senate Committee on Banking, Housing and Urban Affairs, 2–5 February, 1988. See Greenspan (1988).
7 Thus, the "fundamentals" are not the cause of asset price volatility. A more complicated model could make both production technology and portfolio preferences stochastic.
8 This is the case in this model because, though there are two targets and only one instrument, effects of portfolio shifts (if known) on both targets can be neutralized by varying the money supply. In effect, there is no conflict between

the twin objectives of price and output stability. Hence, if the welfare function was maximized initially, it would continue to be so after changing the money supply appropriately.

5

Alternative Empirical Models of the Open Economy

1. Introduction

We have argued in previous chapters that the effect of multiplier uncertainty, far from eliminating the welfare gains from coordination, may in fact increase them. Specifically, the effect of uncertainty itself will be to raise the *ex ante* expected welfare gain from coordinating macroeconomic policies. As discussed in Chapter 3, introducing uncertainty into a framework in which there already exist gains from coordination has potentially ambiguous effects. There is a presumption, however, that uncertainty will raise these gains from coordination as long as transmission effects are more uncertain than domestic multipliers. Ultimately, though, whether uncertainty raises or lowers the gains from coordination is an empirical matter which cannot be resolved by theoretical arguments alone. A second shortcoming of a purely theoretical discussion is that we are forced to use the *ex ante* expected utility as our welfare criterion; this is the appropriate criterion when policymakers are assumed to know the correct probability distribution function of the models. But we might also be interested in the actual, *ex post*, welfare attained when policymakers are systematically wrong in their beliefs over the true model (i.e. when their subjective priors over the models do not coincide with the objective probabilities of the models being correct). This cannot be done in the theoretical framework because we do not have specific alternative models.

The purpose of this chapter is to estimate a number of different macroeconomic models of the world economy which will be used in Chapter 6 where we present empirical estimates of the gains from coordination under uncertainty. There are, of course, a very large number of possible models of the world economy. Our choice of models is dictated in part by the computational burden of simulating these models when we calculate optimal coordinated and uncoordinated policies, below. Nonetheless, the models included here have been chosen to represent very diverse economic theories and philosophies and they have quite different implications for the role of policy in controlling the economy. Many of the issues involved in formulating econometric models are quite technical so section 2 of this chapter presents a broad overview. Section 3 discusses the actual estimation of the models, while section 4 describes their key properties.

2. Overview

The discipline of macroeconomics dates back to John Maynard Keynes, and the *General Theory* provided the impetus for the collection of data by official agencies that makes possible the construction of empirical macroeconomic models. Since the 1940s such models have helped to guide economic policy choice;[1] since the 1970s vast increases in computing power have led to an explosion in the number of macro models.[2] The number of different models may however give a false impression of diversity, since models built at about the same time are often based on similar theories, are estimated on the same data, and therefore have roughly similar properties. When one surveys models of the post-war period, models are likely to differ due to differences in vintage, and to reflect the changing consensus in macroeconomic theory. In what follows, an attempt is made to identify the main currents that have guided the construction of empirical macromodels, and to represent those currents in a small number of alternative models estimated using the same data set. In this way, one obtains a sense of the degree of uncertainty facing policymakers.

It could be objected that some of the early model vintages are no longer relevant, since our knowledge of economics has increased since then. However, it is not so obviously true that we have progressed very much, as witnessed by the continued existence of Keynesian and classical schools of thought.[3] Another objection is that use of a common data set should permit the application of standard nested or non-nested tests that would allow one to discriminate among the theories. However, the theories are not so narrowly focused that we can unequivocally reject one in favor of another; changes in lag length or the addition of other explanatory variables may make the predictive power of a given theory greater without being inconsistent with it. It will be argued below that the alternative models do give a good sense of the diversity across views of the world, and so it will be of interest to examine their alternative implications for policy and their explanations for the macroeconomic developments of recent decades. Our purpose is not so much to test models but to give an idea of the uncertainty facing policymakers.[4]

Not surprisingly, early post-war models were inspired by the General Theory and Hicks' interpretation of Keynes, the IS-LM model.[5] These formulations concentrated on real output effects, on the assumption that wages and prices were rigid. The Keynesian model was fleshed out in the mid-1950s by an equation for inflation that related the rate of change of wages to the unemployment rate – the so-called Phillips curve (Phillips, 1958). Of early empirical models embodying this framework, those of Klein and various collaborators are especially noteworthy.[6]

The early macroeconomic consensus was soon to be attacked from various sides. Monetarists questioned the lack of emphasis on inflation and monetary policy, but their methodological criticisms were later viewed as less fundamentally about the structure of models than about the values to be assigned to key parameters.[7] However, their concern that the inflationary consequences of expansionary aggregate demand policies were underestimated led to a new consensus that no long-run trade-offs between output and inflation existed – that is, that the Phillips curve was vertical.[8] This was implemented by explicitly including a proxy for inflation expectations on the right-hand side of an equation for the rate of change of wages, and constraining its coefficient to unity.

Another attack, the "rational expectations revolution," was both methodological and inspired by the conviction that activist policy was ineffective.[9] Even if the Phillips curve includes a unit coefficient on expected inflation, there still remains a short-run trade-off between output and inflation that can be exploited by monetary policy if expectations are based on a distributed lag over past inflation. Denying the value of activist policy, Milton Friedman had argued that the money supply should be made to grow at a constant rate – the "k percent rule" (Friedman, 1948). Rational expectations theorists explained the ineffectiveness of monetary policy as follows: if wage bargainers formed their expectations of inflation in a rational way, they would know that the authorities were attempting to exploit the short-run trade-off, and would react accordingly, nullifying the stimulus to output that would otherwise result from expansionary monetary policy. Only unexpected, i.e. non-systematic, policy changes would have real effects. A key to this result is that agents form "rational expectations," in the sense that those expectations are consistent with the implications of the model, rather than being based on some mechanical extrapolation of past data.

Rationality of expectations, as defined above, was soon understood not to be sufficient to eliminate the effectiveness of monetary policy.[10] In the Lucas, and Sargent and Wallace, models, the further assumption is made that wages and prices are perfectly flexible, in that they can move instantaneously to clear markets. Models in which expectations are rational but in which contracts prevent wages from being adjusted instantaneously to new information retain a role for activist monetary policy. One strand of subsequent macroeconomic research has explored the implications of overlapping contracts as a source of imperfect flexibility of wages and prices in the context of rational expectations.[11] Another strand of research has however continued the assumption of nominal flexibility, and instead explored the role of real shocks rather than monetary phenomena as an explanation for macroeconomic fluctuations.[12]

We estimate four structural models (denoted A to D) which try to capture these various ideas about the unemployment/inflation trade-off as well as views on the determination of potential output. The models apply to two regions: the United States and an aggregation of the remaining OECD countries (ROW). Each region has an aggregate demand curve and an aggregate supply function (or a Phillips curve), and a money demand function. The consumer price index is defined to be a weighted average of domestic and foreign prices; and an interest parity condition links the two regions. Model A is a standard Mundell–Fleming model with a forward-looking exchange rate (see Dornbusch, 1976). Prices are sticky and inflation expectations are backward looking so that monetary policy can affect output in the short-run. The unit coefficient on expected inflation in the Phillips curve, however, ensures that there is no long-run trade-off between output and inflation. Model B is similar to model A, but the coefficient on expected inflation is not constrained to unity. As a result, the model implies that there is a long-run trade-off between output and inflation. Model C is quite different from the other models. In the tradition of the New Classical School prices are assumed to be fully flexible so that monetary policy has no effect on output. All of these models assume that potential output may be modeled by a deterministic time trend. Recent work by macro-economists, however, challenges this view. In particular, potential output is thought to exhibit a stochastic trend. This changes the stabilization problem significantly since the bliss level to which output should be targeted shifts stochastically each period. Accordingly, we include a stochastic trend for output in model D. Model D also includes an error correction money demand function rather than the standard Cagan money demand function. Table 5.1 summarizes the features of the four models. For our simulations in Chapter 6 we also want an "agnostic" model; that is, one which imposes no structural restrictions on the parameters. Our last "model," therefore, is a simple vector autoregression (VAR).[13]

Table 5.1 Estimated models

	Sticky prices	Long-run output/inflation trade-off	Potential output	Money demand
Model A	yes	no	deterministic	Cagan
Model B	yes	yes	deterministic	Cagan
Model C	no	no	deterministic	Cagan
Model D	yes	no	stochastic	error correction

3. Estimation

In what follows, we describe the estimation of simple models that contain the main structural features of the mainstream macroeconomic models discussed above. These models are simple enough to be tractable for policy coordination experiments, for instance, yet reflect some of the key structural controversies in economics over the past few decades. The models are specified in terms of a two-country world, where the first country is the United States, the second "country" is proxied by the rest of the industrialized world (ROW). Clearly, we are leaving out an empirically important part of the global economy: the part that includes newly-industrializing economies, mainly in Asia (Korea, Taiwan, Singapore, and Hong Kong), developing countries in Latin America, Asia, and Africa, and centrally planned (or formerly so) economies – countries in eastern Europe, the former USSR, and China.

The structural models

We begin by describing the broad details of the alternative structural models, which are labelled models A through D, and the alternative forms of their equations, which are reported in Table 5.2. The first of the models (Model A) reflects the standard open-economy model that emerged from the neo-classical synthesis and the rational expectations revolution. Mundell (1960) and Fleming (1962) formulated a simple model to examine the transmission of monetary and fiscal policy changes in a world of perfect capital mobility.[14] This model was extended by Dornbusch (1976) to incorporate rational exchange rate expectations. Oudiz and Sachs (1985) use such a model to consider effects of policy coordination, albeit with imposed coefficients. The model has been estimated in various alternative forms by West (1987) Papell (1989), and

Table 5.2 Equations of alternative models

U.S. Aggregate Demand
$$Q = q_0 + q_1(P - E - P^*) + q_2 Q^* + q_3(I - P_{+1} + P) + q_4 T + q_5 G \tag{1}$$
U.S.Money Demand
  Lagged adjustment:
$$M - P^C = m_0 + m_1 Q + m_2 I + m_3(M_{-1} - P^C_{-1}) \tag{2}$$
  Error correction (Model D)
$$\Delta(M - P) = m_0 + m_1 \Delta Q + m_2 \Delta I + m_3 \hat{U}_{-1} \tag{2'}$$
U.S. Output Price
  Phillips Curve ($p_1 = 1$ in Model A)
$$P - P_{-1} = p_0 + p_1(P^C_{-1} - P^C_{-2}) + p_2(Q_{-1} - \hat{Q}_{-1}) + p_3(Q_{-1} - Q_{-2}) \tag{3}$$
  Supply curve (Model C)
$$Q = p_0 + p_1(P^C - P) + \hat{Q} \tag{3'}$$
U.S. Consumer Price
$$P^C = \alpha P + (1 - \alpha)(P^* + E) \tag{4}$$
ROW Aggregate Demand
$$Q^* = q_0^* + q_1^*(P - E - P^*) + q_2^* Q + q_3^*(I^* - P_{+1}^* + P^*) + q_4^* T + q_5^* G^* \tag{5}$$
ROW Money Demand
  Lagged adjustment:
$$M^* - P^{C*} = m_0^* + m_1^* Q^* + m_2^* I^* + m_3^*(M_{-1}^* - P_{-1}^{C*}) \tag{6}$$
  Error correction (Model D)
$$\Delta(M^* - P^*) = m_0^* + m_1^* \Delta Q^* + m_2^* \Delta I^* + m_3^* \hat{U}_{-1}^* \tag{6'}$$
ROW Output Price
  Phillips Curve ($p_1^* = 1$ in Model A)
$$P^* - P_{-1}^* = p_0^* + p_1^*(P_{-1}^{C*} - P_{-2}^{C*}) + p_2^*(Q_{-1}^* - \hat{Q}_{-1}^*) + p_3^*(Q_{-1}^* - Q_{-2}^*) \tag{7}$$
  Supply curve (Model C)
$$Q^* = p_0^* + p_1^*(P^{C*} - P^*) + \hat{Q}^* \tag{7'}$$
ROW Consumer Price
$$P^{C*} = \alpha^* P^* + (1 - \alpha^*)(P - E) \tag{8}$$
Exchange Rate
$$E_{+1} = E - I - I^* \tag{9}$$
Variables
(Unstarred variables refer to the U.S., starred variables to the ROW. All variables are in logarithms except I and T).

E = nominal effective exchange rate (increase indicates dollar depreciation)
G = government spending on goods and services (National Accounts basis)
I = short-term interest rate
M = monetary base
P = GDP deflator
P^C = consumer price index
Q = output (GDP)
$\hat{Q}$ = estimate of potential output))
T = time trend))
$\hat{U}$ = residual from static regression of real money balances ($M - P$) on real output (Q) and the nominal interest rate (I)

Ghosh and Masson (1991). The sharp contrast between forward-looking exchange markets and backward-looking product and labor markets is made for analytical convenience, in order to limit the number of non-predetermined, or "jumping," variables.

The form of the inflation equation can be derived from wage and price equations as follows. Suppose that the change in the log of the wage rate (W) depends on expected inflation (π) and the unemployment rate $(L - E)/L$ where L is labor force and E is employment, and that unemployment is proportional to the gap between the logs of actual and potential output, $Q - \bar{Q}$. So

$$\Delta W = a + b(Q - \bar{Q}) + c\pi + e \tag{1}$$

where a, b, c are coefficients and e is a stationary random variable. The labor force is assumed to grow at exogenous rate η, while productivity grows at rate ρ, so potential output can be written:

$$\Delta \bar{Q} = \beta \tag{2}$$

where $\beta = \eta + \rho$. Output prices are assumed to be equal to a markup over normalized unit labor costs in the previous period, that is (in logs), wages minus normal productivity $\bar{Q} - L$ with the markup assumed to be proportional to the output gap:

$$P = d(Q_{-1} - \bar{Q}_{-1}) + (W_{-1} - \bar{Q}_{-1} + L_{-1}) \tag{3}$$

Substituting (1) and (2) into (3), after differencing the latter, yields

$$\Delta P = a' + d\Delta Q_{-1} + b(Q - \bar{Q})_{-1} + c\pi_{-1} + u \tag{4}$$

where $a' = a - (1 + d)\rho - d\eta$ and $u = e_{-1} - (1 + d)\varepsilon_{-1}$. This is the form of the inflation equation in models A, B, and D.

Models A–C make the further assumption that potential output is a deterministic trend and that actual output exhibits stationary fluctuations around potential output. In this case, potential output can be estimated from a regression of actual output on time:

$$Q = \alpha + \beta T + \delta \tag{5}$$

and $\bar{Q}$ can be proxied by $\hat{Q} = \hat{\alpha} + \hat{\beta}T$.

Model A has the "natural rate" property, in that the long-run growth rate of output is independent of the rate of inflation. The natural rate property is the result of a parameter restriction, that expected inflation affects actual inflation with a coefficient of unity. More generally, expected and lagged actual inflation could have coefficients summing to one, so that the equation contains a unit root: essentially, the equation in this form explains the acceleration of inflation, not its level. Earlier models, which had guided policy in the 1950s and 1960s, had taken for granted that aggregate demand stimulus would durably increase output, at the expense of some additional inflation, but that the increase of inflation was limited. Model B relaxes this natural rate restriction by allowing a freely-estimated coefficient on lagged inflation, which proxies expected inflation in the model.

Model B implies a stable trade-off between inflation and unemployment, in contrast to Model A, which implies that lowering unemployment below the natural rate (or, equivalently, raising output permanently above its full-capacity level) produces accelerating rates of inflation.

Model C departs from the tradition of the Phillips curve, embodied in Models A and B. Lucas (1972) presented a different basis for models of aggregate supply, one in which only inflation surprises are positively related to output stimulus. Nominal variables are perfectly flexible, but output increases are associated with unexpected inflation because individual workers and firms confuse a general price increase with a relative price increase – i.e. they think that demand for their labor or output good has risen. In Model C, aggregate supply depends on the price of domestic output relative to the consumption price (a weighted average of domestic and foreign output prices), plus an error term that reflects the effects of inflation surprises.

Model D incorporates information about the long-run comovements of variables using tests described in the next section. Recently, a considerable literature has considered whether output exhibits stationary fluctuations around a deterministic trend (as is assumed by models A through C), or instead, exhibits a unit root, meaning that the trend in output is stochastic (see Nelson and Plosser; 1982; Campbell and Mankiw, 1987; Stock and Watson, 1988; and Blanchard and Quah, 1989). The significance of the unit root property is that in this case innovations to technology tend to be permanent, and so the path of output is permanently shifted up by such shocks. Unit root tests suggest that output is non-stationary, and therefore Model D allows for permanent as well as transitory shocks to potential output. In particular, Model D assumes that productivity follows a random walk (with drift). In Model D, potential output (in logs) is assumed to be equal to last period's value, plus a constant term, and plus a white noise error ε, $\Delta \bar{Q} = \beta + \varepsilon$, so

$$\bar{Q}_T = \beta T + \sum_{i=0}^{T} \varepsilon_i + \bar{Q}_0 \qquad (5)$$

and is non-stationary. However, the gap between actual output and potential output may still be stationary if there are economic mechanisms that keep them from diverging. One such mechanism is the effect of income on consumption: productivity shocks will be reflected in household income and will therefore tend to have similar effects on consumption, perhaps with a lag. Another is movements in the real exchange rate: the existence of an output gap will tend to keep down increases in prices and costs, improve competitiveness, and thus close the output gap. It is assumed for this model that the output gap is equal to a stationary but possibly serially-correlated error, w:

$$Q - \bar{Q} = w \tag{6}$$

In addition, the error is assumed to be proportional to the change in the unemployment rate UR, so we can use the regression

$$\Delta Q = \beta + \kappa \Delta UR + \varepsilon \tag{7}$$

to get an estimate of the change in potential output,

$$\Delta \hat{Q} = \hat{\beta} + \hat{\varepsilon} \tag{8}$$

The assumption that $\bar{Q} = Q$ in some base year allows us to cumulate changes into a time series for potential output $\hat{Q}$, which then is used in equation (4).

Unit root tests also suggest that real money balances are non-stationary. However, real money balances are co-integrated with real output and the nominal interest rate – that is, a regression of the former on the latter two variables produces residuals that are stationary. Engle and Granger (1987) show that co-integration implies that an error correction model exists between the variables. Consequently, in Model D the money demand equations are specified in this form.

Econometric issues

Before discussing the model estimates, we must first address some econometric issues that are related to the discussion above of deterministic versus stochastic trends. In order for the estimated model to make sense and not yield coefficients that are the result of "spurious regression" (Granger and Newbold, 1974), it should be the case that all the variables entering a given equation are stationary, or, if not, the set of variables is co-integrated. If some of the variables are characterized by stationary fluctuations about different deterministic trends, equations relating the levels of variables should include a time trend, as is done in the aggregate demand equations. If variables are non-stationary and are not co-integrated, then they should be differenced to make them stationary.

Tests for stationarity are reported in Table 5.3. The method of Nelson and Plosser (1982) was used to test for deterministic versus stochastic

Table 5.3 Tests of random walk with drift against a deterministic trend in the regression
$$\Delta x = \alpha + \beta x_{-1} + \mu T + \beta \Delta x_{-1}$$
over the period 1964–88

Dependent Variable	$t(\rho)$	ϕ_3
Q	−3.3*	6.67*
Q^*	−2.7	5.62
P	−2.5	3.97
P^*	−2.5	5.44
I	−3.0	5.37
I^*	−2.3	3.54
$(I - (P_{+1} - P))$	−1.8	1.96
$(I^* - (P^*_{+1} - P^*))$	−2.5	3.96
G	−2.6	4.04
G^*	0.0	11.76**
$M - P$	−2.2	2.73
$M^* - P^*$	−2.6	4.02
E	−3.3*	6.55*
$E - P^* + P$	−2.8	4.64

$t(\rho)$: Test of $\rho = 0$. See Fuller (1976).

ϕ_3: Test of $\rho = 0$ and $\mu = 0$. See Dickey and Fuller (1981), Table V.

* Rejection of random walk at 10 percent significance level.

** Rejection of random walk at 5 percent significance level.

trends, and two alternative Dickey–Fuller tests were applied. Specifically, for a given variable (e.g. the log of output, Q), the following regression is run:

$$\Delta Q = \alpha + \rho Q_{-1} + \mu T + \beta \Delta Q_{-1} + \gamma \Delta Q_{-2} + \ldots + u \qquad (8)$$

where as many lags are included as are needed to remove serial correlation from the residuals. The null hypothesis of a random walk with drift implies that $\rho = 0$ and $\mu = 0$. A significantly negative coefficient ρ indicates stationarity, possibly around a deterministic trend (if μ is different from zero). One of the tests, described in Dickey and Fuller (1979), compares the t-ratio of ρ to critical values tabulated in Fuller (1976). The other test, described in Dickey and Fuller (1981), is a likelihood ratio test of the joint hypothesis $\rho = 0$ and $\mu = 0$.

It can be seen that for most variables it is impossible to reject non-stationarity. Exceptions are U.S. output and the nominal exchange rate; this is surprising since these variables are usually found to be non-stationary, e.g. in the case of U.S. output by Nelson and Plosser (1982), Campbell and Mankiw (1987), and Perron (1988). In contrast, inflation rates and interest rates, usually thought to be stationary series, seem to be non-stationary in our sample. Given the small number of observations, conclusions must be taken with a large grain of salt. Moreover, the use of such test results is subject to controversy. For instance, Sims (1988) has questioned whether the tests usually used may not be biased toward acceptance of non-stationarity. The alternative he proposes, based on Bayesian inference, tends to reject random walk models in favor of deterministic trends; however, his methodology has been challenged by Phillips (1990). Another critique has been made by Cochrane (1991), who argues that tests for unit roots or trend stationarity have arbitrarily low power in finite samples, since a time series process with a unit root can be made arbitrarily close to a stationary process.

Turning to the tests of co-integration reported in Table 5.4, it seems that even if the stationarity of U.S. and ROW output were to be rejected, that variable would be co-integrated with the other variables of the aggregate demand relationship, justifying estimating the equation in the form of (1) of Table 5.2. Though the Augmented Dickey–Fuller test does not permit rejection of non-stationarity for the ROW, the theoretically preferable Johansen (1988) test does. We therefore proceed to estimate both U.S. and ROW aggregate demand in the form of equation (1).

Table 5.4 Tests for cointegration using augmented Dickey–Fuller and Johansen Tests, 1965-89

Variable Set	$t(\rho)$	Trace $(r = 0)$
$Q, Q^*, (E - P^* + P), R, G$	−4.7*	78.6*
$Q, Q^*, (E - P^* + P), R, G, T$	−5.4*	78.6*
$Q^*, Q, (E - P^* + P), R^*, G^*$	−3.0	113.4*
$Q^*, Q, (E - P^* + P), R^*, G^*, T$	−3.0	113.4*
M, P, Q, I	−4.1*	66.4*
$M - P, Q, I$	−2.8	17.1
M^*, P^*, Q^*, I^*	−4.2*	61.6*
$M^* - P^*, Q^*, I^*$	−2.5	30.4*

$t(\rho)$: Test of $\rho = 0$, using the residuals from a regression of the first variable on the remaining ones. See Fuller (1976). Approximate critical values are taken from Engle and Yoo (1987), table 3.

Trace: Test of null hypothesis of no cointegrating vectors, using two lags in VAR. See Johansen (1988). Critical values are tabulated in Tables A1 and A2 of Johansen and Juselius (1990).

* Rejection of null hypothesis of no co-integration, at 5 percent significance level.

As for money demand, the two tests lead to different conclusions concerning co-integration of real money balances[15], output, and the nominal interest rate, when the long-run price homogeneity restriction is imposed. However, the Johansen test permits acceptance of co-integration, at least for the Rest of the World. In any case, homogeneity seems justified on a priori grounds. In Models A–C, therefore, the usual lagged adjustment specification is estimated, while in Model D, the estimated co-integrating vector (with unit price coefficient imposed) is used for the long-run relationship between real money balances, interest rates and output, and a short-run error correction model is estimated jointly with the other equations of the model. The co-integration regressions are as follows:

$$M - P = 3.763 + 1.204Q - 1.547I - 0.023T \tag{9}$$

(sample period: 1960–89, $\bar{R}^2 = 0.902$, $DW = 1.02$, $SEE = 0.031$)

$$M^* - P^* = -6.214 + 1.542\,Q^* - 1.379I^* - 0.028\,T \tag{10}$$

(sample period: 1965–89, $\bar{R}^2 = 0.942$, $DW = 0.81$, $SEE = 0.042$)
Letting $\hat{U}$ be the residual from equation (10), the error correction model took the form:

$$\Delta(M - P) = m_0 + m_1\Delta Q + m_2\Delta I + m_4\hat{U}_{-1} \tag{11}$$

This is equation (2′) of Table 5.2. A similar equation was specified for the ROW.

The results of the stationarity and cointegration tests are somewhat mixed. Clearly the small sample size is a problem, especially considering that the hypotheses relate to long-run relationships among the variables. We therefore feel justified in including in our set of models both those which are consistent with trend stationarity of output and cointegration of the variables that usually appear in money demand equations (Models A–C) and a model in which output includes a unit root and in which the residuals from the long-run money demand relationship are used in an error correction equation (Model D).

Structural model estimates

The models were each estimated using Three-Stage Least Squares, using annual data for the period 1966–88. Data for the United States were obtained directly from the MULTIMOD data base (see Masson, Symansky, and Meredith, 1990); for the Rest of the World (ROW), data were obtained by aggregating the other Group of Seven countries

(Japan, Germany, France, Italy, the United Kingdom, and Canada) and the Smaller Industrial Country region.

The following equations were estimated together (for both the United States and the ROW): aggregate demand, money demand, and the Phillips curve/Lucas supply equation (depending on the model). The quasi-identities for consumer prices and for interest parity (equations 4, 8, and 9) were not included in the estimation. Shares of domestic goods in the consumer price index were calculated from national accounts data as one minus the ratio of imports to domestic absorption: they are equal to 0.899 for the United States and 0.758 for the ROW. For models A–C, trend output growth rates ($\beta = 0.029$, i.e. 2.9 percent per annum, and $\beta^* = 0.033$) were estimated from a prior regression of output on time over 1966–88:[16]

$$Q = 7.292 + 0.029\,T,\ \bar{R}^2 = 0.979,\ SEE = 0.037,\ DW = 0.37$$
$$(0.014)\ (0.008) \tag{12}$$

$$Q^* = 7.796 + 0.033\,T,\ \bar{R}^2 = 0.971,\ SEE = 0.042,\ DW = 0.17$$
$$(0.023)\ (0.001) \tag{13}$$

For Model D, potential output is a random walk with drift, and it was estimated as described above from the following equations:

$$\Delta Q = 0.029 - 0.020\,\Delta UR,\ \bar{R}^2 = 0.835,\ SEE = 0.009,\ DW = 2.11$$
$$(0.002)\ (0.002) \tag{14}$$

$$\Delta Q^* = 0.036 - 0.023\,\Delta UR^*,\ \bar{R}^2 = 0.360,\ SEE = 0.014,\ DW = 1.00$$
$$(0.003)\ (0.006) \tag{15}$$

Variables ΔUR and ΔUR^* are changes in unemployment rates in the U.S. and ROW respectively, with means removed.

Coefficient estimates and fit statistics are given in Table 5.5. Since 3SLS uses the covariance structure of all the equation residuals in estimation, all of the coefficient estimates are affected by a change in any single equation, even if the form of many of the equations does not change across models. This method yields increased efficiency relative, for instance, to Two-Stage Least Squares; the asymptotic properties of 3SLS are identical to Full Information Maximum Likelihood estimation. Another important property of 3SLS is that it yields a full covariance matrix of the parameters, which is needed for assessing the degree of uncertainty when we simulate the models in later chapters.

108 Alternative Empirical Models of the Open Economy

Table 5.5 Coefficients estimated by three–stage least squares and associated fit statistics (coefficient values; standard errors in parentheses)

Coefficient	Model A	Model B	Model C	Model D
q_0	4.888	5.927	9.082	2.592
	(1.248)	(1.429)	(1.454)	(1.474)
q_1	− 0.033	− 0.037	− 0.019	− 0.057
	(0.026)	(0.032)	(0.032)	(0.035)
q_2	0.091	0.000	− 0.241	0.319
	(0.116)	(0.132)	(0.134)	(0.134)
q_3	− 0.389	− 0.560	− 0.646	− 0.139
	(0.183)	(0.208)	(0.219)	(0.201)
q_4	0.019	0.023	0.035	0.009
	(0.005)	(0.006)	(0.006)	(0.006)
q_5	0.286	0.231	0.023	0.373
	(0.071)	(0.084)	(0.084)	(0.091)
m_0	1.085	0.991	1.281	− 0.005
	(0.410)	(0.420)	(0.391)	(0.008)
m_1	0.159	0.170	0.182	0.523
	(0.034)	(0.035)	(0.034)	(0.223)
m_2	− 1.717	− 1.729	− 1.768	− 1.115
	(0.242)	(0.247)	(0.242)	(0.300)
m_3	0.573	0.575	0.500	− 0.788
	(0.082)	(0.084)	(0.080)	(0.167)
p_0	− 2.136	− 2.141	7.277	− 0.009
	(0.649)	(0.516)	(0.007)	(0.005)
p_1	–	0.765	− 0.820	–
		(0.947)	(0.172)	
p_2	0.290	0.294	–	0.187
	(0.089)	(0.072)		(0.090)
p_3	0.525	0.247	–	0.432
	(0.113)	(0.128)		(0.111)
q_0^*	2.411	2.578	5.769	− 1.470
	(2.855)	(2.791)	(3.034)	(2.127)
q_1^*	0.049	0.050	0.037	0.095
	(0.043)	(0.042)	(0.042)	(0.040)
q_2^*	0.033	0.030	− 0.292	0.372
	(0.262)	(0.256)	(0.280)	(0.192)
q_3^*	− 0.743	− 0.771	− 0.792	− 0.662
	(0.205)	(0.202)	(0.211)	(0.184)
q_4^*	0.007	0.008	0.021	− 0.009
	(0.012)	(0.112)	(0.013)	(0.009)
q_5^*	0.848	0.823	0.688	1.074
	(0.185)	(0.182)	(0.190)	(0.159)

Table 5.5 (continued). Coefficients estimated by three-stage least squares and associated fit statistics (coefficient values; standard errors in parentheses)

Coefficient	Model A	Model B	Model C	Model D
m_0^*	−0.019	−0.337	−0.078	−0.019
	(0.278)	(0.346)	(0.387)	(0.013)
m_1^*	0.142	0.308	0.259	1.227
	(0.056)	(0.074)	(0.083)	(0.344)
m_2^*	−1.287	−1.777	−1.369	−0.372
	(0.290)	(0.356)	(0.420)	(0.264)
m_3^*	0.829	0.658	0.678	−0.393
	(0.083)	(0.107)	(0.124)	(0.133)
p_0^*	−0.566	−3.858	7.801	−0.037
	(0.674)	(0.429)	(0.008)	(0.019)
p_1^*	–	0.294	−0.368	–
		(0.670)	(0.353)	
p_2^*	0.069	0.500	–	0.083
	(0.086)	(0.055)		(0.156)
p_3^*	0.666	0.163	–	0.825
	(0.217)	(0.125)		(0.291)

$\bar{R}^2$				
Eqn. 1	0.987	0.986	0.981	0.988
Eqn. 2 or 2'	0.848	0.844	0.837	0.526
Eqn. 3 or 3'	0.489	0.69	0.976	0.548
Eqn. 5	0.993	0.993	0.990	0.993
Eqn. 6 or 6'	0.903	0.893	0.905	0.512
Eqn. 7 or 7'	0.253	0.852	0.971	0.264

S.E.E.				
Eqn. 1	0.020	0.021	0.024	0.019
Eqn. 2 or 2'	0.027	0.027	0.028	0.025
Eqn. 3 or 3'	0.016	0.012	0.027	0.015
Eqn. 5	0.019	0.019	0.022	0.019
Eqn. 6 or 6'	0.046	0.048	0.046	0.030
Eqn. 7 or 7'	0.024	0.011	0.038	0.024

The estimates are generally sensible in terms of the signs and magnitudes of parameters, though individual coefficients are not always significantly different from zero. In what follows, we describe some of the interesting features of the various models, by considering each of the equations in turn.

In the U.S. aggregate demand equation (equation 1 in Table 5.2), the real exchange rate (where an increase in $P - E - P^*$ indicates an appreciation) always has the expected negative coefficient q_1, which is not however significantly different from zero. ROW output is expected to have a positive coefficient q_2, reflecting the effects of increased demand for exports on U.S. output. The value of this coefficient differs greatly in magnitude; only for Model D is it statistically greater than zero; it is negative for Model C. In contrast, the real interest rate has a significantly negative effect q_3 on demand in Models A–C, and a negative, but insignificant effect in Model D. Finally, the effects of exogenous variables time and government spending are both positive in all models; with the latter having similar (and statistically significant) coefficients in all models except Model C.

Turning to U.S. money demand, again there is a large degree of uniformity across models, though the dynamics are quite different for Model D. In each of the other models, there is a lagged dependent variable with a coefficient of about 0.5, implying a mean lag of about 2 years in the adjustment of money balances to their long-run level.[17] In Models A–C, real GDP has a positive effect on money demand that is about 0.2 in the short run and 0.4 in the long run; in Model D, the long-run effect is 1.2 (see equation 9 in the text above). It should be recalled that the monetary aggregate used here is the monetary base; the estimated income elasticity for M1 is typically somewhat higher than the 0.4 estimate of models A–C (see Goldfeld, 1973; Hendry and Ericsson, 1990). Finally, the interest semi-elasticity seems fairly well determined, and equal in the short run to between 1.7 and 1.9 in Models A–C, and 1.1 in Model D. Long-run interest semi-elasticities are 3.5 to 4 for Models A–C, and 1.5 for Model D. Another contrast is the use of the output price to deflate money balances in Model D (as estimates of error correction models performed somewhat better with this definition), not the consumer price, as in Models A–C. It can be observed from the single-equation fit statistics that the standard error of U.S. money demand is somewhat lower for Model D than the other models, which are all fairly similar in terms of fit.

The price (or aggregate supply) equations provide the major contrast across models. The Phillips curve models (A, B, and D) find a strong effect of the lagged output gap on the change in the log of the GDP deflator; this coefficient is equal to about 0.3 in Models A and B, and 0.2 in Model D in which potential output is a random walk. The lagged change in output has a wider range of effects in these models, but the effect is always positive and significant. When the restriction that the coefficient on the lagged rate of change of consumer prices (proxying expectations) equals unity is loosened (Model B), p_1 is estimated to be insignificantly different from 1.0. However, the model with a point estimate of 0.8 has quite different long-run properties from a natural rate model (see section 3 below). Turning to Model C, the ratio of consumer prices to output prices has a significantly negative effect on output, as would be expected from a positively-sloped aggregate supply curve.

Equations for the ROW are broadly similar to the U.S. ones, but with a few contrasts. The ROW aggregate demand equation has an expected positive real exchange rate effect (the mirror image of the negative U.S. effect), but again is not significant, except in Model D; nor is the transmission effect of U.S. output significant – in fact, it is negative for Model C. As was the case for the United States, real interest rates have a significantly negative effect in the ROW, equal to about -0.7. Government spending seems to have a much more powerful effect in the rest of the world than in the United States: q_5^* is estimated to be about 0.8 on average, and to be statistically significant.

ROW money demand gives very similar results for output to those for the United States, but with higher interest semi-elasticities. Coefficients are well determined, though the estimates range more widely. In particular, the short-run effects of output range between 0.1 and 1.2, and of interest rates, between -0.4 and -1.8. Long-run output elasticities are about 0.8 for Models A–C and 1.5 for Model D, while the interest semi-elasticity ranges between -4.3 and -7.5 for Models A–C, and equals -1.4 for Model D. The fit for this latter, more general dynamic specification is considerably better here than for Models A–C.

Turning to ROW price equations, the Phillips curve models are better determined in terms of significant coefficients than Model C; comparing fit statistics of the Lucas supply models with the Phillips curve models is not possible since the dependent variables are not the same. The effects of lagged output and its rate of change vary considerably across the Phillips curve models, however. Only for the non-vertical Phillips curve (Model B) is lagged output significant; this model also gives quite a low value of lagged consumer prices, equal to 0.3 (but still not significantly different from unity). Model C has the expected positively-sloped aggregate supply curve.

A visual impression of the fit of the models can also be gained by Figures 5.1–5.9, which plot the residuals of the various models (including also the quasi-identities, equations 4, 8, and 9). For this purpose, the models have been nested into a more general, common model, such that the dependent variable is the same in each case. In particular, for the Lucas supply curve model, equation 3′ was renormalized on the output price. The errors plotted in Figure 5.1 are the differences between actual and predicted values of the left-hand side variables, when the right-hand side variables take on their historical values.[18]

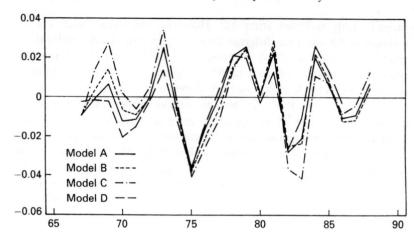

Figure 5.1   Model residuals: U.S. aggregate demand

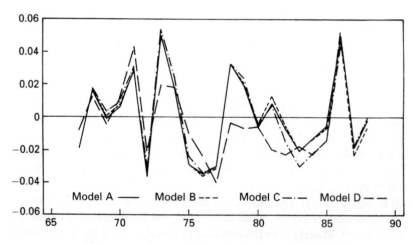

Figure 5.2   Model residuals: U.S. money demand

As expected given their identical form and similarity in estimated coefficients, aggregate demand equations 1 and 5 have very similar residuals across models. It is also interesting that large positive residuals for output are observed for both the United States and the ROW in 1973–74, 1981, and 1984 or 1985, while large negative shocks are observed in 1975. There thus appears to be some symmetry in the shocks

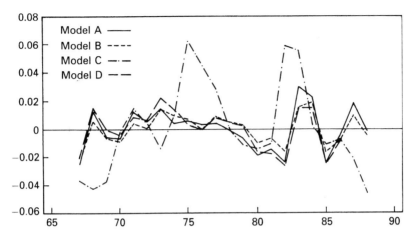

Figure 5.3 Model residuals: U.S. output price

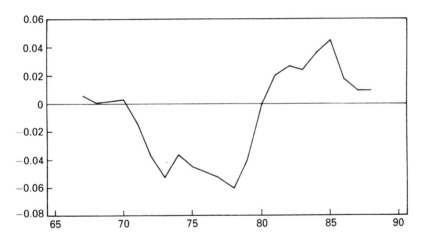

Figure 5.4 Model residuals: U.S. consumer price level (all models)

facing them, though it is also notable that in 1967–68 residuals are roughly zero for the U.S. and negative for the ROW, and the peak residual in 1969–70 is much larger for the ROW.

Money demand equations also give similar residuals across models. It is notable that aside from the 1972–73 period (perhaps associated with a breakdown of Bretton Woods system of fixed but adjustable parities), the ROW money demand equation has exhibited small errors. In contrast,

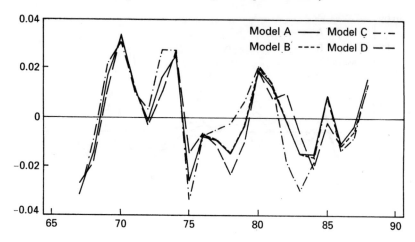

Figure 5.5   Model residuals: ROW aggregate demand

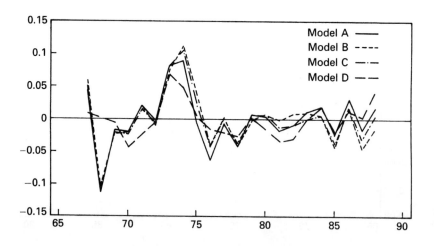

Figure 5.6   Model residuals: ROW money demand

the errors for the U.S. equation are large during the late 1970s and 1980s, a period in which money demand is thought to have been perturbed by financial innovation (see Simpson, 1984).

Price equations 3 and 7 show the greatest variation. Not surprisingly, the renormalized supply equation (Model C) shows the largest errors, while the residuals of the Phillips curve equations are similar, and

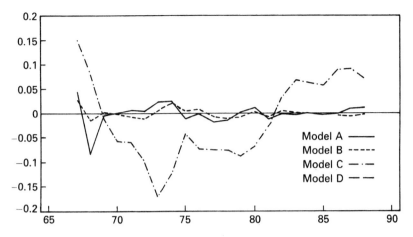

Figure 5.7   Model residuals: ROW output price

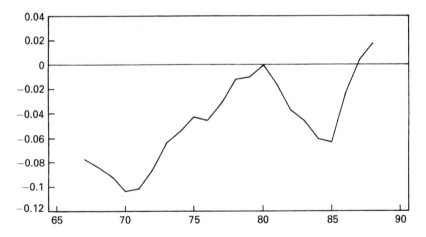

Figure 5.8   Model residuals: ROW consumer price index (all models)

smaller. For the United States, large positive residuals occur in 1974–75 and 1982 – perhaps because the oil price is not explicitly included in the Model.

Residuals of equations 4 and 8 reflect errors related to the approximation embodied in the form of the equation. Reasons for the non-zero errors include the fact that import prices are not identical to

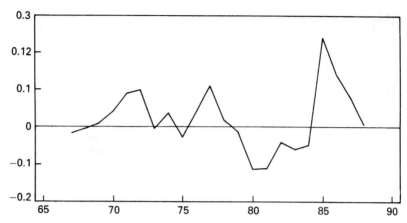

Figure 5.9   Model residuals: exchange rate (all models; increase is a depreciation of the U.S. dollar)

foreign output prices (because of compositional reasons and "pricing to market"), that the share of imports is not constant over time, and that the consumer bundle includes a different mix of traded versus non-traded goods than does output. Residuals for the U.S. equation seem reasonably well behaved, though for the ROW there is a clear trend.

Finally, the interest parity relationship, equation 9, measures differences from interest parity that reflect both expectational errors (i.e. E_{+1} differs from what was expected) and possible risk premia or discounts. Negative effects on the value of the U.S. dollar occur in 1986 (as measured by the positive residual in 1985), positive ones in 1981 and 1982.

A non-structural model

The above models are open to the criticism, made strongly by Sims (1980), that they impose "incredible restrictions," which go beyond those derivable by theory. In any case, the theories themselves are best interpreted as paradigms that highlight particular features of the economy, rather than complete representations of the complex interactions of heterogeneous agents. Taking seriously an attempt to derive macro behavior from micro foundations, with agents that have different preferences, ages, and endowments, would imply that the economy could not behave as a representative agent – and yet our macro theories are derived on the assumption of a representative agent. The restrictions that result from such models cannot be expected to hold in aggregate data. An alternative modeling strategy is to impose the fewest restrictions possible on the data, but simply to regress a set of variables on their lagged values. This strategy – vector autoregression, or VAR – was advocated by Sims, and has found wide use. The length of the autoregression is typically to be determined by the data, for instance, using Akaike's criterion. However, in our estimates we restrict the lags to the set that is included in the reduced form of our structural models. The VAR estimates therefore have the same form as those models, but without any of the exclusion or cross-equation restrictions imposed in the structural models. Estimates of the coefficients of this model are given in Table 5.6. Not surprisingly for a model with few parameter restrictions, estimated standard errors are large, but the overall fit of the equations is very good. The Ljung Box test for serial correlation, $Q(11)$, is distributed as a chi-square with 11 degrees of freedom. It indicates that serially independent residuals cannot be rejected at the 5 percent level (critical value 19.68).

4. Properties of the Models

There are a number of tools that are useful for understanding how the models differ.[19] In this section, we will look at their dynamic properties, and discuss simulations of standardized changes of the monetary and fiscal policy variables.

Since the models are linear, it is straightforward to calculate their eigenvalues. This permits us to characterize the dynamics, at least qualitatively, and to verify that the models are dynamically stable. Since each of the models contains a non-predetermined variable, the exchange rate, stability takes the form of saddle-point stability, provided there are as many roots with modulus greater than unity as non-predetermined variables (see Blanchard and Kahn, 1980). The other roots should be less than unity in modulus. The existence of complex roots indicates a cyclical approach to equilibrium. The presence of unit roots does not actually indicate dynamic instability (the model can be solved with the usual simulation algorithms), but rather dependence of long-run equilibrium on initial conditions. The consequence of permanent productivity shocks to output, for instance, implies that history matters, and that variables do not return to unchanging steady state paths that are independent of their starting points.

The eigenvalues are reported in Table 5.7. It can be seen that there are considerable differences across models, both in the number of roots and in their magnitudes. Model A has one root with modulus greater than unity, which differs from unity by a relatively small amount, indicating

Table 5.6 VAR estimates (1966–88)

| | Dependent Variable | | | | | |
	Q	Q^*	P_{+1}	P^*_{+1}	I	I^*
Q_{-1}	0.564	0.214	0.398	0.153	0.545	0.380
	(0.174)	(0.206)	(0.221)	(0.132)	(0.140)	(0.232)
Q^*_{-1}	0.217	1.003	0.419	0.148	−0.091	−0.185
	(0.230)	(0.272)	(0.292)	(0.175)	(0.186)	(0.307)
P	0.488	0.219	1.054	0.597	1.533	0.605
	(0.358)	(0.423)	(0.453)	(0.271)	(0.288)	(0.477)
P^*	−0.679	0.017	−0.176	0.589	−0.205	1.155
	(0.476)	(0.562)	(0.603)	(0.361)	(0.383)	(0.635)
I_{-1}	−1.276	−0.465	−0.313	−0.265	−0.906	−0.355
	(0.420)	(0.496)	(0.532)	(0.319)	(0.339)	(0.560)
I^*_{-1}	−0.317	−0.522	−0.189	0.030	−0.113	−0.559
	(0.225)	(0.265)	(0.284)	(0.170)	(0.181)	(0.299)
P_{-1}	0.382	0.173	0.255	−0.066	0.129	0.567
	(0.371)	(0.438)	(0.470)	(0.282)	(0.299)	(0.495)
P^*_{-1}	0.217	−0.142	0.091	−0.108	−0.612	−1.595
	(0.448)	(0.529)	(0.567)	(0.340)	(0.361)	(0.598)
Constant	1.949	0.372	−6.404	−2.829	−1.984	0.803
	(2.136)	(2.523)	(2.706)	(1.620)	(1.722)	(0.285)
Time	−0.016	0.010	−0.047	−0.018	−0.040	−0.011
	(0.018)	(0.021)	(0.023)	(0.014)	(0.014)	(0.024)
M	0.010	−0.146	−0.057	−0.139	−0.120	−0.074
	(0.097)	(0.114)	(0.123)	(0.073)	(0.078)	(0.129)
M^*	−0.059	−0.018	0.037	0.226	−0.102	−0.146
	(0.097)	(0.114)	(0.123)	(0.073)	(0.078)	(0.129)
M_{-1}	−0.144	−0.145	0.027	−0.102	−0.057	−0.086
	(0.086)	(0.102)	(0.109)	(0.065)	(0.069)	(0.115)
M^*_{-1}	0.191	−0.089	0.089	0.092	0.132	−0.038
	(0.168)	(0.198)	(0.213)	(0.127)	(0.135)	(0.224)
$\bar{R}^2$	0.998	0.998	1.00	1.00	0.945	0.847
SEE	0.0074	0.0087	0.0094	0.0056	0.0060	0.0099
$Q(11)$	16.98	15.90	5.28	13.87	16.58	16.71

Note: Standard errors in parentheses.

that the future is not discounted at a very high rate; this means that anticipated changes in exogenous variables in the distant future can have large effects today. Similarly, there are two stable roots with modulus close to unity, so that the speed of adjustment to equilibrium in response to contemporaneous shocks may be slow. One pair of roots is complex, indicating cyclical behavior. Model B has similar properties, but smaller

Table 5.7 Eigenvalues of alternative models

Model A	Model B	Model C	Model D	VAR
1.193	1.127	1.368	1.388	$-0.662 \pm 0.144i$
$0.973 \pm 0.172i$	0.872	1.357	0.971	$0.437 \pm 0.569i$
0.978	$0.818 \pm 0.132i$	1.253	$0.914 \pm 0.172i$	$0.154 \pm 0.094i$
-0.740	0.294	0.362	0.549	$0.941 \pm 0.246i$
0.701	-0.291	0.209	$-0.150 \pm 0.076i$	
-0.110	-0.08			

stable roots and hence a quicker adjustment to shocks can be expected. Model C is quite different. For this model, the price level is not a predetermined variable. It can adjust flexibly to equilibrate aggregate demand and supply; moreover, it is the led value that performs this role in the aggregate demand equation, since expected inflation appears in the ex ante real interest rate. Therefore, this model has three unstable roots, not one. The number of eigenvalues is smaller – five instead of seven – and there are no complex roots, reflecting simplified dynamics. Model D contains two pairs of complex roots, probably due to the more complicated dynamics of the money demand equation. Equations for potential output (i.e. specifying them as random walks) have not been included in the model analysis here; the series are taken to be exogenous. If the equations had been included, they would have added two unit roots. The VAR model is dynamically stable, with all roots within the unit circle.

Since the dynamic effects of exogenous variables on the endogenous variables depend on a number of different coefficients, it is useful to perform simulations of standardized changes in the money supply in the different models and compare their effects over time – often called "dynamic multipliers." We report dynamic effects on five variables: logarithms of U.S. and ROW real GDP and their deflators, and the logarithm of the exchange rate. These multipliers are plotted in Figures 5.10–5.13 for the effects on U.S. variables, Figures 5.14–5.17 for the ROW variables, and Figures 5.18–5.19 for the effects on the exchange rate. In each case, the logarithm of the policy variable in question is permanently increased by 0.01 starting in 1967, i.e. the policy variable is increased by (approximately) one percent. That increase is assumed to have been unexpected when it occurred, but to be correctly perceived as permanent.

Effects on endogenous variables can be described qualitatively as follows. Since a change in money is neutral in all the models in the long

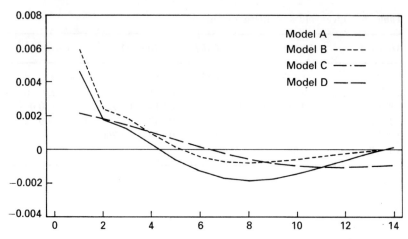

Figure 5.10   Effect on U.S. output of a one percent increase in the U.S. money
supply

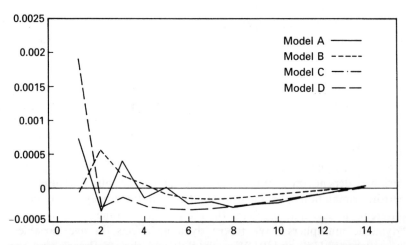

Figure 5.11   Effect on U.S. output of a one percent increase in the ROW money
supply

run (including Model B, in which changes in money growth rates are not
however neutral), in response to a one percent increase in the U.S. money
stock output in both the U.S. and the ROW should return to its baseline
path eventually, and U.S. prices and the exchange rate should eventually
increase by one percent. Similar effects should result from an increase in
the ROW money stock, except that exchange rate effects would be
reversed in sign, and the ROW price level, not the U.S. one, should

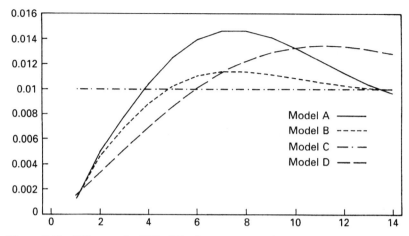

Figure 5.12 Effect on the U.S. CPI of a one percent increase in the U.S. money supply

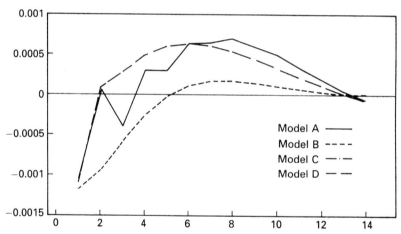

Figure 5.13 Effect on the U.S. CPI of a one percent increase in the ROW money supply

increase. The flexible price, Lucas supply curve model should reach the long-run equilibrium immediately, while for the other models, adjustment may be gradual.

The charts confirm these qualitative effects, but magnitudes of short-run effects and speeds of adjustment differ considerably. The Lucas supply model (Model C) does reach equilibrium immediately. Model B

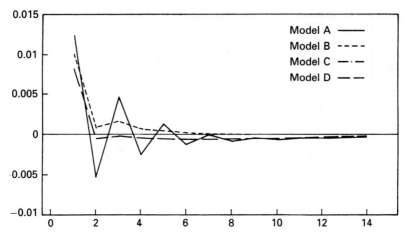

Figure 5.14   Effect on ROW output of a one percent increase in the ROW money
supply

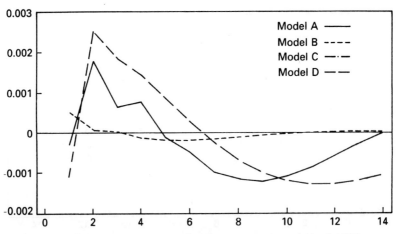

Figure 5.15   Effect on ROW output of a one percent increase in the U.S. money
supply

(which embodies a long-run trade-off between output and inflation) gives
the largest short-run stimulus to output. The slowest return to
equilibrium seems to occur in Model D. By the end of the period
reported in the graph, i.e. 13 years after the shock to money, the price
level is still not at its steady-state level of 0.01 above the initial
equilibrium – though it is returning toward it. In this model, as in the

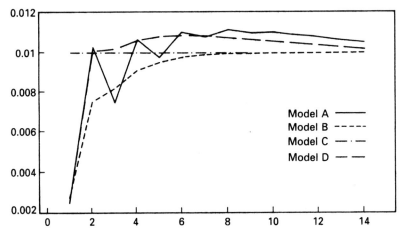

Figure 5.16   Effect on the ROW CPI of a one percent increase in the ROW money supply

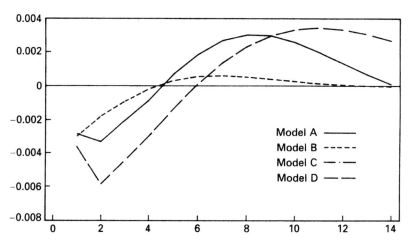

Figure 5.17   Effect on the ROW CPI of a one percent increase in the U.S. money supply

other Phillips curve models, the price level overshoots its long-run equilibrium, as would be expected when the dynamics exhibit cycles. The exchange rate also overshoots in the Phillips curve models, as is standard in models similar to that of Dornbusch (1976): it rises by more than one percent on impact, and then falls back to that level in the long run, after a

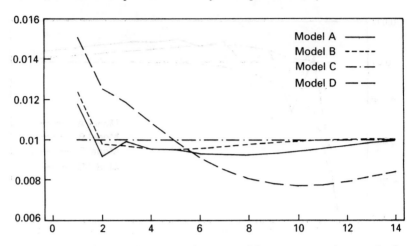

Figure 5.18   Effect on the U.S. exchange rate of a one percent increase in the
U.S. money supply

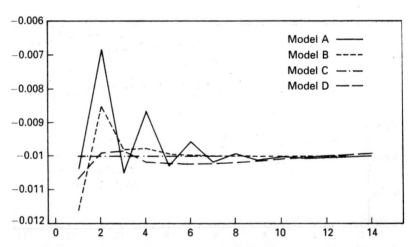

Figure 5.19   Effect on the U.S. exchange rate of a one percent increase in the
ROW money supply

period of *under*shooting. Finally, transmission effects on ROW output
are positive after the first period in the three Phillips curve models, and
zero in the Lucas supply model.

Effects of a ROW money shock are somewhat different in their
dynamic adjustment paths. Models A and B exhibit a saw-tooth pattern,
so that for instance the ROW price and output oscillate. This could

plausibly result from a combination of parameter values that produced the following: an increase in money lowers interest rates and stimulates output in the first period; however, higher output raises prices in the second period, and both factors raise money demand, which tends to dampen or reverse the interest rate decline, appreciating the exchange rate, and reversing the output stimulus. This process of oscillation might occur if the interest rate coefficient in money demand is sufficiently small, and/or the coefficient on lagged money balances is sufficiently high.

Otherwise, the models imply a quicker return to equilibrium for a ROW money shock than a U.S. one. Exchange rate overshooting is less, and in Model D does not occur on impact, though after three years the exchange rate has moved beyond its long-run, one percent depreciation. Transmission effects on U.S. output are generally positive in the Phillips curve models; though for Model B, the effect is a small negative on impact, and for Model A, oscillates between positive and negative. U.S. prices decline in the second period for Models A and B, but rise in Model D and are unaffected in Model C.

Notes

1   An early application of Keynesian economics to model building was by Tinbergen (1939).
2   A survey of empirical macroeconomic models in the Keynesian tradition is given by Bodkin, Klein, and Marwah (1991). Bryant et al. (1988) examine the properties of multi-country models.
3   Phelps (1990) asserts that seven schools of thought represent the current state of economics.
4   Frankel (1988b) and Frankel and Rockett (1988) take the range of reduced-form policy multipliers of existing multi-country models as a measure of uncertainty or disagreement concerning the effects of policy.
5   Hicks (1937).
6   See Klein (1950) and Klein and Goldberger (1955) for early models of the United States economy. The latter model includes a wage equation much like the Phillips curve, in which the change in an index of hourly wages depends on employment and the lagged change in the general price level. Klein et al. (1961) describe a model for the United Kingdom.
7   See Modigliani (1977). Agreement on the basic model structure was termed by Samuelson the "neoclassical synthesis."
8   Friedman (1968).
9   The concept of rational expectations is due to Muth (1961). It was first applied to macroeconomic policy questions by Lucas (1972), (1973) and Sargent and Wallace (1975).
10   See, for instance, Fischer (1977) and Buiter (1979).

11   Taylor (1979), (1980), (1983), and Calvo (1983).

12   This work has come to be known as "real business cycle theory." See Lucas (1981), Kydland and Prescott (1982).

13   In a vector autoregression the vector of endogenous variables, x_t is written as a function of its own lagged values, x_{t-1} : $x_t = Ax_{t+1} + \varepsilon_t$, where the parameters in A are unrestricted. The first-order system is not restrictive since higher order lags can be included by stacking the vector (see Sargent, 1979).

14   Frenkel and Razin (1987) conclude that, even after 25 years, the Mundell–Fleming model constitutes the standard open-economy model.

15   This is the case whether money is deflated by the output price or the consumer price.

16   Standard errors are in parentheses below coefficients.

17   The interpretation of this coefficient – which is very significant statistically – is the subject of some controversy. One explanation is that it reflects price stickiness, rather than actual delays in adjusting nominal money balances. See Laidler (1985).

18   Thus the error in the output equations will include errors in forecasting inflation, that is, differences between *ex ante* and *ex post* real interest rates.

19   See Fair (1984), Kuh, Neese, and Hollinger (1985), and Wallis (1988) for comprehensive discussions.

6

Model Uncertainty and the Gains from Coordination: an Empirical Analysis

1. Introduction

Model uncertainty, by its very nature, is difficult to model. One approach is to survey a wide class of existing empirical models – such as those included in the Brookings study (Bryant *et al.*, 1988) – and capture the degree of model uncertainty by the extent of disagreement across models' multipliers. A second approach, the one adopted here, is to survey the main theoretical frameworks, and apply each to the same data set. Such an approach may, on the one hand, minimize model differences that are due purely to different sample periods or variable definitions; but, on the other hand, it may avoid having models that are similar because they share a mainstream theoretical framework. Accordingly, we restrict our attention to the four models estimated in Chapter 5. Within each model, we can generate parameter uncertainty by allowing the structural parameters of the model to be chosen stochastically according to the variance matrix of the estimated parameters. While this undoubtedly understates the true extent of model uncertainty, we do find that the degree of uncertainty about the multipliers, as measured by the ratio of the mean value of the multiplier squared to the mean squared plus its variance, is at least as great as the disagreement amongst the models surveyed in the Brookings study (compare Table 2.1 above and Table 6.4 below).

A basic question in evaluating policy regimes under uncertainty is whether policymakers are assumed to know the probability distribution underlying that uncertainty.[1] In most of the macroeconomics literature, policymakers are assumed to know all the relevant moments (usually the mean and the variance) of the stochastic processes which affect their targets. In this approach (which has been adopted by Ghosh (1986), Ghosh and Masson (1988), Ghosh and Ghosh (1991), and in the theoretical discussion of Chapter 3), the true model of the world economy is viewed as being drawn stochastically from some set of possible models, each of which has a given objective probability of being the correct description of the world economy at that instant. Policymakers are assumed to know this probability distribution of possible models, though not, of course, the model actually prevailing. We implement this approach by assuming that one of the four structural models is the "underlying" model but that parameter values are not known, only their distribution. This is what we called *parameter* uncertainty in Chapter 2. Thus the true description of the world economy is generated by a particular stochastic realization of the structural parameters. For example, the Mundell–Fleming model with a vertical Phillips curve and the GDP deflator for money balances (Model A) may be the underlying model, with the true model of the world being given by a particular realization of the structural parameters of that model. Since policymakers are assumed to know the variance–covariance matrix of the structural parameters, on average their expectation of the true model will be correct. Since the drawings of the structural parameters are assumed to be independent across time periods, moreover, there is no model learning to be done.

Alternatively, we may assume that policymakers do not even know which is the underlying model, but are forced to formulate some vector of priors over the various models. Policymakers are said to face *model uncertainty* in this case. However, unless this vector of priors happens to assign probability one to the actual "underlying" model, policymakers will be using the wrong model when choosing their policies, even on average. A special case of this approach (in which parameters were non-stochastic) was adopted by Frankel and Rockett (1988), who found that coordination frequently resulted in lower welfare than non-coordination (although there were also cases in which coordination was welfare superior). Once policymakers are using the wrong model (even on average), there is no guarantee that macroeconomic policies, whether coordinated or uncoordinated, will raise welfare. Whether coordination is welfare improving then becomes a matter of pure luck.

In a previous paper (Ghosh and Masson, 1991) we criticized this approach on grounds that economic agents are assumed not to try to learn about the true model, even though their expectations will always be invalidated. Under the assumption that there is a single constant model (i.e. one whose structural parameters do not change from period to period), and that this model is one of the models being entertained by policymakers, we showed that the probability priors over the models quickly converge to the true model if policymakers use Bayesian updating.[2] This fast learning behavior resulted from the very different dynamics implied by the models; in consequence, it would soon become apparent that the wrong model of the economy was being assumed. If the models were made more similar, learning became slower, but differences across models became less important when choosing optimal policies. Thus we argued that the outcomes envisioned by Frankel and Rockett – in which coordination actually reduces welfare – are difficult to reproduce once endogenous model learning is allowed. When the models are very similar coordination improves welfare even with the wrong model. Models that are very different (so that having the wrong model results in welfare deteriorating policies), in contrast, spur rapid model learning.

In this chapter, we examine whether our results in Ghosh and Masson (1991) still hold under more realistic assumptions about the learning process. First, we assume that while there is a single underlying model generating the data, its parameters are stochastic. Thus policymakers never observe the data generated by the "true" model when updating their priors – they only observe the data from stochastic variants of the underlying model. Second, we examine what happens when none of the models being entertained by policymakers is in fact the true model: policymakers in this instance are assumed to believe that the economy is described by one of the four structural models, (with various probabilities attached to each of them), while the actual data-generating process follows a non-structural vector autoregression.

The plan of this chapter is as follows. Section 2 discusses general issues concerning the simulations. In particular, we show that a dynamic model, with a forward-looking exchange rate, introduces problems of time inconsistency that need to be taken into account in setting both the coordinated and the uncoordinated monetary policies. In addition, the simulation algorithm we use to compute the gains from coordination under uncertainty is described. The section is quite technical and may be omitted by readers who are primarily interested in the final results. Section 3 reports some basic simulations when there is no uncertainty. Section 4 calculates the effects of multiplier uncertainty on the gains from coordination when policymakers know which of the four models is the underlying model, but face uncertainty because the structural parameters change stochastically from period to period (that is, there is parameter uncertainty but not model uncertainty). Section 5 compares the coordinated and the uncoordinated regimes when policymakers do not know which, if any, of the four structural models is generating the data, and either have fixed priors over the models or try to update their priors in a Bayesian fashion. Section 6 concludes.

2. Time Consistency in Dynamic Models

Models which incorporate forward-looking expectations embody the property that announcements of future policy changes can have real economic effects in the current period. Consequently, governments will be tempted to manipulate expectations by announcing a particular course for future monetary policy. Once the future arrives, however, bygones are bygones and the government will have an incentive not to follow through on its previously announced policies. By announcing that it will tighten policies in the future, for example, the government is able to appreciate the exchange rate in the current period and thereby reduce current inflation. In future periods, however, the government will be tempted to renege on its promise to tighten monetary policy since the gains of lower inflation have mostly been achieved, and lowering monetary growth would create unemployment. Monetary policy, in this case, is said to be *time inconsistent* (see Kydland and Prescott, 1977; Calvo, 1978). More formally, if x_t is the state vector of the economy (including if necessary current realizations of stochastic shocks) then a policy sequence is said to be *time consistent* if the government announces, in period t, that it will set the money supply to $\hat{m}_{t+j}(x_{t+j})$ in period $t+j$ and when period $t+j$ arrives it does indeed find setting $m_{t+j} = \hat{m}_{t+j}(x_{t+j})$ to be optimal.

We have already seen in Chapter 2 that in the non-cooperative equilibrium each government tries to manipulate the exchange rate in order to export inflation, whereas in the cooperative equilibrium no such incentive exists. Thus the time consistency problem is likely to be particularly important in the non-cooperative equilibrium. Indeed, one can show that the symmetric cooperative monetary strategy will be time consistent, in our models, while the non-cooperative strategy is not.[3]

While policymakers would (in general) find it beneficial to announce dynamically inconsistent policies, a rational private sector will foresee this incentive to cheat and only time-consistent policies will be considered credible. In what follows, therefore, we focus exclusively on the level of welfare attainable when governments are restricted to time-consistent policies.

Monetary policy will be time consistent if the government in period t, takes as *given* the optimal policies of all future governments when choosing its own policy. Future governments will have no incentive to deviate from the announced sequence of policies since, by definition, these policies represent their optimal choices when the time comes. To calculate the optimal time consistent we use dynamic programming techniques (see Bellman and Kalaba, 1964). Under dynamic programming, the logic of solving an intertemporal optimization problem is turned on its head: rather than start with the first period and work forwards, we start with the final period and work backwards. This makes a great deal of sense since, in order to choose the optimal policy for period t, we need to know what all future policies will be. With an infinite horizon model, of course, there is no final period; the trick here is to specify a finite (T) period game, and then take the limit as $T \Rightarrow \infty$.

The algorithm we use follows Oudiz and Sachs (1985), extended to deal with model uncertainty (see Ghosh and Masson, 1988)[4]. Given a T period horizon, each government's objective function may be written:

$$\mathcal{V} = \text{Max} - \tfrac{1}{2} \sum_{t=0}^{T} \delta^t E\{\tau_t' \Omega \tau_t\} \qquad (1)$$

$$\mathcal{V}^* = \text{Max} - \tfrac{1}{2} \sum_{t=0}^{T} \delta^t E\{\tau_t' \Omega^* \tau_t\} \qquad (2)$$

where τ_t is a vector of target variables, δ is the discount rate, and Ω and Ω^* are matrices which weight the target variables. In each period, all lagged values of variables appearing in the structural equations are obviously pre-determined, that is, their value cannot change in the current period. The current values of certain variables are also pre-determined: in the Keynesian models (A, B and D), for example, the current period price level is pre-determined. We let x_t denote the vector of all pre-determined variables which enter the structural equations, and we let e_t denote the jumping variables (the exchange rate in all of the models, and prices in Model C). We let τ_t denote the vector of variables which the policymakers wish to target; these target variables can be written as a linear combination of x_t, e_t, and the policy instruments, U_t. Given this notation, each of the four models can be written:

$$\begin{bmatrix} x_{t+1} \\ e_{t+1}^e \end{bmatrix} = \begin{bmatrix} A^i & B^i \\ D^i & F^i \end{bmatrix} \begin{bmatrix} x_t \\ e_t \end{bmatrix} + \begin{bmatrix} C^i \\ G^i \end{bmatrix} U_t + \begin{bmatrix} H^i \\ J^i \end{bmatrix} \varepsilon_t \qquad (3)$$

for i ranging over the possible models $i = 1, ...k$, and where x_t is the state vector, e_{t+1}^e denotes the expected value of the jumping variables, $U_t \equiv \{u_t\ u_t^*\}'$ is a stacked vector of home and foreign policy instruments, and ε_t is an unobserved vector white noise shock, distributed $N(0, \Sigma^i)$ (Σ^i is the variance covariance matrix).[5] $\{A^i(\Phi^i), B^i(\Phi^i), C^i(\Phi^i), D^i(\Phi^i), F^i(\Phi^i), G^i(\Phi^i), H^i(\Phi^i), J^i(\Phi^i)\}$ are coefficient matrices associated with model i whose value depends upon the realization of the structural parameters of model i. For notational convenience we suppress the dependence of these matrices on the structural parameters Φ^i. Policymakers are assumed to have inherited a vector of priors Π_t that give the subjective probability that model i is the true model of the world economy. Although nothing in the logic of the algorithm dictates that the priors of the home and foreign governments (and those of the private sector) be equal, computational constraints force us to assume identical priors for all three players in the simulations reported below. The structural equations of the model that map the state variables and the forward-looking variables into a vector of targets τ are written:[6]

$$\tau_t = L^i x_t + M^i e_t + N^i U_t + K^i \varepsilon_t \qquad (4)$$

To solve the model, we begin with the last period, T. We assume that by this date, the exchange rate has stabilized so that the expected future exchange rate equals the current exchange rate: $e_{T+1} = e_T$. Substituting this terminal condition for the exchange rate into (3) lets us write the period T exchange rate, under each model, as a function of the inherited state vector, x_t, and the policy instruments, U_t:[7]

$$e_T = E\{(I - F^i)^{-1}(D^i x_T + G^i U_T)\} \qquad (5)$$

where the expectation is taken both over the i possible models (using the priors Π_t) and the structural parameters Φ^i (using the variance–covariance matrix of the parameters). We write the target vector τ_T as a function of the inherited state vector x_T, the control variables U_T, and the shock ε_T. Substituting (5) into (4) gives the period T target vector:

$$\tau_T = (L^i + M^i E\{(I - F^i)^{-1}D^i\})x_T + (N^i + M^i E\{(I - F^i)^{-1}G^i\})U_T \qquad (6)$$

The home country's objective function in the final period is given by:

$$\mathcal{V}_T(x_T, \Pi_T) = \mathrm{Max} - \tfrac{1}{2}E\{\tau_T' \Omega \tau_T\} \qquad (7)$$

with an analogous objective function for the foreign country.

In the non-cooperative regime, each country maximizes its own welfare function, taking as given the policy of the other country. This yields two simultaneous equations which may be solved to yield the non-cooperative policy setting. The linear-quadratic structure of the model implies that the optimal policies will be a linear function of the state vector, and a non-linear function of the inherited priors:

$$U_T = \Gamma_T^N(\Pi_T)x_T \qquad (8)$$

In the cooperative regime, a single global social planner maximizes:

$$\mathcal{V}^G = \chi \mathcal{V} + (1 - \chi)\mathcal{V}^*$$

Again, the optimal policies will be a linear function of the state vector:

$$U_T = \Gamma_T^C(\Pi_T)x_T \qquad (9)$$

If we are simulating the effects of a fixed rule, such as nominal income targeting, then as long as the rule can be written as a function of the state variables, the monetary policies under such a rule are written:[8]

$$U_T = \Gamma_T^R x_T \tag{10}$$

Substituting (8), (9) or (10) into (6) gives the state vector under each of the models:

$$\tau_T = \{(L^i + M^i E\{(I - F^i)^{-1} D^i\}) + (N^i + M^i E\{(I - F^i)^{-1} G^i\})\Gamma_T\} x_T \tag{11}$$

where Γ denotes Γ^C, Γ^N or Γ^R as appropriate. Substituting the target vector into the objective function, and taking expectations of the different models and the stochastic structural parameters, Φ, gives the period T value function:

$$\mathcal{V}_T(x_T, \Pi_T) = x_T' S(\Pi_T) x_T \tag{12}$$

From (5) we can also solve for the period T exchange rate:

$$e_T = E\{(I - F^i)^{-1}(D^i + G^i \Gamma_T)\} x_T = \Lambda_T(\Pi_T) x_T \tag{13}$$

Now consider period $T - 1$ to which the state vector x_{T-1} has been bequeathed. The objective function for period $T - 1$ is given by:

$$\mathcal{V}_{T-1}(x_{T-1}, \Pi_{T-1}) = \text{Max} - \tfrac{1}{2} E\{\tau_{T-1}' \Omega \tau_{T-1}\} + \delta E\{x_T' S_T(\Pi_{T-1}) x_T\} \tag{14}$$

We first solve for e_{T-1}:

$$e_{T-1} = E\{(\Lambda_T B^i - F^i)^{-1}((D^i - \Lambda_T A^i)x_{T-1} + (G^i - \Lambda_T C^i)U_{T-1})\} \tag{15}$$

From (15) and (3) we find the implied value of the bequeathed state vector (under each model, and for each value of the structural parameters):

$$\begin{aligned} x_T = &\{A^i + B^i E((\Lambda_T B^i - F^i)^{-1}(D^i - \Lambda_T A^i))\} x_{T-1} \\ &+ \{C^i + B^i E((\Lambda_T B^i - F^i)^{-1}(G^i - \Lambda_T C^i))\} U_{T-1} \end{aligned} \tag{16}$$

Likewise, the target vector for period $T - 1$ is given by:

$$\begin{aligned} \tau_{T-1} = &\{L^i + M^i E((\Lambda_T B^i - F^i)^{-1}(D^i - \Lambda_T A^i))\} x_{T-1} \\ &+ \{N^i + M^i E((\Lambda_T B^i - F^i)^{-1}(G^i - \Lambda_T A^i))\} U_{T-1} \end{aligned} \tag{17}$$

Substituting (16) and (17) into the objective function, and solving for the optimal policies, yields:

$$U_{T-1} = \Gamma_{T-1}(\Pi_{T-1})x_{T-1} \tag{18}$$

where, again, Γ denotes the optimal rule under cooperation or non-cooperation or the fixed rules, as appropriate. Finally, substituting for the optimal policies gives the value function for period $T - 1$,

$$\mathcal{V}_{T-1}(x_{T-1}, \Pi_{T-1}) = x'_{T-1}S_{T-1}(\Pi_{T-1})x_{T-1} \tag{19}$$

Likewise, for the foreign country,

$$\mathcal{V}^*_{T-1}(x_{T-1}, \Pi_{T-1}) = x'_{T-1}S^*_{T-1}(\Pi_{T-1})x_{T-1} \tag{20}$$

and the exchange rate in period $T - 1$ is:

$$e_{T-1} = \Lambda_{T-1}(\Pi_{T-1})x_{T-1} \tag{21}$$

To solve the infinite horizon game we simply continue this process of backward recursion until the sequences of the value and policy functions converge and become stationary:

$$\Gamma_T(\Pi), \ \Gamma_{T-1}(\Pi), \cdots \Rightarrow \Gamma(\Pi)$$
$$S_T(\Pi), \ S_{T-1}(\Pi), \cdots \Rightarrow S(\Pi)$$
$$\Lambda_T(\Pi), \ \Lambda_{T-1}(\Pi), \cdots \Rightarrow \Lambda(\Pi)$$

Once these functions have been obtained the world economy can be simulated forward under the different monetary regimes. In the simplest case of no uncertainty, no additive stochastic shock, and a single model with fixed parameters we need only specify an initial state vector x_0 to simulate the model. In period 1, for example, the state vector is given by:

$$x_1 = A^i x_0 + B^i \Lambda x_0 + C^i \Gamma x_0 \tag{22}$$

where model i is the model under consideration. The target vector is:

$$\tau_1 = L^i x_1 + M^i \Lambda x_1 + N^i \Gamma x_1 \tag{23}$$

where Λ and Γ are evaluated at the probability prior which gives a weight of unity to model i. Substituting the target vector into the objective function, and accumulating over time, gives the present discounted value of welfare for any given initial state vector, x_0, and model, i. When there is additive uncertainty, the expressions for x_1 and τ_1 simply become:

$$x_1 = A^i x_0 + B^i \Lambda x_0 + C^i \Gamma x_0 + H^i \varepsilon_0 \tag{24}$$

$$\tau_1 = L^i x_1 + M^i \Lambda x_1 + N^i \Gamma x_1 + K^i \varepsilon_0 \tag{25}$$

To calculate the expected level of welfare with additive shocks we simply take the average level of welfare over different realizations of the path of ε. Likewise, when the individual structural parameters are uncertain, we simulate the model forward for different realization of the structural parameters and calculate the expected level of welfare under the different stochastic realizations.

When the underlying model is assumed not to be known, we need to specify a vector of priors over the i models, where $i = 1, ...k$; and a true model which will generate the data, say model j. If the priors, Π_t, are not updated then the forward simulation for period 1 is given by:

$$x_1 = A^j x_0 + B^j \Lambda(\Pi_0) x_0 + C^j \Gamma(\Pi_0) x_0 + H^j \varepsilon_0 \qquad (26)$$

$$\tau_1 = L^j x_1 + M^j \Lambda(\Pi_0) x_1 + N^j \Gamma(\Pi_0) x_1 + K^j \varepsilon_0 \qquad (27)$$

and we take averages over the realizations of the structural parameters of model j. The state vector for period 2 is given by:

$$x_2 = A^j x_1 + B^j \Lambda(\Pi_0) x_1 + C^j \Gamma(\Pi_0) x_1 + H^j \varepsilon_1 \qquad (28)$$

and so forth.

If agents are assumed to engage in learning about the true model, then the vector of priors is updated by comparing an "observation vector," to that implied by each model ω_t^i, which is a function of the inherited state variables, the current exchange rate, monetary policies, and the stochastic shock:

$$\omega_{t+1}^i = W_x^i x_t + W_e^i e_t + W_u^i U_t + W_\varepsilon^i \varepsilon_t \qquad (29)$$

Given an observation vector ω_{t+1}, the implied value of shock under each model is:

$$\bar{\varepsilon}_t^i = (\bar{W}_\varepsilon^i)^{-1} \{ \omega_{t+1} - (\bar{W}_x^i + \bar{W}_e^i \Lambda(\Pi_t) + \bar{W}_u^i \Gamma(\Pi_t)) x_t \} \qquad (30)$$

where $\bar{W}_\varepsilon^i$, $\bar{W}_x^i$, $\bar{W}_e^i$, $\bar{W}_u^i$ are the matrices W_ε^i, W_x^i, W_e^i, W_u^i evaluated at the *mean value of the structural parameters* of model i. The subjective priors are then updated using Bayes' theorem:

$$\Pi_{t+1}^i = \frac{Pr(\bar{\varepsilon}^i \mid \Sigma^i) \Pi_t^i}{\left\{ \sum_{l=1}^{k} Pr(\bar{\varepsilon}^l \mid \Sigma^l) \Pi_t^l \right\}} \qquad (31)$$

where $Pr(\cdot)$ is the probability that a vector shock, distributed $N(0, \Sigma^i)$ assumes the value ε^i. In period 2, the state variables are given by:

$$x_2 = A^j x_1 + B^j \Lambda(\Pi_1) x_1 + C^j \Gamma(\Pi_1) x_1 + H^j \varepsilon_1 \qquad (32)$$

and the whole process is repeated.

3. Policy Coordination in a Deterministic Setting

In addition to the model parameters, the simulation analysis requires specification of the policymakers' discount factors, the utility weights on each target, and the relative weight each country receives in the social planner's objective function. The discount factor was taken to be $\delta = 0.95$ (i.e. a discount rate of 5 percent per annum). The utility weights were taken from the revealed preference estimates of Oudiz and Sachs (1984) with policymakers assumed to target inflation and output.[9] The objective functions are as follows for the United States (unstarred) and the rest of the world (starred):

$$\mathcal{V} = \text{Max} - \tfrac{1}{2}\sum_{t=0}^{\infty} 0.95^t E\{0.07 y_t^2 + 0.49(\Delta p_t^C)^2\} \tag{1}$$

$$\mathcal{V}^* = \text{Max} - \tfrac{1}{2}\sum_{t=0}^{\infty} 0.95^t E\{0.045 y_t^{*2} + 0.50(\Delta p_t^{C*})^2\} \tag{2}$$

where y is the deviation of output and Δp^C the consumer price inflation rate, each measured as a deviation from baseline. The utility function weights estimated by Oudiz and Sachs imply a high relative weight on inflation for each of the regions. Although their estimates are not independent of the model they assumed, the effects of model uncertainty on the gains from coordination are probably fairly robust to plausible changes in the utility function weights since such changes affect the gains from coordination both with and without model uncertainty. The world objective function is:

$$\mathcal{V}^G = \chi\mathcal{V} + (1 - \chi)\mathcal{V}^* \tag{3}$$

In the simulations reported below, $\chi = 0.5$; each country is given equal weight in the world objective function, which is used to evaluate the outcomes under the different policy regimes.

The optimal policies are designed to stabilize output and inflation against the specific random shocks applied to the models; as such these policies are not easily interpreted. To obtain some intuition about the workings of the different models, therefore, in this section we consider the policy game between the two regions when each region has inherited a 10 percent inflation shock ($p_1 = p_1^* = 0.1$; $p_0 = p_0^* = 0$). The assumption of a symmetric shock is made in order to simplify interpretation of the dynamic paths; in our simulations below no such symmetry is imposed. In addition to the cooperative and non-cooperative regimes, we also report the performance of five "model independent" fixed policy rules.

Like the cooperative and non-cooperative policies, these rules map the state vector, x, into each country's monetary policies, m and m^*. Unlike the cooperative and non-cooperative strategies, however, the fixed rules do not depend upon the economic models which policymakers believe describe the world economy. Simple rules have been justified as being possibly more robust to model misspecification as well as easier to monitor and explain to the public (Currie and Levine, 1985).

Our first rule is the simplest one, a fixed money target often associated with Milton Friedman (1948). Since all variables are measured as a deviation from the baseline the monetary target is to keep m and m^* equal to zero. The second rule is the international nominal income targeting rule (see Frankel, 1991), which is implemented here such that the money supply in both countries is reduced by 0.05 percent for each percentage point above baseline that nominal income rises. The third and fourth rules are nominal exchange rate targeting and real exchange rate targeting (see Williamson and Miller, 1987) respectively. The final rule, which we call the synthetic fixed rule, is a combination of these rules with the money supply in each country being a decreasing function of output and producer prices, and an increasing function of nominal interest rates. (Table 6.1 summarizes the various fixed rules). Although we do not formally optimize over the parameters in these fixed rules, they are chosen to give reasonably good performance in the face of structural parameter uncertainty under each of the four models (A to D).

Table 6.2 reports the welfare levels attained under each of the policy regimes. The welfare levels are reported in terms of permanent GDP losses for each country. A value of 5 percent, for example, implies a level of disutility equal to the disutility associated with output being 5 percent lower than its full employment level forever in each of the two regions. Full policy coordination, of course, attains the lowest level of disutility with the Nash policy setting doing slightly worse. The gains from coordination are modest but measurable for Models A, B and D, amounting to between 2.5 and 8.4 percent. Note that the welfare gain equals the difference between the welfare levels attained under coordination and non-coordination, and is expressed in terms of GDP equivalents.[10] There are no welfare gains under Model C, since an inflationary shock produces no welfare loss under either regime: it is instantaneously dissipated because prices are fully flexible.

Figures 6.1, 6.2, and 6.3 show the sum of the levels of output in the home and foreign countries under the cooperative and non-cooperative strategies for Models A, B and D.[11] Notice that the initial fall in output is much larger under the non-cooperative regime than under cooperation. As argued by Buiter and Miller (1982), and Oudiz and Sachs (1985), the cumulative loss in output is the same under each regime in a natural rate

Table 6.1 Coefficients of model independent rules

	y	y^*	p	p^*	i	i^*	e
Money Target							
m	0.0	0.0	0.0	0.0	0.0	0.0	0.0
m^*	0.0	0.0	0.0	0.0	0.0	0.0	0.0
Nominal Income							
m	−0.05	−0.05	−0.05	−0.05	0.0	0.0	0.0
m^*	−0.05	−0.05	−0.05	−0.05	0.0	0.0	0.0
Nominal Exch.							
m	0.0	0.0	0.0	0.0	0.0	0.0	−0.1
m^*	0.0	0.0	0.0	0.0	0.0	0.0	0.1
Real Exch.							
m	0.0	0.0	0.1	0.0	0.0	0.0	−0.1
m^*	0.0	0.0	0.0	0.1	0.0	0.0	0.1
Synthetic							
m	0.1	0.1	−0.1	−0.1	0.05	0.05	0.0
m^*	0.1	0.1	−0.1	−0.1	0.05	0.05	0.0

Table 6.2 Level of disutility for 10% inflation shock

Model	Money	NIT	N.Exch	R.Exch	Syn.	COOP	NASH	GAIN
A	25.3	24.8	24.1	24.1	11.5	8.2	8.5	2.5
B	9.7	9.7	9.0	9.0	9.5	8.4	9.5	4.4
C	0.0	0.0	0.0	0.0	0.0	0.0	0.0	0.0
D	14.4	14.3	13.9	12.0	13.4	8.5	12.0	8.4

Notes: GAIN is COOP versus NASH, calculated as the square root of the difference in squared disutilities. Welfare loss in terms of GDP equivalent.

model (all except Model B). The steeper fall in output under non-coordination, however, leads to lower welfare because the welfare function is convex. (Ignoring discounting, a 4 percent fall in output in a single period, for example, results in lower welfare than two periods each with a 2 percent fall in output.) Figures 6.4, 6.5, and 6.6 show the dynamics of inflation under the two regimes. Notice that inflation does not fall much faster under the non-cooperative regime because, as explained in Chapter 3, each government's attempt to export inflation via a competitive appreciation of the exchange rate is (mainly) vitiated by the actions of the other country. The monetary policies under non-cooperation, of course, are significantly more contractionary initially than under cooperation (Figures 6.7, 6.8 and 6.9).

For Models A and D (though not for Model B) the various fixed rules perform rather poorly compared to either the coordinated or non-coordinated monetary policies (Table 6.2, and Figures 6.10–6.24). This finding is consistent with Canzoneri and Minford's results that strategic behavior pays. For Model B, the fixed rules compare more favorably, and the two exchange rate targeting rules actually outperform the non-cooperative regime. The performance of the fixed rules can be somewhat improved for any specific shock (such as the 10 percent inflation shock considered here) by making them more responsive to the state vector, but then their performance becomes much worse in response to random shocks.

The fixed rules perform particularly poorly for Model A. This is because there are two eigenvalues of Model A which are are very close to unity (a complex pair with modulus 0.987) so that with relatively un-activist policies, the effect of the inflationary shock persists for many periods. Nonetheless, the synthetic rule does reasonably well in stabilizing output and inflation, and does much better than any of the other rules. However, for none of the models is it better than the Nash equilibrium.

4. Model Uncertainty and the Gains from Coordination

We next calculate the welfare gains from coordination when there is not a single, initial inflationary shock, but rather a vector of shocks to aggregate demand, money velocity, inflation, and the exchange rate. Shocks are drawn from a normal distribution with mean zero and the empirically estimated variance–covariance matrix of the residuals. For the moment we are still assuming that there is no model uncertainty (so each model is evaluated at the mean value of the parameter estimates). Unlike the single, one-time shock considered above, however, the policy conflict between the two countries no longer disappears over time. Canzoneri and Henderson, among others, have conjectured that the potential welfare gains from coordination are much larger when there are on-going conflicts between the two countries, and this is confirmed by our results, discussed below. (The conflict here arises from each government trying to manipulate the exchange rate in order to raise its own welfare. With a one-time shock, inflation eventually dissipates and

140   *Model Uncertainty and the Gains from Coordination*

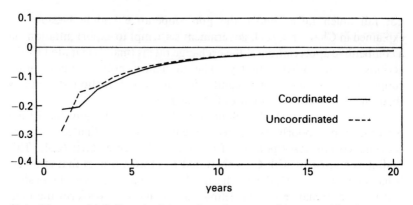

Note: 10 percent inflation shock to each region; sum of home and foreign output levels.

Figure 6.1   Coordinated and uncoordinated regimes: output levels – Model A

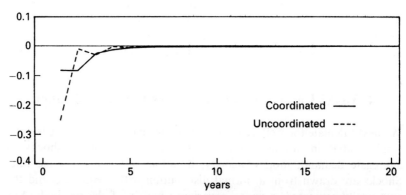

Note: 10 percent inflation shock to each region; sum of home and foreign output levels.

Figure 6.2   Coordinated and uncoordinated regimes: output levels – Model B

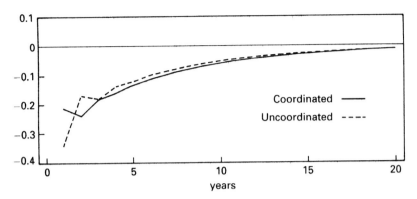

Note: 10 percent inflation shock to each region; sum of home and foreign output levels.

Figure 6.3 Coordinated and uncoordinated regimes: output levels – Model D

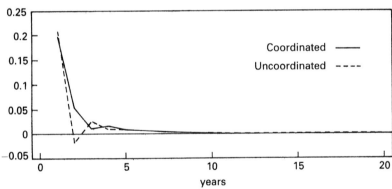

Note: 10 percent inflation shock to each region; sum of home and foreign inflation rates.

Figure 6.4 Coordinated and uncoordinated regimes: inflation rates – Model A

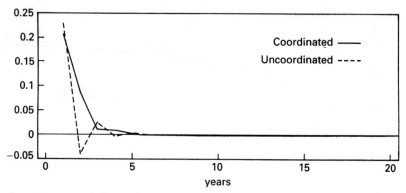

Note: 10 percent inflation shock to each region; sum of home and foreign inflation rates.

Figure 6.5   Coordinated and uncoordinated regimes: inflation rates – Model B

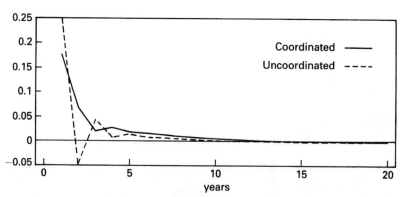

Note: 10 percent inflation shock to each region; sum of home and foreign inflation rates.

Figure 6.6   Coordinated and uncoordinated regimes: inflation rates – Model D

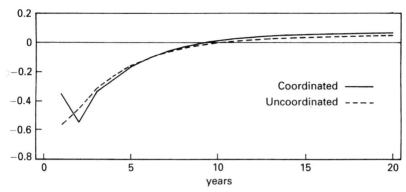

Note: 10 percent inflation shock to each region; sum of home and foreign money supplies.

Figure 6.7 Coordinated and uncoordinated regimes: money supplies – Model A

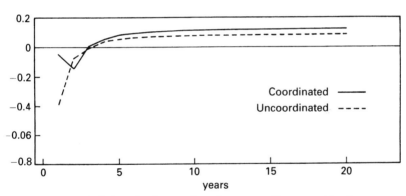

Note: 10 percent inflation shock to each region; sum of home and foreign money supplies.

Figure 6.8 Coordinated and uncoordinated regimes: money supplies – Model B

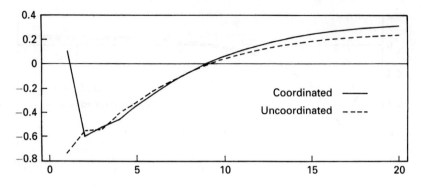

ote: 10 percent inflation shock to each region; sum of home and foreign money supplies.

Figure 6.9   Coordinated and uncoordinated regimes: money supplies – Model D

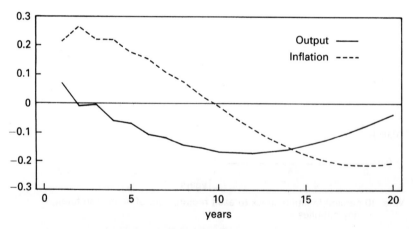

Note: 10 percent inflation shock to each region.

Figure 6.10   Money target – Model A

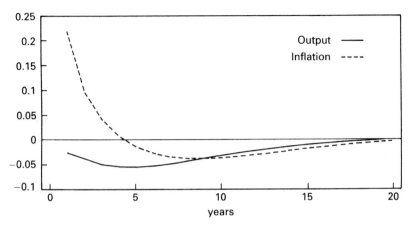

Note: 10 percent inflation shcok to each region.

Figure 6.11 Money target – Model B

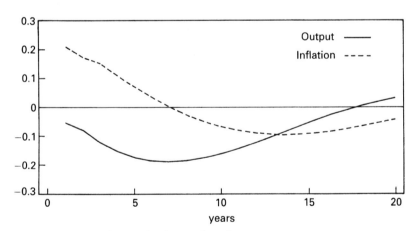

Note: 10 percent inflation shock to each region.

Figure 6.12 Money target – Model D

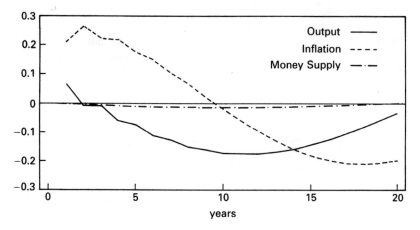

Note: 10 percent inflation shock to each region.

Figure 6.13   Nominal income target – Model A

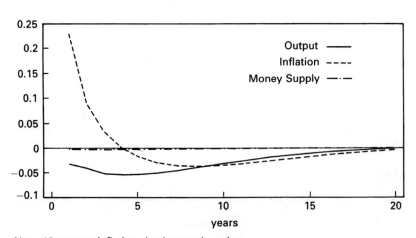

Note: 10 percent inflation shock to each region.

Figure 6.14   Nominal income target – Model B

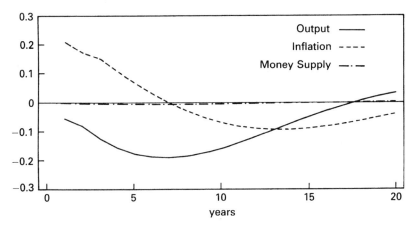

Note: 10 percent inflation shock to each region.

Figure 6.15 Nominal income target – Model D

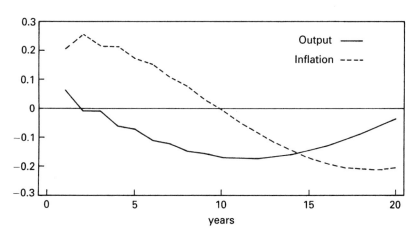

Note: 10 percent inflation shock to each region.

Figure 6.16 Nominal exchange rate target – Model A

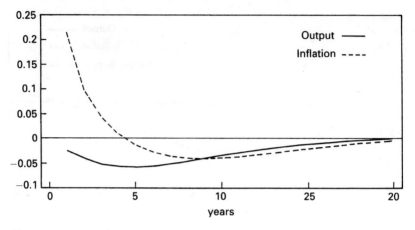

Note: 10 percent inflation shock to each region.

Figure 6.17   Nominal exchange rate target – Model B

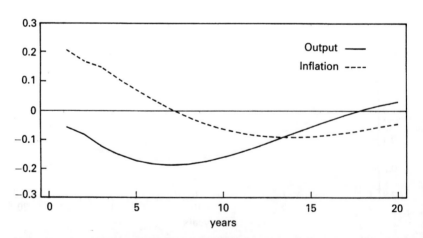

Vote: 10 percent inflation shock to each region.

Figure 6.18   Nominal exchange rate target – Model D

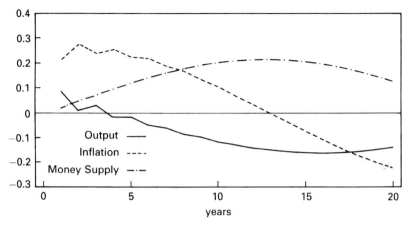

Note: 10 percent inflation shock to each region.

Figure 6.19 Real exchange rate target – Model A

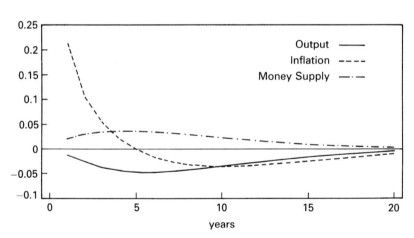

Note: 10 percent inflation shock to each region.

Figure 6.20 Real exchange rate target – Model B

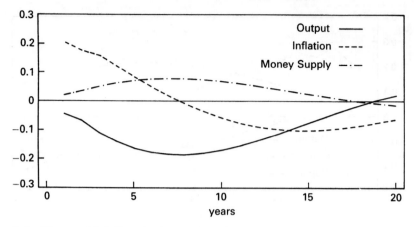

Note: 10 percent inflation shock to each region.

Figure 6.21   Real exchange rate target – Model D

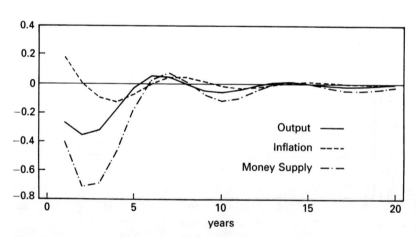

Note: 10 percent inflation shock to each region.

Figure 6.22   Synthetic rule – Model A

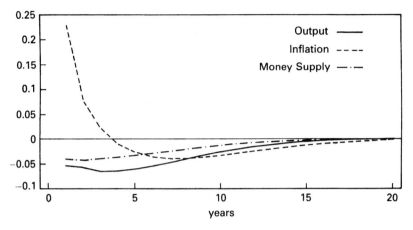

Note: 10 percent inflation shock to each region.

Figure 6.23 Synthetic rule – Model B

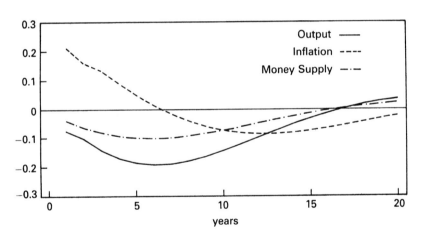

Note: 10 percent inflation shock to each region.

Figure 6.24 Synthetic rule – Model D

152   *Model Uncertainty and the Gains from Coordination*

both governments become content with the long-run equilibrium value of the exchange rate so that there are no long-run conflicts in targets.)

The top half of Table 6.3 reports the average welfare levels under the various regimes when there are continuous random shocks, conditional on each of the four models being "true". The largest welfare gains from coordination arise under Model D where the estimated welfare gains are equivalent to about 8 percent of GDP in each year, forever. This is significantly larger than the estimates of Oudiz and Sachs who found welfare gains of only 1 percent of GDP per year. Again, there are no gains from coordination under Model C because monetary policy cannot affect output given the New Classical structure of Model C (there are still measured welfare losses under each regime because output fluctuates in response to random supply shocks). The performance of the various fixed rules is roughly similar with the synthetic rule doing somewhat, but not very significantly, better than any of the others.

We next introduce model uncertainty. For each of the four models in turn we make the structural parameters stochastic, using the estimated variance–covariance matrix of the parameters from the three-stage least squares estimation. As discussed in Chapter 3, model uncertainty can either raise or lower the gains from coordination depending, *inter alia*, on whether the uncertainty concerns domestic or transmission multipliers, and the extent of the uncertainty. To give some indication of the degree and nature of the model uncertainty, Table 6.4 gives the ratio of the mean multiplier squared to the sum of the mean multiplier squared and the

Table 6.3 Welfare with and without model uncertainty

Model	Money	NIT	N.Exch	R.Exch	Syn.	COOP	NASH	GAIN
No model uncertainty								
A	23.0	22.8	29.0	25.6	20.5	14.9	16.1	5.7
B	9.2	9.2	9.0	9.0	9.2	8.7	9.7	4.1
C	3.3	3.3	3.3	3.3	3.3	3.3	3.3	0.0
D	11.8	12.6	12.3	12.0	12.3	8.2	11.8	8.5
With model uncertainty								
A	54.1	60.5	56.1	58.4	44.6	25.4	27.1	9.0
B	12.5	12.5	12.1	12.0	12.5	11.6	13.9	7.5
C	3.3	3.3	3.3	3.3	3.3	3.3	3.3	0.0
D	19.2	18.4	17.9	18.2	18.4	12.6	20.2	15.6

Note: GAIN is COOP versus NASH, calculated as the square root of the difference in squared disutilities. Welfare loss in terms of GDP equivalent.

variance of the multiplier. If there is no model uncertainty then this statistic equals unity; it becomes smaller as the the degree of uncertainty rises. It bears emphasizing that the uncertainty ratios calculated are not for the true reduced-form multipliers since, via the forward-looking exchange rate, those depend upon the entire sequence of future monetary policies and hence are not regime independent. Instead, therefore, we report the uncertainty surrounding the impact multiplier ignoring the effects of the exchange rate; in terms of the state space representation (2.3) we are giving the uncertainty surrounding the coefficients in the "C" matrix. As Table 6.4 indicates, for most of the models, the degree of uncertainty surrounding the transmission effects (U.S. on ROW and ROW on U.S.) is significantly larger than the uncertainty about domestic multipliers. It seems likely, therefore, that model uncertainty will raise the gains from coordination.[12]

For Models A, B and D, introducing model uncertainty *raises* the welfare gains from coordination, from 5.7 percent to 9.0 percent under Model A, from 4.1 percent to 7.5 percent under Model B, and from 8.5 to 15.6 percent under Model D (see lower panel of Table 6.3). (The welfare gains remain zero under Model C.) Model uncertainty also raises the welfare losses under the various fixed rules considerably, particularly

Table 6.4 A measure of multiplier uncertainty for the effects of a money supply change on domestic and foreign variables

	U.S. on U.S.	*U.S. on ROW*	*ROW on U.S.*	*ROW on ROW*
Model A				
Output	0.68	0.04	0.17	0.71
Prices	0.63	0.04	0.16	0.62
Model B				
Output	0.77	0.03	0.06	0.80
Prices	0.68	0.03	0.06	0.70
Model C				
Output	1.0	1.0	1.0	1.0
Prices	0.98	1.0	1.0	0.88
Model D				
Output	0.23	0.27	0.71	0.92
Prices	0.19	0.17	0.66	0.65

Note: The uncertainty measure is calculated as $\mu^2/(\mu^2 + \sigma^2)$ where μ is the mean effect of the multiplier and σ^2 its variance. A value of 1 indicates no uncertainty; a value of zero, infinite uncertainty. Prices are the domestic output price.

under Model A. In part this is because the fixed rules do not modify the degree of activism according to the model uncertainty, as would be required for optimal control. However, with model uncertainty the synthetic rule does better than the Nash for all models except Model A, suggesting that a properly designed fixed rule could be robust to parameter variations.

5. Model Uncertainty, Learning, and the Gains from Coordination

We saw above how the welfare gains from coordination may be enhanced by the presence of model uncertainty. Policymakers were assumed to have sufficient knowledge of the structure of the world economy that their views about the true model are correct on average – though not, of course, for any particular realization of the structural parameters. A recent paper by Jeffrey Frankel and Katherine Rockett (1988) considered a somewhat different scenario. Suppose that policymakers have completely the wrong model of the world economy.[13] Not even on average (or indeed ever) will they have the correct model. Would policy coordination still raise welfare relative to non-coordination? Using the models surveyed in the Brookings study (see Chapter 3, above), Frankel and Rockett found that coordination would often lower welfare relative to non-coordination (although in many cases it did outperform non-coordination). This result stems from their assumption that the subjective probabilities over the true model used by policymakers in choosing their optimal policies do not coincide with the objective probabilities governing the realizations of the models. In much of their discussion, for example, policymakers are assumed to believe dogmatically, but wrongly, in one model of the world economy. Even when Frankel and Rockett extend their basic framework and assume that policymakers assign equal probability to any of their ten models being the correct model, there is only one model generating the data; therefore, the subjective probabilities (0.1 for each model) do not equal the objective probabilities that each model is correct (which are 1 for the true model and 0 for all of the others).

In an earlier paper (Ghosh and Masson, 1991), one of our criticisms of their approach was that policymakers were assumed never to update their priors, even though they found their expectations consistently invalidated. Accordingly, we included some learning behavior in the simulations. As discussed in the introduction, we found in our simulations that once learning is possible, the coordinated regime never results in a lower level of welfare than the uncoordinated regime. In essence, the models must be very different before the error in setting policies in the coordinated regime is even potentially worse than the disutility from not coordinating. If the models are very different, however, it soon becomes apparent which is the true model of the economy (at least when there is a finite set of distinct models).

One troubling aspect of our previous experiment was the speed with which policymakers (endogenously) learnt the true model. We found that within one or two periods the probability priors converged on the true model. In part, this is because the structural parameters of each model were held constant at their mean level so that comparing actual observations on macroeconomic variables (the observation vector, ω) to the predicted outcomes from each model is very simple: the true model's predictions differ only by the additive error term ε_t. In the learning experiments conducted below, therefore, we make the learning more difficult (and realistic) by letting the structural parameters vary stochastically within each model. In order to learn the true model, therefore, policymakers must now compare the actual observation vector, ω_t, to the predicted vector from each model, where the prediction must be done using the *mean* of the estimated parameters (since policymakers do not know the current realization of the structural parameters).

Thus we assume that policymakers have some vector of prior probabilities that each of the four models is the model actually generating the data. One of the four models, with its parameters stochastically chosen period by period, is then used to generate the outcomes in the forward simulation of the model and to generate the observation vector. We begin with the case in which there is no learning behavior (the priors remain fixed at their initial values). Tables 6.5–6.8

Table 6.5 Welfare levels under Model A (fixed probability priors)

Priors										
A	*B*	*C*	*D*	*Money*	*NIT*	*N. Exch.*	*R. Exch.*	*Syn.*	*COOP*	*NASH*	*GAIN*
1.0	0.0	0.0	0.0	54.1	60.5	56.1	58.4	44.6	25.4	27.1	9.0
0.7	0.1	0.1	0.1	57.4	54.9	60.2	61.0	62.2	23.3	29.0	17.2
0.4	0.2	0.2	0.2	57.6	60.4	57.7	58.2	60.8	25.7	29.4	13.9
0.1	0.3	0.3	0.3	54.1	59.0	53.1	54.7	42.6	expl.	expl.	neg.
0.9	0.1	0.0	0.0	54.8	55.4	56.9	59.2	44.6	27.4	26.7	−6.1
0.9	0.0	0.1	0.0	58.4	55.8	60.4	61.5	45.9	23.6	30.8	19.8
0.9	0.0	0.0	0.1	56.1	59.5	57.4	59.5	45.1	28.0	27.4	−6.2
0.1	0.9	0.0	0.0	55.6	57.2	57.1	58.5	43.8	expl.	expl.	neg.
0.1	0.0	0.9	0.0	61.8	56.9	64.0	60.7	46.7	expl.	expl.	neg.
0.1	0.0	0.0	0.9	47.6	64.1	44.0	49.9	39.7	expl.	expl.	neg.

Notes: GAIN is COOP versus NASH, calculated as the square root of the difference in squared disutilities. Welfare loss in terms of GDP equivalent.

Table 6.6 Welfare levels under Model B (fixed probability priors)

Priors											
A	B	C	D	Money	NIT	N. Exch.	R. Exch.	Syn.	COOP	NASH	GAIN
0.0	1.0	0.0	0.0	12.5	12.5	12.1	12.0	12.5	11.6	13.9	7.5
0.1	0.7	0.1	0.1	12.5	12.5	12.1	12.1	12.3	12.3	13.1	4.6
0.2	0.4	0.2	0.2	12.5	12.5	12.3	12.3	12.3	12.0	13.3	5.7
0.3	0.1	0.3	0.3	12.6	12.6	12.5	12.3	12.5	12.0	12.6	3.9
0.1	0.9	0.0	0.0	12.5	12.5	12.1	12.0	12.3	11.6	13.3	6.1
0.0	0.9	0.1	0.0	12.3	12.3	12.1	12.0	12.1	13.6	15.3	6.9
0.0	0.9	0.0	0.1	12.6	12.6	12.3	12.1	12.6	11.3	13.6	7.5
0.9	0.1	0.0	0.0	12.8	12.8	12.3	12.1	12.5	13.8	13.8	1.5
0.0	0.1	0.9	0.0	12.1	12.3	12.3	12.1	12.1	12.3	12.3	0.7
0.0	0.1	0.0	0.9	14.6	14.8	14.1	12.1	14.4	expl.	expl.	pos.

Notes: GAIN is COOP versus NASH, calculated as the square root of the difference in squared disutilities. Welfare loss in terms of GDP equivalent.

Table 6.7 Welfare levels under Model C (fixed probability priors)

Priors											
A	B	C	D	Money	NIT	N. Exch.	R. Exch.	Syn.	COOP	NASH	GAIN
0.0	0.0	1.0	0.0	3.3	3.4	3.3	3.3	3.4	3.3	3.3	0.0
0.1	0.1	0.7	0.1	3.4	3.4	3.4	3.4	3.6	3.3	3.3	0.0
0.2	0.2	0.4	0.2	3.4	3.4	3.4	3.4	3.6	4.6	4.3	−1.4
0.3	0.3	0.1	0.3	3.8	3.8	3.6	3.6	3.9	7.2	expl.	pos.
0.1	0.0	0.9	0.0	3.3	3.4	3.3	3.3	3.4	3.4	3.4	0.0
0.0	0.1	0.9	0.0	3.3	3.4	3.3	3.3	3.4	3.3	3.3	0.0
0.0	0.0	0.9	0.1	3.4	3.4	3.4	3.4	3.4	3.4	3.4	0.0
0.9	0.0	0.1	0.0	3.9	3.9	3.8	3.4	4.1	9.5	expl.	pos.
0.0	0.9	0.1	0.0	3.4	3.4	3.4	3.4	3.6	expl.	11.2	neg.
0.0	0.0	0.1	0.9	5.6	5.6	5.4	3.8	5.7	7.4	4.3	−5.9

Notes: GAIN is COOP versus NASH, calculated as the square root of the difference in squared disutilities. Welfare loss in terms of GDP equivalent.

report the welfare levels under the various regimes when one of the models A to D is the model generating the actual outcomes. The simulations are reported for a given initial prior vector over the four models. Since the value functions and optimal policies depend upon these initial priors the dynamic programming algorithm described above had to be solved on a grid of priors, $(\pi^1, \pi^2, \pi^3, \pi^4)$. A grid spacing of 0.1 was used, so (given the adding up constraint that $\Sigma \Pi^i = 1$) a total of 273 cases needed to be solved for each regime.

Table 6.8 Welfare levels under Model D (fixed probability priors)

Priors				Money	NIT	N. Exch.	R. Exch.	Syn. COOP	NASH	GAIN
A	B	C	D							
0.0	0.0	0.0	1.0	18.4	18.4	17.9	18.2	18.4 12.6	20.2	15.6
0.1	0.1	0.1	0.7	18.4	18.4	17.7	18.2	18.2 14.4	16.6	8.2
0.2	0.2	0.2	0.4	18.4	18.4	17.7	18.5	18.2 15.6	17.1	7.1
0.3	0.3	0.3	0.1	18.5	18.5	17.7	18.9	18.4 16.7	17.5	4.9
0.1	0.0	0.0	0.9	18.2	18.2	17.9	18.0	18.2 13.6	18.4	12.3
0.0	0.1	0.0	0.9	18.4	18.4	17.7	18.0	18.4 13.6	18.5	12.6
0.0	0.0	0.1	0.9	18.5	18.4	17.7	18.4	18.4 15.4	17.1	7.5
0.9	0.0	0.0	0.1	17.9	18.0	17.7	18.0	17.2 18.7	17.7	−5.7
0.0	0.9	0.0	0.1	18.5	18.5	17.7	18.2	18.4 16.9	18.9	8.2
0.0	0.0	0.9	0.1	19.2	19.2	17.7	19.5	18.9 22.6	22.6	1.3

Notes: GAIN is COOP versus NASH, calculated as the square root of the difference in squared disutilities. Welfare loss in terms of GDP equivalent.

Several conclusions emerge from these tables. First, and not surprisingly, as long as agents assign sufficiently high probability to the true model, the coordinated regime nearly always outperforms all of the other regimes. Second, even in the cooperative regime, the level of welfare attained is not necessarily increasing in the probability assigned to the true model. This is because the models incorporate a forward-looking private sector which is also assumed to have priors over the four models (in our simulations, these equal the policymakers' priors). As the priors change, therefore, the structural model facing the policymakers – including the private sector's behavior – changes as well. Since the constraints facing the policymakers change across different initial priors, the simulations with different initial priors are not strictly comparable. Third, once policymakers assign sufficiently low probability to the true model *both* the coordinated and the uncoordinated regimes can lead to very high welfare losses, yielding (eventually) explosive behavior of the economies (marked "expl."). In some of these cases coordination is still better than non-coordination but in others the Nash regime does better (the sign in the column marked "Gain" shows whether coordination leads to greater or lower welfare when both regimes result in explosive behavior). Once policymakers are using the wrong model there is no *a priori* theoretical reason why coordination should do better or worse than non-coordination. Some of these "explosive" cases arise from the very different form of the Phillips curve in the four models. Recall that in Model A there is no long-run output/inflation trade-off, while Model B, with its lower than unit coefficient on the consumer price inflation term in the Phillips curve, implies that such a trade-off exists. When policymakers assume that this trade-off exists when in fact it does not (e.g. when they assign 0.9 probability to Model B when Model A is the true model in Table 6.5) explosive behavior of the economy results. Conversely when this long-run output/inflation trade-off exists but policymakers assume that it does not (Table 6.6), no such explosive behavior occurs. Placing a high probability prior on Models A, B, or D when Model C is the true model similarly leads to explosive behavior (Table 6.7) as policymakers try to stabilize fluctuations in output using the money supply when such stabilization is impossible. Fourth, the model independent rules, such as nominal income targeting or the synthetic rule, never result in explosive behavior. The outcomes under these rules are very similar across different initial probability priors. Indeed, the outcomes differ down the table simply because the private sector's expectations of the future exchange rate depend upon their priors over the true models. Since none of these fixed rules results in explosive behavior, the occasionally extremely poor outcomes in the cooperative and non-cooperative regimes must be the result of the monetary policies followed, rather than the incorrect priors held by the private sector. Notice, moreover, that under Model B, the fixed rules are always better than the non-cooperative regime because they rule out the over-activist use of competitive depreciations (which, given the non-accelerationist model, policymakers will otherwise try to exploit in an extreme way).

The simulations reported in Tables 6.5–6.8 suggest that adopting a rule which is model independent is by far the safest policy when there is uncertainty about the true model. It should be noted, however, that even these fixed rules may require some form of implicit or explicit coordination. Otherwise, given that one government is following the fixed rule, the other government will have the incentive to deviate (at least marginally) from it. It may also be possible to improve upon the fixed rules generally considered in the literature, such as nominal income targeting, or fixed money targets; our synthetic rule, for example, generally performs better than the other rules.

It seems somewhat implausible, however, that policymakers would not update their priors when they find that effects of their policies are consistently invalidated.[14] In a second set of simulations, therefore, we assume that agents update their priors over the models in the Bayesian fashion described above. Specifically, agents are assumed to observe levels of output, interest rates, producer prices, and the exchange rate to update their priors over the four models. The Bayesian updating is complicated by the assumption that within each model the structural parameters change stochastically each period, thus agents never actually observe the "true" model. The results of these simulations are reported in Tables 6.9–6.12. The important conclusion which emerges is that

Table 6.9 Welfare levels under Model A (Bayesian updating)

Priors				Money	NIT	N. Exch.	R. Exch.	Syn.	COOP	NASH	GAIN
A	B	C	D								
1.0	0.0	0.0	0.0	54.1	60.5	56.1	58.4	44.6	25.4	27.1	9.0
0.7	0.1	0.1	0.1	54.1	54.9	56.1	58.4	44.6	25.3	26.7	8.9
0.4	0.2	0.2	0.2	54.1	55.1	56.1	58.4	44.6	25.1	26.6	8.7
0.1	0.3	0.3	0.3	54.1	55.1	55.9	58.4	44.6	25.3	27.1	8.5
0.9	0.1	0.0	0.0	54.1	54.9	55.9	58.4	44.6	25.4	26.7	9.0
0.9	0.0	0.1	0.0	54.3	54.9	55.9	58.4	44.6	25.3	27.1	8.5
0.9	0.0	0.0	0.1	54.1	55.1	55.9	58.4	44.4	25.4	27.1	9.0
0.1	0.9	0.0	0.0	54.1	54.9	56.1	58.4	44.6	25.6	27.1	8.9
0.1	0.0	0.9	0.0	54.3	54.9	56.1	58.4	44.6	25.1	26.6	8.7
0.1	0.0	0.0	0.9	54.1	54.9	55.9	58.4	44.6	25.7	27.1	8.5

Notes: GAIN is COOP versus NASH, calculated as the square root of the difference in squared disutilities. Welfare loss in terms of GDP equivalent.

Table 6.10 Welfare levels under Model B (Bayesian updating)

Priors				Money	NIT	N. Exch.	R. Exch.	Syn.	COOP	NASH	GAIN
A	B	C	D								
0.0	1.0	0.0	0.0	12.5	12.5	12.1	12.0	12.5	11.6	13.9	7.5
0.1	0.7	0.1	0.1	12.8	12.8	12.3	12.1	12.5	12.8	14.3	6.2
0.2	0.4	0.2	0.2	12.8	12.8	12.3	12.1	12.5	12.8	14.1	5.7
0.3	0.1	0.3	0.3	12.8	12.8	12.3	12.1	12.5	13.0	13.9	5.1
0.1	0.9	0.0	0.0	12.8	12.5	12.3	12.1	12.5	12.8	14.3	6.4
0.0	0.9	0.1	0.0	12.5	12.6	12.1	12.0	12.3	11.6	13.8	7.4
0.0	0.9	0.0	0.1	12.6	13.0	12.1	12.1	12.5	11.6	13.9	7.7
0.9	0.1	0.0	0.0	12.8	12.5	12.3	12.3	12.5	13.1	14.1	5.2
0.0	0.1	0.9	0.0	12.3	12.6	12.1	12.0	12.3	11.8	13.9	7.4
0.0	0.1	0.0	0.9	12.6	14.8	12.3	12.1	12.5	11.8	14.1	7.9

Notes: GAIN is COOP versus NASH, calculated as the square root of the difference in squared disutilities. Welfare loss in terms of GDP equivalent.

coordination is now *never* worse than non-coordination, and the explosive behavior of the economies is completely eliminated under either regime. In some instances, moreover, the fixed rules perform better than the Nash equilibrium so that the losses from beggar-thy-neighbor policies are greater than the losses from model independent rules. Figures 6.25–6.28 illustrate the learning process over time under the coordinated regime (the policy regime makes little difference to the speed of learning). Although the learning is much slower than in our earlier simulations (Ghosh and Masson, 1991) it is still quite fast: starting with a prior of 0.4

160   *Model Uncertainty and the Gains from Coordination*

Table 6.11 Welfare levels under Model C (Bayesian updating)

A	B	C	D	Money	NIT	N. Exch.	R. Exch.	Syn.	COOP	NASH	GAIN
0.0	0.0	1.0	0.0	3.3	3.4	3.3	3.3	3.4	3.3	3.3	0.0
0.1	0.1	0.7	0.1	3.3	3.4	3.3	3.3	3.4	3.3	3.3	0.0
0.2	0.2	0.4	0.2	3.3	3.4	3.3	3.4	3.4	3.4	3.4	0.0
0.3	0.3	0.1	0.3	3.4	3.4	3.4	3.4	3.4	3.4	3.4	0.8
0.1	0.0	0.9	0.0	3.4	3.4	3.3	3.3	3.4	3.8	3.8	0.0
0.0	0.1	0.9	0.0	3.3	3.4	3.3	3.3	3.4	3.3	3.3	0.0
0.0	0.0	0.9	0.1	3.3	3.4	3.3	3.3	3.4	3.3	3.3	0.0
0.9	0.0	0.1	0.0	3.4	3.4	3.4	3.4	3.4	3.4	3.4	0.5
0.0	0.9	0.1	0.0	3.3	3.4	3.3	3.4	3.4	3.4	3.4	0.0
0.0	0.0	0.1	0.9	3.4	3.4	3.4	3.3	3.4	3.4	3.4	0.0

Notes: GAIN is COOP versus NASH, calculated as the square root of the difference in squared disutilities. Welfare loss in terms of GDP equivalent.

Table 6.12 Welfare levels under Model D (Bayesian updating)

A	B	C	D	Money	NIT	N. Exch.	R. Exch.	Syn.	COOP	NASH	GAIN
0.0	0.0	0.0	1.0	18.4	18.4	17.9	18.2	18.4	12.6	20.2	15.6
0.1	0.1	0.1	0.7	18.2	18.2	17.7	18.2	18.2	13.0	19.8	14.9
0.2	0.2	0.2	0.4	18.4	18.4	17.7	18.4	18.2	13.0	20.0	15.3
0.3	0.3	0.3	0.1	18.4	18.4	17.7	18.0	18.4	13.0	19.8	15.1
0.1	0.0	0.0	0.9	18.4	18.4	17.9	18.2	18.4	13.1	20.0	15.3
0.0	0.1	0.0	0.9	18.4	18.4	17.7	18.2	18.4	12.6	20.2	15.6
0.0	0.0	0.1	0.9	18.4	18.4	17.7	18.2	18.4	12.6	20.0	15.4
0.9	0.0	0.0	0.1	18.4	18.2	17.7	18.2	18.2	12.9	20.2	15.6
0.0	0.9	0.0	0.1	18.4	18.4	17.7	18.2	18.4	12.6	20.0	15.4
0.0	0.0	0.9	0.1	18.7	18.5	17.7	18.4	18.5	12.6	20.2	15.7

Notes: GAIN is COOP versus NASH, calculated as the square root of the difference in squared disutilities. Welfare loss in terms of GDP equivalent.

on the true underlying model, for example, the probability priors have generally converged to the true underlying model within 6 years.[15] There are, however, instances in which the priors "converge" to the wrong model. When Model B is the true model, certain simulations result in priors converging to Model A (as illustrated in Fig. 6.26). This behavior presumably reflects the overall similarities of Models A and B. Interestingly, however, we have not found a case in which the priors converge to Model B when Model A is the true model.[16]

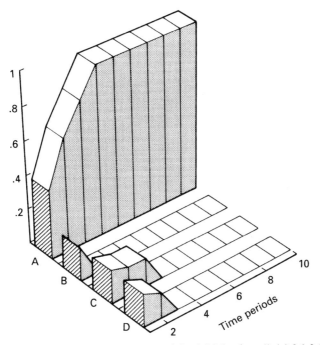

Figure 6.25 Model A is the true model – initial priors (0.4,0.2,0.2,0.2)

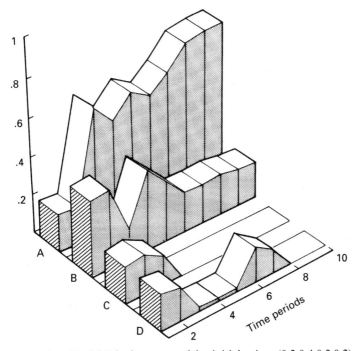

Figure 6.26 Model B is the true model – initial priors (0.2,0.4,0.2,0.2)

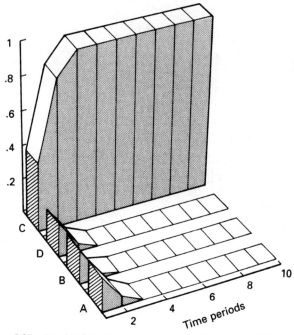

Figure 6.27 Model C is the true model – initial priors (0.2,0.2,0.4,0.2)

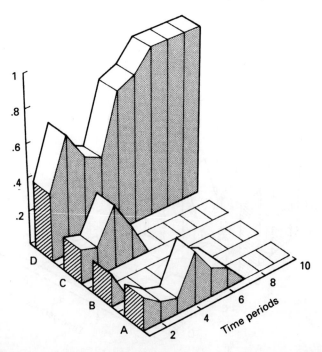

Figure 6.28 Model D is the true model – initial priors (0.2,0.2,0.2,0.4)

In order to gauge the sensitivity of the results, we increased the variance of the shocks, and the variance of the drawings of the structural parameters. We continued to find, however, that the performance of the cooperative regime is superior to non-coordination. The *ex post* performance of the coordinated regime depends upon two factors: the robustness of the optimal policy to model errors, and the rate of learning of the model. Clearly, the more diverse the models are, the more likely the optimal policy based on the "wrong" priors will result in lower welfare (although there is no presumption that the coordinated regime is more vulnerable than non-coordination). The intuition as to why coordination does so well once there is endogenous model learning is straightforward: if the models are very different then the implied observation vector of each model is also very different, and the updated priors assigned to the false models will be correspondingly low. Thus, although greater diversity between the models makes more likely the possibility of welfare-deteriorating policies, it also serves to increase the rate of learning.

Of course, these simulations assume that *one* of the four models being used by policymakers is the true *underlying* model but policymakers do not know which one it is.[17] In a final set of simulations we allow for the possibility that *none* of the models is generating the true data (even on average). We still need some way of generating the data which will be used to calculate the expected level of welfare (and to generate the observation vector which policymakers will use for Bayesian updating). In order to be as agnostic as possible about the structure of this model, we use an atheoretical vector autoregression (parameter estimates of this VAR as given in Table 5.6).

Tables 6.13 and 6.14 report the welfare levels attained under each regime when policymakers keep their priors over the four models (A to D) fixed, and when they try to update those priors using Bayesian updating, respectively. Policymakers cannot learn the true model, of course, since the actual model generating the data (the VAR) is not included in policymakers' set of models. We find that coordination does *much* better than non-coordination, but not significantly better than most of the fixed rules. In fact, when policymakers believe either Model A or Model C with probability one, coordination does slightly worse than the fixed rules. Figure 6.29 shows the evolution of the probability priors vector when the true model is the VAR model. Not surprisingly the priors do not exhibit stable behavior over time and do not converge on any one model.

The experiments with the VAR model may represent a "worst case" scenario in the sense that, of the structural models being used by policymakers, none is even approximately correct. Presumably, with careful modeling effort, it should be possible to capture at least *some* of

164   *Model Uncertainty and the Gains from Coordination*

Table 6.13 Welfare levels under VAR model (fixed priors)

A	B	C	D	Money	NIT	N. Exch.	R. Exch.	Syn.	COOP	NASH	GAIN
1.0	0.0	0.0	0.0	5.8	5.8	5.1	5.1	5.3	8.5	104.4	103.9
0.7	0.1	0.1	0.1	5.3	5.3	5.3	4.9	5.1	5.4	133.6	133.4
0.4	0.2	0.2	0.2	4.9	4.8	5.3	4.9	4.6	4.9	90.7	90.5
0.1	0.3	0.3	0.3	4.6	4.6	4.4	4.8	4.4	4.9	67.7	67.6
0.0	1.0	0.0	0.0	5.7	5.7	5.1	5.1	5.6	5.1	31.5	31.0
0.1	0.7	0.1	0.1	5.1	4.9	4.8	4.8	4.9	6.1	101.6	101.5
0.2	0.4	0.2	0.2	4.8	4.8	4.6	4.8	4.6	5.1	65.3	65.1
0.3	0.1	0.3	0.3	4.6	4.6	4.6	4.8	4.4	4.9	65.4	65.3
0.0	0.0	1.0	0.0	4.4	4.4	4.4	4.8	4.3	11.2	11.2	0.0
0.1	0.1	0.7	0.1	4.4	4.4	4.4	4.8	4.3	5.1	70.7	70.5
0.2	0.2	0.4	0.2	4.4	4.4	4.4	4.8	4.3	4.9	72.2	72.0
0.3	0.3	0.1	0.3	5.2	5.2	4.8	4.9	4.4	5.1	110.8	110.7
0.0	0.0	0.0	1.0	6.1	6.1	5.4	5.6	5.9	5.2	156.2	156.2
0.1	0.1	0.1	0.7	5.4	5.4	4.9	5.1	5.2	5.1	95.0	94.9
0.2	0.2	0.2	0.4	4.8	4.8	4.6	4.9	4.6	4.8	85.6	85.4
0.3	0.3	0.3	0.1	4.6	4.6	3.6	4.8	4.4	5.4	70.0	69.8

Notes: GAIN is COOP versus NASH, calculated as the square root of the difference in squared disutilities. Welfare loss in terms of GDP equivalent.

Table 6.14 Welfare levels under VAR model (Bayesian updating)

A	B	C	D	Money	NIT	N. Exch.	R. Exch.	Syn.	COOP	NASH	GAIN
1.0	0.0	0.0	0.0	5.7	5.7	5.1	5.1	5.3	8.5	104.4	103.9
0.7	0.1	0.1	0.1	5.6	5.6	5.2	5.4	5.3	5.2	135.9	135.9
0.4	0.2	0.2	0.2	5.6	5.6	5.2	5.4	5.3	5.1	126.4	126.2
0.1	0.3	0.3	0.3	5.6	5.6	5.1	5.4	5.4	5.1	92.2	92.0
0.0	1.0	0.0	0.0	5.7	5.7	5.1	5.1	5.6	5.1	31.4	31.0
0.1	0.7	0.1	0.1	5.6	5.6	5.2	5.4	5.2	5.2	130.2	130.2
0.2	0.4	0.2	0.2	5.6	5.6	5.1	5.4	5.2	5.1	85.9	85.8
0.3	0.1	0.3	0.3	5.6	5.6	5.1	5.4	5.2	5.1	89.7	89.5
0.0	0.0	1.0	0.0	4.4	4.4	4.4	4.8	4.3	11.2	11.2	0.0
0.1	0.1	0.7	0.1	5.6	5.6	5.1	5.4	5.2	5.1	104.4	104.3
0.2	0.2	0.4	0.2	5.6	5.6	5.1	5.4	5.2	5.1	101.1	101.0
0.3	0.3	0.1	0.3	5.6	5.6	5.1	5.4	5.4	4.9	133.9	133.8
0.0	0.0	0.0	1.0	6.1	6.1	5.4	5.6	5.9	5.2	156.2	156.2
0.1	0.1	0.1	0.7	5.6	5.6	5.1	5.4	5.4	5.4	143.3	143.1
0.2	0.2	0.2	0.4	5.6	5.6	5.1	5.4	5.2	5.1	128.9	128.7
0.3	0.3	0.3	0.1	5.6	5.6	5.1	5.4	5.2	5.4	94.6	94.5

Notes: GAIN is COOP versus NASH, calculated as the square root of the difference in squared disutilities. Welfare loss in terms of GDP equivalent.

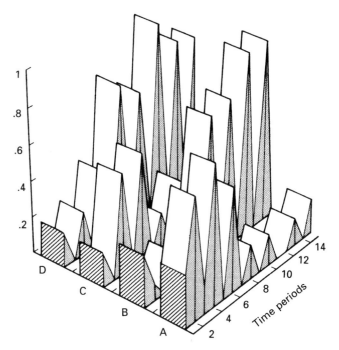

Figure 6.29 VAR Model is the true model – initial priors (0.3,0.3,0.2,0.2)

the true structural features of national economies. It is perhaps encouraging for the case for coordination that even in this "worst case" scenario, coordinated policies seldom do significantly worse than fixed rules, and always perform much better than non-cooperative discretionary policies. But the results also suggest that the possibility of designing simple fixed rules for international economic policy coordination – rather than fully optimal policy rules – should be explored. Agreement on such rules would have the advantage of being more easily monitored, a question discussed in Chapter 8 below.[18]

6. Conclusions

This chapter has presented some empirical estimates of the effects of model uncertainty on the gains from coordination. If policymakers are assumed to have the correct model on average, then model uncertainty increases the gains from coordination. When policymakers are not certain of the underlying model and do not try to learn about the true model, both coordination and non-coordination may result in lower welfare than simple fixed rules. In our simulations, under the assumption that policymakers update their priors in a Bayesian fashion, coordination always does better than non-coordination, even if the set of models under consideration does not include the true model. In the latter case, however, coordination does not perform significantly better than the fixed rules. International agreement on such rules may therefore be an adequate substitute for fully optimal, coordinated policies, which are in any case an unrealistic objective. The simulations do suggest that whether governments adopt fixed rules, or attempt full coordination, they will achieve much higher levels of welfare than they would in the Nash regime.

We would not like to exaggerate the importance of these results. We have assumed a limited set of possible models and imposed a particular learning mechanism (i.e. Bayesian updating), so it is hard to make very general claims about the desirability of policy coordination in the face of uncertainty. At the very least, however, all of our results suggest that countries would be no worse off by coordinating their macroeconomic policies so long as policymakers do not stick dogmatically to incorrect models.

There are historical instances, moreover, of policymakers learning about the functioning of the economy and adapting their policies accordingly. Thus the examples in which policymakers assume that a long-run inflation-output trade-off exists when in fact the structural model does not embody this trade-off have some relevance to the history of demand management in the postwar period. Early models of the "Phillips curve" (see, for example, A. W. Phillips, 1958, Richard Lipsey, 1960) implied that there was a trade-off between the rate of change of wages or prices and the unemployment rate or output. These models no doubt helped induce central banks and treasuries to engage in demand expansion, in an attempt to buy more output growth at what was judged to be an acceptable inflation cost. The experience of accelerating inflation in the late 1960s forced economists and policymakers to reconsider those models, and there has been a profound shift in policy away from short-term fine-tuning and to a concern for the medium-term inflation consequences of policy. Moreover, the rationale for the policy changes has been acceptance of natural-rate models, which do not allow for monetary stimulus to have permanent positive effects on the level of activity. Friedman (1977, p. 470) commented on the change in policy in his Nobel lecture:

> Government policy about inflation and unemployment has been at the center of political controversy. Ideological war has raged over these matters. Yet the drastic change that has occurred in economic theory has not been a result of ideological warfare. It has not resulted from divergent

political beliefs or aims. It has responded almost entirely to the force of events: brute experience proved far more potent than the strongest of political or ideological preferences.

The fact that governments adapt their views of the world to economic reality removes some of the force to the critique of policy coordination based on model uncertainty. Nevertheless, in the short run – which is, after all, the relevant horizon for most policymakers – it is possible to be very wrong both in assessing the state of the economy and in gauging the effects of policy. Beyond the short run, historical experience suggests that policymakers exhibit flexibility; both in their views of the world and in the choice of policy rules. The policy regime is not chosen once and for all.

Notes

1   Knight (1921) would describe this as a situation of "risk" rather than uncertainty.
2   In that study, there were only three possible models. See, also, Kemball-Cook (1992) for a similar analysis.
3   Cooperation does not always result in time-consistent policies. See, for example, Rogoff (1985).
4   This backward recursion algorithm for dynamic games (without model or parameter uncertainty) is also used by McKibbin and Sachs (1986, 1991).
5   The realized values of x_t, e_t and ε_t will, of course, depend upon the true model. To keep the notation from becoming too confusing we do not use i superscripts on these variables.
6   Since the expected value of the shocks ε_t^i is zero, certainty equivalence implies that they have no effect on the optimal policies. To simplify the exposition they are ignored in our derivations.
7   We think of the exchange rate as being set in the asset markets before the current realization of the shock is known to either speculators or to policy makers. Therefore we take the expected value over the models in equation (5).
8   The rules we consider are model independent so that Γ^R is not a function of Π. Rules which depend on the subjective probability priors, of course, can also be simulated.
9   The current account objective in Oudiz and Sachs (1984) was ignored. The utility-function weights were those reported in table 11 of their paper; for the rest of the world, weights for Japan and Germany were averaged.
10   Welfare gain $= \sqrt{\left(\mathcal{E}^{N2} - \mathcal{E}^{C2}\right)}$ where $\mathcal{E}^C$ is the GDP equivalent welfare loss under coordination and $\mathcal{E}^N$ is the GDP equivalent welfare loss in the non-cooperative regime.
11   The levels of output (and inflation) in each country follow a more complicated path as the cooperative planner redistributes the burden of the

inflationary shock between the two countries in order to maximize the equally weighted sum of the two countries' welfare. Figures for Model C are not shown since output remains at the baseline level throughout the simulation.

12   Recall from Chapter 3 that transmission uncertainty necessarily raises the gains from coordination while the effects of domestic multiplier uncertainty are potentially ambiguous (but certainly reduce welfare gains for sufficiently high degrees of uncertainty).

13   Actually, they could be correct – they have a 1 in 10 chance of having the correct model.

14   More precisely, the error implied by any incorrect model will have a non-zero mean.

15   With Bayesian updating, priors never actually converge to 1.0; convergence here means convergence to within the numerical accuracy of the simulation algorithm. Of course, policymakers still face model uncertainty since the structural parameters within each model continue to be stochastic.

16   This is of importance because setting policies in the belief that model B – with its long-run output/inflation trade-off – is the true model while in fact model A is the correct one can lead to explosive behavior of the economy. Because model A imposes a unit coefficient on the inflation term of the Phillips curve it makes sharp predictions about the evolution of producer prices; therefore, it is relatively simple to detect the true model when model A is generating the data.

17   To reiterate, in these simulations policymakers eventually discover the underlying structure of the correct model of the world economy, but never learn the precise values of its coefficients.

18   Since the fixed rules are not constrained to be time consistent there is an issue of whether the superiority of these rules arises from their potential time inconsistency. Thus a direct comparison with either the coordinated or the unco-ordinated policies may not be strictly valid. For the models being used here it seems unlikely that time consistency issues would have very significant effects on the ranking of the various policies.

7
Cooperation versus Coordination

1. Introduction

Although the terms cooperation and coordination are often used interchangeably, it is useful, for analytical purposes, to distinguish between the two concepts. The term coordination, as used by game-theorists, refers to the joint maximization of a common welfare function (which is usually taken to be a weighted average of each country's objective function). Cooperation is a much wider term; it may take the form of meetings to discuss policy issues, the exchange of information between governments or central banks, as well as formal coordination in the sense used above (see Artis and Ostry, 1986).

Though politicians often appear reluctant to embrace actual policy coordination as a means of improving economic welfare, there seems to be almost universal agreement that the international exchange of information is beneficial. In fact, with a few notable exceptions – such as the 1978 Bonn Summit and the 1985 Plaza Agreement – the main outcome of most economic summits, or meetings of finance ministers and central bank governors, seems to be an exchange of views about the problems afflicting each country's economy, and the policies that each government intends to pursue. There are, indeed, many institutions, such as the the Organization for Economic Cooperation and Development, the Bank for International Settlements, and the International Monetary Fund, whose functions and mandate specifically include the international exchange of information.

Some would go further, arguing that international cooperation which is limited to information exchange actually captures most of the welfare benefits associated with international policy coordination, without incurring the technical and political difficulties of achieving coordinated policy agreements. Thus, while it may not quite yield the level of welfare theoretically attainable under coordination, information exchange may be a more practical goal for summit meetings. Feldstein (1983), for example, writes:

> These meetings inevitably alter the way officials think about their own macroeconomic policies and increase their understanding of the policies being pursued by other governments. Such an exchange of information is clearly desirable and can help each country pursue its own policies more wisely . . . . In practice, despite its aspirations, international coordination may produce results that are not as satisfactory as those that result from each country's uncoordinated pursuit of national self interest.

It is even conceivable that there is a trade-off between information exchange and attempts at formal coordination since conspicuous failure at the latter could endanger the working relations between policymaking officials and thus reduce the effectiveness of these forums in fostering a frank exchange of views. It is perhaps no coincidence that the period of "going it alone" by the major industrialized countries in the early 1980s followed closely on the Bonn summit which many policymakers felt had been a failure.

Since information exchange is the most prevalent and important form of international cooperation it is perhaps surprising that, to date, there has been little formal analysis of the benefits of inter-governmental information exchange. Most studies that address this issue at all simply assert that there may be large welfare gains from information exchange (see, for example, Horne and Masson (1988), Artis and Ostry (1986), Canzoneri and Minford (1988), and Canzoneri and Henderson (1991)). Hughes Hallett (1986) studies an "isolationist" regime in which policymakers simply assume that there are no spillovers from abroad; using an empirical model he finds that taking account of such spillovers provides substantial welfare gains.

In this chapter we take a closer look at whether information exchange could really substitute for macroeconomic *coordination* (in the sense of maximizing a global welfare function). Although information exchange is obviously a prerequisite to successful international coordination, simple common sense arguments suggest that we treat any claims that information exchange could substitute for coordination with a healthy dose of skepticism. In fact, we will show a rather surprising result: it is possible that information exchange without coordination can actually lower both countries' welfare. Thus the value to information exchange itself may actually be *negative* (even though the information is correct).[1] This is profoundly disturbing since much of international cooperation probably consists of information exchange rather than formal coordination. Of course, in most cases information exchange does not lower welfare: we show that sharing information about certain shocks will make both countries better-off. In order to know whether information exchange will be useful when governments are not *coordinating* their policies we need to know both the reason why the uncoordinated equilibrium is inefficient relative to the coordinated regime, and what governments will do with this additional information.

It is useful to introduce some terminology at the outset. The situation we envisage is one in which each government observes some shock which is not observed by the other government (including, possibly, shocks to its preferences). Countries are said to be *coordinating* their policies if each chooses its national policies to maximize the global welfare function. (As shown in Chapter 3, this is also equivalent to requiring each government to take into account the response of the other government when choosing its own policy.) Implicitly, of course, countries must fully share any private information that they may have. In the *uncoordinated* equilibrium, we assume that there is a truthful and credible exchange of all information but that each government maximizes its own objective function in a Nash equilibrium. Finally, the *isolationist* regime involves neither the exchange of information nor the coordination of policies.

We distinguish between two types of inefficiency of the uncoordinated equilibrium. The uncoordinated equilibrium will be said to suffer from a *bias of commission* when governments are undertaking policies more forcefully than they would in the coordinated equilibrium. The model of Chapter III in which the uncoordinated equilibrium involved overly-contractionary policy in face of positive inflationary shocks (overly-expansionary in the case of negative shocks) would be a bias of commission. Such a bias arises when the objectives of the two governments are in direct conflict: in the model of Chapter 3, each government is trying to appreciate its bilateral exchange rate so that the two countries' objectives are mutually incompatible. In this chapter we shall encounter a second type of inefficiency, which we term a bias of *omission*, in which governments share a common objective but, because each one fails to take account of the benefit on the other country of its own policies, it does not pursue the policy sufficiently vigorously. Suppose, for example, that both governments agree that exchange rate *stability* is desirable (relative to a situation in which the exchange rate changes – regardless of whether this involves an appreciation or a depreciation). Each government may be willing to undertake some monetary or exchange rate policy to achieve that stability, but in general this will be at the cost of another of its objectives. Accordingly, because in the uncoordinated equilibrium neither government takes account of the positive externality on the other country of its exchange rate policy, it "under provides" the stabilization policy. The situation is precisely akin to the under-provision of public goods in a competitive equilibrium.

Once this distinction about the nature of the inefficiency of the un-coordinated equilibrium has been made, it is simple to see why information exchange is welfare improving when there is a bias of *omission* but welfare *deteriorating* when there is a bias of *commission*. When there is a bias of omission, knowledge about the shock observed by the foreign government to the common objective allows the home government to react to this shock. Since the uncoordinated equilibrium has a bias of too little policy intervention, this raises welfare. When the uncoordinated equilibrium has a bias of *commission*, in contrast, knowledge about the shock observed by the other government results in each country pursuing its inefficient policies even more vigorously, thereby *lowering* welfare.

2. The Framework

We use the same model as the one developed in Chapter 3, but augment it to include the effects of sterilized intervention, and shocks to the interest parity condition. We choose to focus on sterilized intervention for two reasons. First, most of the coordination – in the narrow sense – which has taken place in practice has taken the form of foreign exchange intervention. We assume that intervention is sterilized because, as a matter of operating practice, central banks of the major industrialized countries generally sterilize their interventions in the foreign exchange market. (They can, of course, alter overall monetary policy separately as well.) Second, because central banks rarely publicly reveal the amount of intervention that they are undertaking, it is plausible that they would not necessarily know how much intervention other central banks are doing. The assumption that governments do not observe each other's policy actions (unless there is explicit information exchange) is important for the strict logic of the model since, otherwise, knowing the foreign country's objective function, the home government could infer the shock observed by the foreign government simply by observing its policy actions. (Likewise, of course, the foreign government would be able to infer the shock observed by the home government.) Of course, in practice, it is unlikely that one could infer the shock observed by the government by observing its policy actions since the government could be responding to a variety of different shocks. It bears emphasizing, moreover, that the results we obtain hold for other types of monetary control and different shocks from those considered here (see Ghosh, 1991b).

Recall from Chapter 2 that the output price in the current period is pre-determined (and can therefore be normalized to zero); thus, aggregate demand can be written as an increasing function of the nominal exchange rate, and a decreasing function of the real interest rate:

$$y = \delta e + \gamma y^* - \sigma(i - p_{+1}) + u \tag{1}$$

$$y^* = -\delta e + \gamma y - \sigma(i^* - p^*_{+1}) + u^* \tag{2}$$

Money demand, in inverted form, is written:

$$i = \xi y - \varepsilon m \tag{3}$$

$$i^* = \xi y^* - \varepsilon m^* \tag{4}$$

Both m and m^* are set to zero since we are focusing on purely sterilized intervention. We augment the interest parity condition to include the effects of sterilized intervention and stochastic shocks:[2]

$$e = e_{+1} + i^* - i + \Delta - \Delta^* + z - z^* \tag{5}$$

Where Δ (Δ^*) is the amount of intervention undertaken by the home (foreign) central bank and z (z^*) is the shock to the interest parity condition observed by the home (foreign) central banks. These shocks could represent shifts in portfolio balances or currency substitution. If the United States is the home country and Germany the foreign country, then Δ (Δ^*) represents a purchase (sale) of DM assets and a simultaneous sale (purchase) of dollar assets by the Federal Reserve (Bundesbank). Notice that if both central banks are buying the same currency then Δ and Δ^* will be *negatively* correlated.[3]

If the stochastic shocks are serially uncorrelated then the (expected value of the) real exchange rate in period $t + 1$ will be equal to its baseline value of zero. Using this fact, it is shown in the appendix to this chapter that a transformation of variables allows us to write the reduced forms for output as:

$$y = \Delta - \Delta^* + z - z^* + u + \eta u^* \tag{6}$$

$$y^* = \Delta^* - \Delta + z^* - z + u^* + \eta u \tag{7}$$

where $0 \leq \eta \leq 1$.

In addition to wanting to prevent deviations of output from its potential level (which is normalized to zero here), central banks are assumed to be averse to intervening in the foreign exchange market.[4] This certainly appears to be the case in practice, since even the central banks of the major industrialized countries are concerned about the possibility of losses on their intervention. The losses of the Deutsche Bundesbank in 1987, amounting to some DM 9bn, for example, had to be absorbed into the public sector deficit and caused considerable embarrassment to the government (see Obstfeld, 1988). Likewise, in the United States, exchange intervention operations have been sharply criticized by such bodies as the Shadow Open Market Committee. Of course, the central bank may also make profits on foreign exchange intervention but there is a curious asymmetry: the central bank can be (and frequently is) criticized for making losses but (to our knowledge) no central bank has been criticized for failing to make potential profits. There may be limits, moreover, to the amount of debt that the capital markets can absorb and, therefore, on the amount of intervention which can be sterilized. Such limits were clearly reached in 1971 when the Bundesbank was intervening to support the dollar. It seems unrealistic, therefore, to suppose that central banks would be either willing or able to undertake arbitrarily large amounts of exchange intervention.

This reluctance on the part of central banks may be judged by the disagreements between the G-5 countries at the Plaza meeting on how much of the "burden" of intervention each party had to bear (Funabashi, 1988, pp. 27–29): Germany, in particular, reportedly drew criticism for failing to do its fair share. Since successful intervention imposes no financial burden on the central bank, this wrangling over each country's share in the intervention can only be attributed to an inherent reluctance to intervene in the foreign exchange market. Interestingly, the central banks which were intervening in support of their currency appear to have been as reluctant to bear the "burden" of intervention as central banks which were intervening to depreciate their currency (mainly the U.S. at the time of the Plaza). Thus a symmetric penalty function in the amount of foreign exchange intervention may be a reasonable specification of the central bank's preferences.

Accordingly, each central bank's objective function is written:

$$\mathcal{V} = \text{Max} -\tfrac{1}{2}E\{y^2 + \omega\Delta^2\} \tag{8}$$

$$\mathcal{V}^* = \text{Max} -\tfrac{1}{2}E\{y^{*2} + \omega\Delta^{*2}\} \tag{9}$$

Note that we use the *ex ante* expected utility criterion for evaluating the three different regimes. This is appropriate since we are interested in the average performance of these regimes, rather than the welfare level attained for any particular realization of the stochastic shocks.

3. Bias of Omission

Suppose, initially, that there are no aggregate demand shocks; the only shocks to the economy are those affecting the exchange rate directly, z and z^*. The home country is assumed to observe z before choosing its optimal intervention, Δ. It does not, however, observe either z^* or Δ^*, except as part of an explicit inter-governmental exchange of information. Likewise, the foreign country does not observe z or Δ before choosing Δ^*. The shocks z and z^* are normally distributed with zero mean, a common variance σ_z^2, and contemporaneous correlation coefficient ρ_z.

In the *coordinated* regime, both governments share their information about the shocks they have observed and then choose their intervention policies in order to maximize the global objective function:

$$\mathcal{V}^G = \tfrac{1}{2}\{\mathcal{V} + \mathcal{V}^*\} \tag{1}$$

where each country is assumed to receive equal weight. The global social welfare function can therefore be written:

$$\mathcal{V}^G = -\left(\tfrac{1}{4}\right)E\{(\Delta - \Delta^* + z - z^*)^2 + \omega\Delta^2 \\ + (\Delta^* - \Delta + z^* - z) + \omega\Delta^{*2} \mid z, z^*\} \tag{2}$$

The home country's first-order condition implies:

$$\partial\mathcal{V}^G/\partial\Delta = 0 \Rightarrow \Delta = \frac{2(z^* - z) + 2\Delta^*}{2 + \omega} \tag{3}$$

while that of the foreign country gives the following reaction function:

$$\partial\mathcal{V}^G/\partial\Delta^* = 0 \Rightarrow \Delta^* = \frac{2(z - z^*) + 2\Delta}{2 + \omega} \tag{4}$$

Solving these two reaction functions simultaneously gives the coordinated outcome (see Figure 7.1):

$$\Delta^C = -\Delta^{C*} = \frac{2(z^* - z)}{4 + \omega} \tag{5}$$

Shocks which would lead to a depreciation of the dollar $(z^* - z) < 0$, for example, require both governments to buy dollar assets and sell DM assets $(\Delta < 0, \Delta^* > 0)$. The implied levels of output in each country are therefore:

$$y = \frac{\omega(z - z^*)}{4 + \omega} \quad \text{and} \quad y^* = \frac{\omega(z^* - z)}{4 + \omega} \tag{6}$$

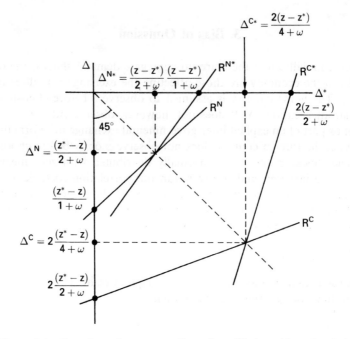

Figure 7.1   Coordinated vs. uncoordinated equilibrium: bias of omission
$(z - z^*) > 0$

Substituting the optimal policies into the objective function, and taking expectations over the distribution of z and z^*, gives the welfare level under coordination:

$$\mathcal{V}^C = \mathcal{V}^{C*} = -\left(\tfrac{1}{2}\right)\frac{2(1 - \rho_z)\sigma_z^2}{4 + \omega} \tag{7}$$

Consider, next, the uncoordinated regime wherein governments exchange information about the realizations of the shocks z and z^* and about the intervention they will undertake, but they do not coordinate their intervention. (To keep the notation consistent with Chapter 3 we denote this uncoordinated equilibrium by the letter N.) The home country maximizes $\mathcal{V}$, taking as given Δ^*, and with the knowledge of the realizations of z and z^*. The home country's objective function is given by:

$$\mathcal{V} = \text{Max} - \left(\tfrac{1}{2}\right)E\{(\Delta - \Delta^* + z - z^*)^2 + \omega\Delta^2 \mid z, z^*\} \tag{8}$$

Solving the analogous optimization problem for the foreign country yields the following reaction functions:

$$\Delta = \frac{\Delta^* - z + z^*}{1 + \omega} \tag{9}$$

and

$$\Delta^* = \frac{\Delta - z^* + z}{1 + \omega} \tag{10}$$

which are depicted in Figure 7.1 (the figure assumes that $z - z^* > 0$). The resulting uncoordinated equilibrium is, therefore, given by:

$$\Delta^N = -\Delta^{N^*} = \frac{z^* - z}{2 + \omega} \tag{11}$$

and the associated level of output in each country is:

$$y = \frac{\omega(z - z^*)}{2 + \omega} \quad \text{and} \quad y^* = \frac{\omega(z^* - z)}{2 + \omega} \tag{12}$$

Substituting (11) and (12) into the objective functions gives the level of welfare attained in the uncoordinated regime:

$$\mathcal{V}^N = \mathcal{V}^{N^*} = -\left(\tfrac{1}{2}\right) \frac{2\omega(1 - \rho_z)\sigma_z^2(1 + \omega)}{(2 + \omega)^2} \tag{13}$$

Comparing (13) and (7) shows that the uncoordinated equilibrium is inefficient compared to the coordinated equilibrium: $\mathcal{V}^C = \mathcal{V}^{C^*} > \mathcal{V}^N = \mathcal{V}^{N^*}$ so that there are gains from coordination. The benefits from coordination arise because each country, acting independently, fails to take into account the benefits to the other country of its own efforts at stabilizing the exchange rate. Thus the uncoordinated equilibrium suffers from a bias of *omission*: each country undertakes too little stabilizing intervention relative to the coordinated optimum (see Figure 7.1).

Since the optimal policies are responding to stochastic shocks, one way to compare them is to assume a specific realizations of those shocks. Suppose that the realization of the interest parity shocks is such that $z - z^* > 0$ (the dollar is depreciating). The welfare effect of a small perturbation in the foreign intervention policy on the home country in the uncoordinated equilibrium is then:

$$\partial \mathcal{V} / \partial \Delta^* = \left(\tfrac{1}{2}\right)(\Delta^N - \Delta^{N^*} + z - z^*) = \left(\tfrac{1}{2}\right)\frac{\omega(z - z^*)}{2 + \omega} > 0 \tag{14}$$

Thus when the dollar is depreciating the Bundesbank could raise U.S. welfare by buying more dollars. Likewise, the effect on the foreign country of a perturbation in the home country's intervention policy is given by:

$$\partial \mathcal{V}^*/\partial \Delta = \left(\tfrac{1}{2}\right)(\Delta^{N^*} - \Delta^N + z^* - z) = \left(\tfrac{1}{2}\right)\frac{\omega(z^* - z)}{2 + \omega} < 0 \qquad (15)$$

so that the Federal Reserve would raise Germany's welfare by purchasing more dollars as well. Given the way we have defined the intervention policies, Δ and Δ^*, this implies that the intervention strategies should have a larger *negative* covariance.

Since the *ex ante* expected value of Δ and Δ^* is zero in each regime we consider (Δ and Δ^* are responding to shocks whose mean value is zero), only the second moments are required to characterize each regime. It turns out, in fact, that we only need the covariance between the two central banks' intervention policies to compare the different regimes.[6]

From (8), under coordination, this covariance is given by:

$$\mathrm{cov}(\Delta^C, \Delta^{C^*}) = \frac{-8(1 - \rho_z)\sigma_z^2}{(4 + \omega)^2} \qquad (16)$$

If we calculate the covariance between Δ^N and Δ^{N^*} we see that though it is of the same sign as $\mathrm{cov}(\Delta^C, \Delta^{C^*})$ it is too small in magnitude relative to the covariance in the coordinated equilibrium:

$$\mathrm{cov}(\Delta^N, \Delta^{N^*}) = \frac{-2\sigma_z^2(1 - \rho_z)}{(2 + \omega)^2} \qquad (17)$$

Thus when the dollar is depreciating both the Federal Reserve and the Bundesbank should be buying more dollars than they would in the uncoordinated equilibrium.

The third regime we consider is the *isolationist* regime in which there is neither information-sharing nor coordination of macroeconomic policies. The home (foreign) government observes neither z^* (z) nor Δ^* (Δ) when choosing its own intervention strategy. The home central bank's optimization problem is now given by:

$$\mathcal{V} = \mathrm{Max} - \left(\tfrac{1}{2}\right)E\{(\Delta - \Delta^* + z - z^*)^2 + \omega\Delta^2 \mid z\} \qquad (18)$$

which is analogous to (11) except for the conditioning information set which now consists of z alone (z^* in the case of the foreign country). The resulting first-order condition is:

$$E\{((\Delta - \Delta^* + z - z^*) + \omega\Delta) \mid z\} = 0 \qquad (19)$$

Similarly, the foreign central bank's first-order condition is given by:

$$E\{((\Delta^* - \Delta + z^* - z) + \omega\Delta^*) \mid z^*\} = 0 \qquad (20)$$

Since we assume that z and z^* are joint Normally distributed the expectation of z^* (z) conditional on z (z^*) is simply ρz (ρz^*). Although the home central bank does not observe Δ^*, it does know that the foreign central bank has only observed z^* and therefore Δ^* can only be a function of z^*. Suppose the home central bank conjectures that the foreign central bank's intervention policy can be written $\Omega^*(z^*)$ for some function $\Omega^*(\cdot)$. Since we have a linear-quadratic model it is natural to restrict attention to policies which are linear in the observed shocks. We therefore assume that the optimal policy is given by $\Omega^* z^*$ for some constant Ω^*.

The home country's first-order condition (19) becomes:

$$\Delta = \frac{\{(1 + \Omega^*)\rho_z - 1\}z}{1 + \omega} \tag{21}$$

If the foreign central bank conjectures that the home central bank's intervention policy may be written $\Delta = \Omega z$ for some constant Ω, then (20) becomes:

$$\Delta^* = \frac{\{(1 + \Omega)\rho_z - 1\}z^*}{1 + \omega} \tag{22}$$

For each central bank's conjectures to be consistent, the following conditions must hold:

$$\Omega = \frac{(1 + \Omega^*)\rho_z - 1}{1 + \omega} \tag{23}$$

$$\Omega^* = \frac{(1 + \Omega)\rho_z - 1}{1 + \omega} \tag{24}$$

Solving these two equations simultaneously gives:

$$\Omega = \Omega^* = \frac{\rho_z - 1}{1 + \omega - \rho_z} \tag{25}$$

Therefore, the intervention strategy in the isolationist regime is:

$$\Delta^I = \frac{(\rho_z - 1)z}{1 + \omega - \rho_z} \quad \Delta^{I*} = \frac{(\rho_z - 1)z^*}{1 + \omega - \rho_z} \tag{26}$$

Substituting these into the reduced forms for output yields:

$$y = \frac{\omega(z - z^*)}{1 - \rho_z + \omega} \quad \text{and} \quad y^* = \frac{\omega(z^* - z)}{1 - \rho_z + \omega} \tag{27}$$

Each country's expected welfare level is therefore:

$$V^I = V^{I*} = -\tfrac{1}{2}\frac{(1 - \rho_z)\omega(1 - \rho_z + 2\omega)\sigma_z^2}{(1 - \rho_z + \omega)^2} \tag{28}$$

Subtracting (28) from (13) shows (after tedious algebraic manipulations) that:

$$\mathcal{V}^N - \mathcal{V}^I \propto \{3(1 - \rho_z^2)\omega^3 + 2(1 - \rho_z)(4 - (1 - \rho_z)^2)\omega^2 \\ + 2(1 - \rho_z)^2(1 + \rho_z)\omega\} \geq 0 \tag{29}$$

Thus information sharing, even without coordination, raises welfare in this example. The inequality in (29) will be strict unless $\rho_z = \pm 1$. This is intuitively clear since a perfect correlation across the shocks observed by each central bank means that there is no need for any information exchange: observing $z(z^*)$ would be equivalent to observing $z^*(z)$.

The intuition for why information-sharing raises welfare in this particular example is straightforward. In the uncoordinated regime, each central bank is insufficiently activist in offsetting shocks to the exchange rate because it fails to take into account the welfare benefits to the other country. This inefficiency is exacerbated in the isolationist regime simply because the home (foreign) central bank cannot offset the shock $z^*(z)$ since, by assumption, it does not observe the shock abroad. (When the shocks are correlated each central bank has an estimate of the shock observed by the foreign country but it is only an imperfect estimate unless there is perfect positive or negative correlation.)

Again to characterize the inefficiency of the isolationist regime it is sufficient to compare the covariance between Δ and Δ^* in each of the three regimes (see Gal-Or, 1986 for a similar argument in an industrial organization context). From (29), in the isolationist regime,

$$\text{cov}(\Delta^I, \Delta^{I^*}) = \frac{\rho_z \sigma_z^2 (1 - \rho_z)}{(1 - \rho_z + \omega)^2} \tag{30}$$

Thus from (16), (17), and (30):

$$\text{cov}(\Delta^I, \Delta^{I^*}) > \text{cov}(\Delta^N, \Delta^{N^*}) > \text{cov}(\Delta^C, \Delta^{C^*}) \tag{31}$$

Greater interventionism of the coordinated regime implies a larger negative covariance between the intervention strategies (that is, a shock which would depreciate the dollar would elicit a large purchase of dollar assets in exchange for Deutschemark assets by both the Federal Reserve and the Bundesbank). Without coordination, intervention strategies are less activist – because in weighing the benefits of exchange rate stability against the cost of intervention neither central bank takes into account the benefit to the other country of its intervention – so the covariance is less negative. Finally, the isolationist regime implies even lower activism as central banks do not observe all of the shocks to the exchange rate: The covariance between Δ and Δ^* is even less negative (and could even be positive, so that central banks would be intervening at cross purposes).

As discussed in the Introduction, the result that sharing information raises welfare has almost universal appeal. As shown below, however, the result is highly specific to the shock being considered; when the uncoordinated equilibrium has a bias of *commission* rather than one of *omission*, information exchange will lower welfare.[7]

4. Bias of Commission

We now drop the interest parity shocks and examine the welfare ranking of the three regimes when there are only aggregate demand shocks. The home (foreign) country does not observe u^* or Δ^* (u or Δ) before choosing its own intervention. The reduced forms for home and foreign output remain given by (2.6)–(2.7) with $z = z^* = 0$. As above, the coordinated regime involves a single social planner choosing Δ and Δ^* in order to maximize $\frac{1}{2}(\mathcal{V} + \mathcal{V}^*)$:

$$\mathcal{V}^G = \text{Max} - \tfrac{1}{4}\{((\Delta - \Delta^*) + u + \eta u^*)^2 + \omega \Delta^2 + ((\Delta^* - \Delta) + u^* + \eta u)^2 + \omega \Delta^{*2}\} \tag{1}$$

Solving the resulting first-order conditions for Δ and Δ^* yields the optimal coordinated intervention strategies:

$$\Delta^C = -\Delta^{C^*} = \frac{(1 - \eta)(u^* - u)}{(4 + \omega)} \tag{2}$$

Notice that the globally optimal strategy involves reacting only to the difference between u and u^*. The reason is apparent from the reduced forms for output; adding them together yields:

$$y + y^* = (1 + \eta)(u + u^*) \tag{3}$$

Therefore, intervention cannot affect the level of world output; it can only change the distribution of that output between the home and foreign countries. As a result, the optimal policy simply involves offsetting the difference between u and u^*: when the shocks hitting the two countries are equal, no intervention should be undertaken.

The level of output in each country at the coordinated equilibrium may be obtained by substituting for Δ^C and Δ^{C^*}:

$$y^C = \frac{(2 + \omega + 2\eta)u + (2 + (2 + \omega)\eta)u^*}{4 + \omega}$$

$$y^{C^*} = \frac{(2 + \omega + 2\eta)u^* + (2 + (2 + \omega)\eta)u}{4 + \omega} \tag{4}$$

and the expected utility level attained by each country is:

$$V^C \big|_{\rho_u=0} = -\frac{(2+\omega+2\eta)^2 + (2+(2+\omega)\eta)^2 + (1/\omega)2(1-\eta)^2}{2(4+\omega)^2}$$

(5)

where, to simplify the algebra, we have set ρ_u, the correlation coefficient between the two demand shocks, equal to zero.[8] Again, for future reference, it is useful to calculate the covariance in the intervention policies:

$$cov(\Delta^C, \Delta^{C^*}) = \frac{-2(1-\eta)^2}{(4+\omega)^2}$$

(6)

In the uncoordinated regime, the home (foreign) central bank maximizes $V(V^*)$ taking as given the intervention policies of the other. The resulting reaction functions are:

$$\Delta = \frac{\Delta^* - (u + \eta u^*)}{1+\omega}$$

(7)

$$\Delta^* = \frac{\Delta - (u^* + \eta u)}{1+\omega}$$

(8)

So that the uncoordinated regime is given by:

$$\Delta^N = -\frac{(\omega+1+\eta)u + (\eta\omega+1+\eta)u^*}{\omega(2+\omega)} \quad \text{and}$$

$$\Delta^{N^*} = -\frac{(\omega+1+\eta)u^* + (\eta\omega+1+\eta)u}{\omega(2+\omega)}$$

(9)

Since $\eta \geq 0$, intervention in the uncoordinated regime does not respond exclusively to the difference between u and u^*. Herein lies the inefficiency of this regime relative to coordination. The inefficiency is one of *commission* since central banks are undertaking intervention operations "in excess" of what they would do in the optimal, coordinated regime. Figure 7.2 depicts the coordinated and uncoordinated equilibria (the figure assumes that $\eta = 0$ and $u = u^* > 0$). In effect, each central bank tries to manipulate the exchange rate in order stimulate (or dampen in the case of positive shocks) the level of its own output. Suppose, for example, that both u and u^* are positive. Then from (7) and (8) both Δ and Δ^* are negative: the U.S. Fed is buying dollars and selling DM assets (to appreciate the dollar and dampen U.S. aggregate demand) while at the same time the Bundesbank is buying DM assets and selling dollar assets. The two central banks are therefore intervening at *cross* purposes with

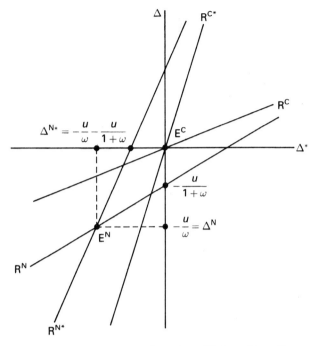

Figure 7.2 Coordinated vs. uncoordinated equilibrium: bias of commission

little net effect on the exchange rate, but a high cost of intervention. This is reflected in the welfare level attained in the uncoordinated equilibrium, which is lower than that of the coordinated equilibrium:

$$
\begin{aligned}
\mathcal{V}^N\big|_{\rho_u=0} &= \mathcal{V}^{N^*}\big|_{\rho_u=0} \\
&= -\tfrac{1}{2}\frac{\{(1+1/\omega)((1+\eta+\omega)^2 + (1+\eta+\eta\omega)^2)\}\sigma_u^2}{(2+\omega)^2}
\end{aligned}
\tag{10}
$$

The covariance between each country's intervention is given by:

$$
\mathrm{cov}(\Delta^N, \Delta^{N^*}) =
$$
$$
\frac{\{2(\omega+1+\eta)(1+\eta+\eta\omega) + \rho_u((1+\omega+\eta)^2 + (1+\eta+\eta\omega)^2)\}}{\omega^2(2+\omega)^2}
$$

$$
\tag{11}
$$

which is necessarily *positive* if ρ_u is zero.

Finally, in the isolationist equilibrium neither central bank knows that shock observed by the other, or the intervention being undertaken. The first-order conditions are:

$$\Delta = \frac{E\{\Delta^* - (u + \eta u^*) \mid u\}}{1 + \omega} \tag{12}$$

$$\Delta^* = \frac{E\{\Delta - (u^* + \eta u) \mid u^*\}}{1 + \omega} \tag{13}$$

Let $\Omega\,(\Omega^*)$ denote the foreign (home) central bank's conjecture of the home (foreign) central bank's intervention policy, then solving for the optimal policies gives:

$$\Omega = \Omega^* = \frac{-(1 + \eta \rho_u)}{1 - \rho_u + \omega} \tag{14}$$

Hence:

$$\Delta^I = \frac{-(1 + \eta \rho_u)u}{1 - \rho_u + \omega} \quad \text{and} \quad \Delta^\Gamma = \frac{-(1 + \eta \rho_u)u^*}{1 - \rho_u + \omega} \tag{15}$$

Substituting for Δ and Δ^* from (18) gives the level of output in each country:

$$y = \frac{(\omega - (1 + \eta)\rho_u)u + (1 + \eta + \eta\omega)u^*}{1 + \omega - \rho_u} \tag{16}$$

$$y^* = \frac{(\omega - (1 + \eta)\rho_u)u^* + (1 + \eta + \eta\omega)u}{1 + \omega - \rho_u} \tag{17}$$

which yields a level of welfare:

$$\mathcal{V}^I \mid_{\rho_u=0} = \mathcal{V}^\Gamma \mid_{\rho_u=0} = -\frac{1}{2}\frac{\{\omega(\omega + (1 + \eta + \eta\omega)^2 + 1\}\sigma_u^2}{(1 + \omega)^2} \tag{18}$$

The covariance between the intervention strategies is given by:

$$\text{cov}(\Delta^I, \Delta^\Gamma) = \frac{\rho_u(1 - \omega)^2}{(1 - \rho_u(1 - \omega))^2} \tag{19}$$

Comparing the isolationist regime to the uncoordinated equilibrium shows that *not* sharing information will raise welfare: $\mathcal{V}^I > \mathcal{V}^N$. (Proving this inequality involves a great deal of tedious algebra; here we present the benchmark case of $\rho_u = 0$):[9]

$$\begin{aligned}\mathcal{V}^I - \mathcal{V}^N &\propto \{2(1 + \eta)^2 + 4\eta^2\omega + (5 + \eta(\eta + 8))\omega^2 \\ &\quad + 2((1 - \eta^2) + 3\eta)\omega^3 + \eta(2 - \eta)\omega^4\} > 0\end{aligned} \tag{20}$$

While the isolationist regime is better than the uncoordinated regime, it is, of course, strictly worse than full coordination.

We can see how information sharing may reduce welfare by considering the case in which the two shocks are uncorrelated. In that case, both Δ^N and Δ^{N^*} – the intervention policies of the uncoordinated regime – are necessarily positively correlated and, on average, the two central banks are intervening at cross-purposes. From the reaction functions (7) and (8), moreover, we see that the more intervention the foreign central bank does, the more intervention the home central bank will do as well. Suppose, for example, that the Fed is intervening to *appreciate* the dollar. When the shocks are uncorrelated we know from (11) that the Bundesbank will, on average, be trying to *depreciate* the dollar on such occasions. If the Fed knows that the Bundesbank is intervening at cross-purposes, however, it will be tempted to intervene even more strongly. Similarly, when the Bundesbank knows that the Fed is intervening to depreciate the dollar it will intervene more vigorously to appreciate the dollar. The result is a large "cost" of intervention (as captured by the terms $\omega\Delta^2$ and $\omega\Delta^{*2}$) but little net effect on the exchange rate. If neither central bank knows when the other is intervening, however, there will be less intervention undertaken at cross-purposes, and both central banks will be better-off. In fact, from (19) we see that when ρ_u equals zero, the intervention strategies of the two central banks are uncorrelated in the isolationist regime.

As above, the ranking of the three regimes can be characterized in terms of the covariance between the two countries' intervention strategies. Thus when ρ_u equals zero, the intervention is *negatively* correlated in the coordinated equilibrium, *uncorrelated* in the isolationist regime, and *positively* correlated in the uncoordinated regime. More generally, we have:

$$\operatorname{cov}(\Delta^C, \Delta^{C^*}) < \operatorname{cov}(\Delta^I, \Delta^{I^*}) < \operatorname{cov}(\Delta^N, \Delta^{N^*}) \tag{21}$$

Notice that the ranking between $\operatorname{cov}(\Delta^I, \Delta^{I^*})$ and $\operatorname{cov}(\Delta^N, \Delta^{N^*})$ relative to $\operatorname{cov}(\Delta^C, \Delta^{C^*})$ is reversed between (3.31) and (21) so that information-sharing without full coordination reduces welfare when there are aggregate demand shocks.

5. Conclusions

In this chapter we examined the benefits of inter-governmental information exchange, using a very stark, and perhaps overly simplistic model of official exchange market intervention. Our main result – that information exchange could actually lower welfare – is certainly surprising. Actual instances in which information exchange has lowered welfare are, of course, difficult to identify. And while central banks are unlikely to deliberately intervene at cross-purposes, public statements made by either the treasury or the central bank of one country are sometimes viewed as counterproductive by the central bank of the other country. Such was the case when the Japanese were trying to prevent any further appreciation of the yen in January 1987. Finance minister Miyazawa and Bank of Japan Governor Sumita let the markets know that the Bank of Japan would intervene to prevent the dollar from depreciating further "regardless of the cost." The very next day the *New York Times* reported an unidentified U.S. official as wanting a further decline of the dollar, whereupon there was an immediate rash of dollar sales against both the mark and the yen (Funabashi, 1988, p. 164).[10]

The question is whether knowledge that other central banks were intervening (or trying to influence the market through public statements or by leaking information) in the opposite direction would have led to even more vigorous intervention or instead, to each central bank stopping its intervention policies. In our uncoordinated regime, each central bank would have re-doubled its efforts in a futile attempt to move the exchange rate in the direction it desired. If central banks recognize the futility of this and instead agree to intervene in one direction to achieve a common objective (or agree not to intervene at all) then they are, at least implicitly, coordinating their policies.

It bears emphasizing that this result is not specific to the model we have chosen. Rather than assume that the policy instruments are sterilized intervention, for example, we could have assumed that each central bank is choosing its money supply. While it is less likely that each central bank does not observe the others' money supply, it is not implausible that one central bank will not know the overall monetary stance of the other central banks at the time that it must choose its own monetary policy. Moreover, notice that the shocks u and u^* could equally well be shocks to the *desired* output level (that is, they could reflect the preferences of the central bank). In general such preferences cannot be observed by foreign central banks. But sharing information about such shocks does not improve welfare unless there is policy coordination as well. If knowledge about the intentions or actions of other governments leads each government to pursue its own objectives more vigorously – and those objectives are in direct conflict – then information-sharing will lower welfare.

Of course, our results are not an argument against international economic cooperation. On the contrary, the real message of the model is that the information-sharing aspects of international cooperation, though an essential prerequisite to coordination, may be a very poor substitute for coordination itself.

Appendix

This appendix derives some of the algebraic expressions used in the text.

Section 2: Reduced forms for output

Using the constancy of the real exchange in the face of temporary shocks we can write the expected future nominal exchange rate as:

$$e_{+1} = 2\theta e + \psi(y - y^*) \tag{A1}$$

Substituting (A1) into (5) of the text, and using (3) and (4) gives:

$$e = \frac{(\psi - \xi)(y - y^*) + (\Delta - \Delta^* + z - z^*)}{1 - 2\theta} \tag{A2}$$

Subtracting the foreign aggregate demand function from that of the home country, and substituting (A2) and the two countries' Phillips curves, yields:

$$y - y^* = \frac{(2\delta + \sigma)(\Delta - \Delta^* + z - z^*) + (1 - 2\theta)(u - u^*)}{(1 - 2\theta)(1 + \gamma) + (\xi - \psi)(2\delta + \sigma)} \tag{A3}$$

Adding the two aggregate demand functions gives:

$$y + y^* = \frac{u + u^*}{1 - \gamma + \sigma(\xi - \psi)} \tag{A4}$$

Adding and subtracting (A3) and (A4) yields:

$$y = \frac{1}{2}\left\{ \frac{(2\delta + \sigma)(\Delta - \Delta^* + z - z^*) + (1 - 2\theta)(u - u^*)}{(1 - 2\theta)(1 + \gamma) + (\xi - \psi)(2\delta + \sigma)} \right. \\ \left. + \frac{u + u^*}{1 - \gamma + \sigma(\xi - \psi)} \right\} \tag{A5}$$

and

$$y^* = \frac{1}{2}\left\{ \frac{(2\delta + \sigma)(\Delta^* - \Delta + z^* - z) + (1 - 2\theta)(u^* - u)}{(1 - 2\theta)(1 + \gamma) + (\xi - \psi)(2\delta + \sigma)} \right. \\ \left. + \frac{u + u^*}{1 - \gamma + \sigma(\xi - \psi)} \right\} \tag{A6}$$

which can be written:

$$y = \Delta - \Delta^* + u + \eta u^* \tag{A7}$$

$$y^* = \Delta^* - \Delta + u^* + \eta u \tag{A8}$$

by the following change of variables. Let $\Delta', \Delta^*, z', z^*, u'$ and $u^{*'}$ be the original variables then we define:

$$\Delta = \frac{(2\delta + \sigma)\Delta'}{(1 - 2\theta)(1 + \gamma) + (\xi - \psi)(2\delta + \sigma)} \tag{A9}$$

$$z = \frac{(2\delta + \sigma)z'}{(1 - 2\theta)(1 + \gamma) + (\xi - \psi)(2\delta + \sigma)} \tag{A10}$$

$$u = \frac{(1 - 2\theta)u'}{(1 - 2\theta)(1 + \gamma) + (\xi - \psi)(2\delta + \sigma)} + \frac{u'}{1 - \gamma + \sigma(\xi - \psi)} \tag{A11}$$

and

$$\eta = \frac{(1 - 2\theta)\gamma + (\delta + \sigma\theta)(\xi - \psi)}{(1 - 2\theta) + (\delta + \sigma(1 - \theta))(\xi - \psi)} \tag{A12}$$

with analogous expressions for Δ^*, z^* and u^*.

Section 4: Expressions for $\mathcal{V}^C, \mathcal{V}^N,$ and $\mathcal{V}^I$ when $\rho_u \neq 0$.

$$\mathcal{V}^C = -\left\{ \frac{(2 + \omega + 2\eta)^2 + (2 + (2 + \omega)\eta)^2}{2(4 + \omega)^2} + \frac{2\rho_u(2 + \omega + 2\eta)(2 + (2 + \omega)\eta)}{2(4 + \omega)^2} + \frac{(1/\omega)2(1 - \eta)^2(1 - \rho_u)}{2(4 + \omega)^2} \right\}\sigma_u^2 \tag{A13}$$

$$\mathcal{V}^N = -\left\{ \frac{(1 + 1/\omega)((1 + \eta + \omega)^2}{2(2 + \omega)^2} + \frac{(1 + \eta + \eta\omega)^2 + 2\rho_u(1 + \eta + \omega)(1 + \eta + \eta\omega)}{2(2 + \omega)^2} \right\}\sigma_u^2 \tag{A14}$$

$$\mathcal{V}^I = -\left\{ \frac{(\omega - (1 + \eta)\rho_u)^2 + (1 + \eta + \eta\omega)^2}{2(1 + \omega - \rho_u)^2} + \frac{2\rho_u(\omega - (1 + \eta)\rho_u)(1 + \eta + \eta\omega) + \omega(1 + \eta\rho_u)^2}{2(1 + \omega - \rho_u)^2} \right\}\sigma_u^2 \tag{A15}$$

Notes

1   There are several papers in the industrial organization literature which examine the incentives of duopolies to share information about demand shocks and supply cost shocks. See Novshek and Sonnenschein (1982), Clarke (1983), Vives (1984), Fried (1984) and Gal-Or (1986).

2   See Ghosh (1992) and Frankel and Dominguez (1990) for econometric evidence on the effectiveness of sterilized intervention.

3   This is just an arbitrary normalization but one which keeps the algebra simple by making the model completely symmetric.

4   We drop the inflation objective to simplify the algebra below. Since we are assuming sterilized intervention we could view the central bank as setting the money supply in order to achieve an inflation target.

5   If $z - z^* < 0$ then both central banks should purchase more DM assets, of course.

6   The covariance, unlike the correlation coefficient, tells us enough about both the magnitude of Δ and Δ^* under each regime and their co-variation to characterize the regime completely.

7   Even in the case analyzed here, it is also possible that concealing information would benefit one of the countries, for a given realization of the stochastic shocks. If governments have to choose between a *regime* of sharing information or not sharing information (as we assume here) then the information-sharing regime is preferable when the uncoordinated equilibrium has a bias of omission.

8   In the appendix to this chapter we give expressions for V^C, V^N and V^I when ρ_u is non-zero.

9   The inequality $V^I \geq V^N$ will be strict unless $\rho_u = \pm 1$.

10   There are often interventions which unintentionally work at cross purposes to the actions of other central banks. For example, countries in the European Monetary System (EMS) will often be forced to sell DM in exchange for their own currencies. If the U.S. Fed is trying to buy DM in order to appreciate the DM against the dollar then the sales of DM by European central banks will partially offset the Fed's efforts.

8

On the Sustainability of Cooperative Agreements

1. Introduction

The results presented thus far give a relatively sanguine picture of the viability of international coordination when there is macroeconomic uncertainty. Indeed, certain types of uncertainty actually raise the benefits of such coordination. In this chapter, and the next, we examine some of the difficulties associated with reaching a cooperative agreement, and in sustaining it, once we admit the possibility that governments either intentionally misrepresent their views and objectives, or defect from previously negotiated agreements.

If macroeconomic policies are to be successfully coordinated then governments must enjoy the trust of their economic partners. Yet depending upon the nature of the contract, verifying compliance with an international policy agreement may be impossible. If the agreement is specified in terms of outcomes for certain target variables and these targets are observable, then, of course, it is easy to verify whether the agreed targets were achieved. But since there will always be uncertainty about the link between policy instruments and final targets, such verification does not ensure that each government made *bona fide* attempts at attaining those objectives. One then runs the risk either of falsely accusing one party of failing to abide by the agreement or of permitting such wide tolerances within the agreement that each government feels free to cheat, or at least interpret the agreement in the way which is most favorable to its own interests.

On the other hand, specifying an agreement in terms of the actual instrument settings does not necessarily solve this problem, since the choice of the optimal instrument settings will generally depend upon *forecasts* (including forecasts of the behavior of autonomous parts of the government, such as Congress in the case of U.S. fiscal policy). If each government has the best forecast of its own economy, then such forecasts are essentially private information and verifying honesty again becomes problematic (see Canzoneri, 1985 for a similar problem in a closed economy game between the central bank and wage-setters). Thus Germany and the United States may report to each other that they are expecting inflationary pressures in their respective economies. But these forecasts will usually contain elements of private information (that is, the German government will have a better forecast of German inflation and the U.S. government will have a better forecast of U.S. inflation) so that they are not really observable by the other. If the U.S. reports that it is expecting a shock which will add 3 percent to the annual inflation rate, it will be difficult to establish *ex post* that the mathematical expectation of the shock, conditional on the information available to the government when the forecast was made, was in fact only one percent.[1]

Suppose that the United States and Germany, each facing its own inflationary shock, agree not to try to export their inflation to each other by an excessive tightening of their monetary policies. If Germany then ends up with a higher than expected inflation rate, and the United States with a lower inflation rate, there will be a suspicion that the Americans either failed to stick to the cooperative agreement or exaggerated the size of the inflationary shock. While governments are unlikely to accuse each other of having "cheated," there would almost certainly be a period during which coordination is viewed with disappointment if not outright suspicion. It may be some time before coordination is attempted again. Arguably, this is what happened in the aftermath of the Bonn locomotive experiment.

We certainly admit that it is an open question whether governments deliberately renege on agreements. Putnam and Henning (1989), for example, argue that most governments view the political cost of losing credibility as outweighing potential economic benefits. Presumably, the greater the visibility of the agreement the greater the political cost of reneging. This suggests that G-7 summit meetings should enjoy the greatest degree of commitment. But as von Furstenberg and Daniels (1992) have shown, most targets specified in summit communiques are not achieved. Von Furstenberg and Daniels assign a score of +1 if the target is achieved or exceeded; a score of −1 if the outcome is exactly the opposite to what was intended and a score of 0 if there is no change. Thus if growth is currently 1 percent and the goal is to raise growth to 3 percent by the next year, then the summitteers get a score of +1 if growth is 3 percent or higher, a score between 0 and 1 if growth is between 1 percent and 3 percent, a score of 0 if growth remains at 1 percent, a score between 0 and −1 if growth is between 1 percent and −1 percent, and a score of −1 for growth rates below −1 percent. Using this scoring method, von Furstenberg and Daniels grade some two hundred agreements in which specific targets can be identified over the fifteen summit meetings (from the 1975 Rambouillet Summit to the 1989 Paris Summit). The *average* score (see Table 8.1) is less than one-third and ranges from about 0.86 (for the 1987 Venice Summit) to −0.45 (for the 1988 Toronto Summit). Thus intentionally or not, governments have a rather poor record of adhering to stated summit goals.

Table 8.1 Degree of compliance with summit targets

Summit	Date	Number of scores	Average
Rambouillet	11/75	9	0.408
			(0.669)
San Juan	6/76	16	0.351
			(0.575)
London I	5/77	10	0.381
			(0.596)
Bonn I	7/78	26	0.343
			(0.693)
Tokyo I	6/79	15	0.623
			(0.640)
Venice I	6/80	14	0.159
			(0.610)
Ottawa	7/81	12	0.266
			(0.815)
Versailles	6/82	15	0.823
			(0.316)
Williamsburg	5/83	19	0.066
			(0.662)
London II	6/84	20	0.352
			(0.578)
Bonn II	5/85	14	0.200
			(0.674)
Tokyo II	6/86	4	0.765
			(0.237)
Venice II	6/87	8	0.857
			(0.259)
Toronto	6/88	14	−0.450
			(0.628)
Paris	7/89	13	0.187
			(0.701)
All combined		209	0.317
			(0.688)

Source: von Furstenberg and Daniels (1992), table 4.
Note: standard errors in parentheses.

Why is the coordinated regime particularly susceptible to defection? The uncoordinated regime is a Nash equilibrium and therefore, by definition, represents each country's best response, given the actions of the other government. As a result, the uncoordinated equilibrium is inherently stable: once attained, neither government will unilaterally deviate from it. The coordinated regime, in contrast, has no such property: if the home government believes that the foreign government will continue to choose the coordinated policy settings, then it will be tempted to deviate from the coordinated strategy itself. Of course, the foreign government has the same incentive to deviate from the cooperative agreement. Unless there is some mechanism to prevent governments from doing so the coordinated regime soon unravels.

There are really two ways in which cooperation may be sustained. The first is institutional: regimes may be sustained by international treaties, agreements, and institutions. The Bretton Woods arrangement of adjustable pegs and the EMS are examples of systems with institutional enforcement mechanisms. In practice, though, the difficulty of writing rules to cover every contingency means that institutional enforcement mechanisms can only support very simple policies which are not well suited to take account of new contingencies. Both Bretton Woods and the EMS, for example, specify a simple goal: maintain a fixed parity (though there are "escape clauses" whereby a country facing fundamental disequilibrium can devalue).

Second, governments which are not myopic may abide by the cooperative agreement out of self-interest. Suppose that a defection from the coordinated regime is "punished" by a reversion to the non-cooperative regime for a specified length of time. In the game theory literature, this is known as a "trigger" mechanism: when either government is suspected of cheating on the cooperative agreement, a reversionary period is triggered in which governments do not cooperate. Since cooperation yields a higher level of welfare than non-cooperation, each government must trade off the benefits of cheating on the cooperative agreement against the cost of triggering a reversionary period in which it will only attain the level of welfare associated with the non-cooperative equilibrium. The "folk-theorem" of repeated games suggests that such trigger mechanisms can sustain the cooperative regime without any explicit enforcement penalties between governments.

Put somewhat more realistically, each government has the incentive to misrepresent either its forecasts or its policies in order to shift the cooperative agreement in its own favor. In doing so, however, it will have to take into account that a disappointed partner country is unlikely to strike agreements in the future. Drawing on the game theory literature (especially Green and Porter, 1984; and Friedman, 1971), Canzoneri and

Henderson (1991) argue that cooperative agreements in international monetary relations may be sustainable because far-sighted governments recognize the costs of cheating.[2] This chapter examines whether these arguments carry over once various types of uncertainty are introduced.

We begin in section 2 by giving an overview of the main arguments of the chapter. In section 3 we consider the design of trigger mechanisms when there is no uncertainty (or only additive uncertainty of the simplest kind, with both countries observing the shock). The results in this case are similar to those obtained by Canzoneri and Henderson. In section 4 we assume that the realization of the stochastic shock is common knowledge but that the macroeconomic policies themselves cannot be observed. This may be unrealistic for certain policy instruments – such as the money supply – but not for others, such as sterilized intervention, or indeed when the overall monetary stance is the policy "instrument." In section 5, moreover, we show that exactly the same results are obtained if it is assumed that macroeconomic policies can be observed but that each country is subject to shocks (or private forecasts of shocks) which cannot be verified by the other government. Section 6 shows how model uncertainty makes the design and implementation of trigger strategies significantly more difficult. Section 7 provides some concluding remarks.

2. An Overview

Political scientists have long been interested in identifying conditions under which governments will abide by cooperative agreements, though often their interest lies more in the implications of economic might and interdependence for political power rather than the effects of political power on the viability of coordination.[3] While there are many schools of thought on the nature of international economic relations, perhaps the most prominent, and relevant to our discussion, are the *Realists* and the *Liberal Institutionalists*.[4] At the risk of gross over-simplification, Realists may be characterized as believing that countries are in a constant state of conflict and competition: cooperation, though beneficial, is seldom achieved as countries fight over the potential gains and try to achieve short-term advantages. International institutions, moreover, can do little to achieve any form of cooperation. Liberal Institutionalists, however, reject this anarchical view of international relations and, while recognizing that nations will want to act in their own self-interest, claim that the cooperation between sovereign, individualistic states is not impossible.

The arguments used by Liberal Institutionalists rely on the "folk-theorem" of repeated games. In the coordinated regime of the typical anti-inflation game we have been considering, each government agrees not to try to export its inflation by appreciating its exchange rate. But if the foreign government abides by this agreement, then the home government could achieve a large coup by aggressively tightening its own money supply, since this would result in a sharp appreciation of the exchange rate. The foreign government, of course, has a similar incentive to cheat (to keep the discussion simple we shall adopt the viewpoint of the home government, with the understanding that similar motivations apply to the foreign government). But if the game is repeated, and the home government knows that once it deviates from the cooperative agreement it will never be trusted again, then it will have to trade-off the short-term gain against the lower welfare of being in the uncoordinated regime in future periods. The length of time that the foreign government refuses to coordinate with the home government, following a defection from the cooperative agreement, is called the *punishment period*. The punishment period may be infinite so that a single deviation from a cooperative agreement results in never being trusted again, but this is unlikely. During the punishment period *both* countries suffer since they each get the welfare associated with the uncoordinated regime rather than the higher utility attained under coordination. Thus the foreign government will probably not be able to make a credible threat to the effect that it will *never* coordinate again if it catches the home government cheating on the current agreement. By the same token, however, the home government is unlikely to believe that there will not be at least some length of time during which the foreign government will be unwilling to coordinate again. Suppose, therefore, that the punishment interval lasts for T periods. In assessing whether or not to cheat, the home government must then weigh the utility gain from cheating in the current period against the present value of the welfare loss from not being able to coordinate for the next T time periods. If the instantaneous utility gain is not too large, the rate of discounting not too high, and the punishment period sufficiently long, coordination can be sustained by governments making a rational decision about whether to renege on the coordinated agreement and without any external mechanism.

Now suppose that governments cannot directly observe each other's money supplies but they do observe the realized rate of inflation. The assumption that money supplies cannot be observed is clearly unrealistic. As explained below, however, one gets identical results if coordination must be done based upon forecasts of economic variables and, as is presumably the case, each government's true forecast cannot be observed. Suppose further that the realized rate of inflation is the sum of the effects of monetary policy and an unobserved shock. If the home government cheats on the cooperative agreement then it appreciates its exchange rate and the foreign country's inflation rate is higher (and the home country's inflation lower) than it would have been had the home government stuck to the agreement. Conversely, if the foreign government cheats then its own inflation rate will be lower (and that of the home country higher) than it would have been under the coordinated agreement. So the governments could agree to a *trigger* strategy: the punishment period is triggered whenever either the home country's inflation rate or the foreign country's inflation rate is lower than it should be under the coordinated agreement.

The trick lies in choosing the appropriate trigger level.[6] To prevent cheating, the trigger level should be chosen so that a deviation from the cooperative agreement *increases* the probability of triggering the punishment period. For in deciding whether to cheat, each government will weigh the marginal gain in the current period against the marginal disutility of cheating which, in turn, is equal to the probability of triggering the punishment period multiplied by the difference in utility achieved under the coordinated regime and the uncoordinated one. If the trigger is such that even a small deviation from the cooperative policy settings results in a large increase in the probability of triggering the punishment period, then governments will not cheat. The rate at which this probability changes is given by the derivative of the probability distribution function which, by definition, is equal to the height of the probability density function. If the inflation rate is Normally distributed then its density function is the familiar bell-shaped curve. The mean, or center, of this distribution would then be the inflation rate which would result if governments followed the cooperative strategy and the exogenous shock to inflation were equal to zero. Inflation rates to the left of the center imply either a negative exogenous shock or a defection from the cooperative regime by the government.

Let the minimum increase in probability required to prevent cheating be $\bar{\Psi}'$, or, in terms of the density function, $\bar{\psi}$. Now by moving the trigger level closer to the center of the distribution we can increase the height of the density function until it reaches $\bar{\psi}$. Of course, the trigger point can be made closer to the center which would certainly prevent cheating, but in that case we increase the probability of triggering the punishment period even when the government is not cheating. Figure 8.1 illustrates how the trigger point should be chosen. The shaded area is equal to the probability that the punishment period is tripped by the exogenous shock so we want to minimize this area while ensuring that the height of the density function at the trigger point exceeds $\bar{\psi}$, the minimum required to prevent cheating.

If the trigger point is chosen correctly then, by construction, governments do not find it optimal to deviate from the cooperative

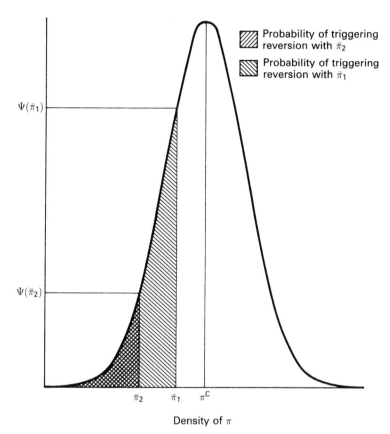

Figure 8.1 Tight vs. loose trigger

agreement. Yet there will be occasions on which the exogenous shock will be sufficiently negative that the punishment period is triggered even though neither government is cheating. Thus the *possibility* of cheating on the cooperative agreement leads to occasional breakdowns in the coordination process *even though neither government cheats in equilibrium.* This seems to characterize the coordination cycle quite well. There is an attempt at coordination and perhaps it succeeds, or at least the economic outcomes are favorable regardless of whether they are the result of the coordination. The aftermath of the Plaza Agreement would be such a case, when the dollar indeed depreciated as desired by policymakers. There is then another, possibly more ambitious attempt at coordination which, for a variety of reasons, fails to deliver such favorable outcomes. The target of exchange rate stability at the Louvre Accord might be an example. Following this "failure" there may be an extended period of time when governments appear to be largely uninterested in coordination. Finally, a new problem or tension arises in the world economy and the cycle begins afresh.

This type of endogenous breakdown in policy coordination is likely to be particularly prevalent when there is multiplier uncertainty. As we explain below, multiplier uncertainty makes detection of a deviation from the agreement very difficult. Technically, multiplier uncertainty lowers the height of the density function so that the trigger point must be moved closer to the mean to be equal to the minimum required $\bar{\psi}$. This, in turn, implies that there is a larger trigger area in which the exogenous shock trips the punishment period. In other words, to sustain the cooperative agreement when there is multiplier uncertainty governments must be willing to trigger the punishment period whenever there is even a small deviation from the expected outcomes (even though in equilibrium governments are not cheating). But this means that exogenous shocks themselves will lead to frequent breakdowns in policy coordination. Thus multiplier uncertainty makes it very difficult to sustain the coordinated regime.

3. Trigger Mechanisms in a Deterministic Setting

As long as monetary policy remains under the control of sovereign policymakers, the only realistic "punishment" one government can inflict on another for deviating from a cooperative agreement may be to refuse to coordinate macroeconomic policies in the future. In the game-theoretic literature, this is known as a trigger strategy (see Friedman, 1971 and Friedman, 1986): when either government is suspected of having cheated on a cooperative equilibrium, a reversionary period is triggered during which governments do not cooperate. One inefficiency of trigger mechanisms is that both governments suffer when either deviates from the cooperative policy setting. Nonetheless, without specific institutional arrangements, trigger mechanisms may be the only way to ensure incentive compatibility.

A second difficulty with trigger strategies has been stressed by Canzoneri and Henderson (1991) who examine the role of such mechanisms in sustaining international coordination. For a trigger strategy to work at all, the policymaker's horizon must either be infinite or the final period of the game must be unknown (i.e. in every period there must be some probability that the interaction between the two governments will continue in the next period). Although administrations are usually elected for finite terms, this assumption is not particularly problematic in the context of international coordination unless policymakers are so cynical as to seek to maximize social welfare during their tenure alone.

A more troubling requirement for the viability of the trigger mechanism is the need for the threat of triggering the non-cooperative equilibrium when either government cheats to be credible. After one (or both) governments has cheated, bygones are bygones, and coordination would again be optimal. Thus it may be difficult to pre-commit to *not* coordinating when either government has cheated. Yet if such pre-commitment is not possible, then there is no punishment mechanism and the coordinated equilibrium will not be sustainable. Again, in the context of international policy agreements this may prove not to be an insurmountable obstacle: if either government is caught "cheating" (or if the coordinated outcome appears very inequitable), domestic political pressures are likely to ensure a lengthy period of non-coordination.

We assume that the governments can commit not to coordinate for T periods once either government is caught cheating.[7]

The governments' objective functions are assumed to be given by:

$$V = \text{Max} - \tfrac{1}{2}\sum_{t=0}^{\infty}\delta^t E\{y_t^2 + \omega\pi_t^2\} \quad 0 < \delta < 1 \tag{1}$$

$$V^* = \text{Max} - \tfrac{1}{2}\sum_{t=0}^{\infty}\delta^t E\{y_t^{*2} + \omega\pi_t^{*2}\} \quad 0 < \delta < 1 \tag{2}$$

where δ is the government's discount rate, and the instantaneous utility functions are:

$$U = \text{Max} - \tfrac{1}{2}\{y_t^2 + \omega\pi_t^2\} \tag{3}$$

$$U^* = \text{Max} - \tfrac{1}{2}\{y_t^{*2} + \omega\pi_t^{*2}\} \tag{4}$$

As discussed in Chapter 3, the reduced form of the model is assumed to be:

$$y = \alpha m + \beta m^* + q \tag{5}$$

$$y^* = \alpha m^* + \beta m + q^* \tag{6}$$

$$\pi = \phi m + \eta m^* + s \tag{7}$$

$$\pi^* = \phi m^* + \eta m + s^* \tag{8}$$

We assume that the shocks q and q^* are not observed before the optimal policies must be chosen so that governments are only responding to s and s^*. In this section we also assume that the shocks are perfectly correlated across countries: $q = q^*$ and $s = s^*$.

We begin by calculating the instantaneous utility level under different regimes. As discussed in Chapter 3, the cooperative equilibrium is found by choosing m and m^* to maximize:

$$\mathcal{U}^G = \tfrac{1}{2}\{\mathcal{U} + \mathcal{U}^*\} \tag{9}$$

The resulting monetary policies are given by:

$$m^C = m^{C^*} = \frac{-\omega(\phi + \eta)s}{(\alpha + \beta)^2 + \omega(\phi + \eta)^2} \tag{10}$$

Substituting these policies into the objective function gives the welfare level for any particular realization of the shock s:

$$\mathcal{U}^C(s) = \mathcal{U}^{C^*}(s) = -\tfrac{1}{2}\frac{\omega(\alpha + \beta)^2 s^2}{(\alpha + \beta)^2 + \omega(\phi + \eta)^2} \tag{11}$$

while the *ex ante* expected level of welfare, denoted by a tilde ($\tilde{\ }$), may be found by taking expectations of (11) over the distribution of s:

$$\tilde{\mathcal{U}}^C(\sigma_S^2) = \tilde{\mathcal{U}}^{C^*}(\sigma_S^2) = -\tfrac{1}{2}\frac{\omega(\alpha + \beta)^2 \sigma_S^2}{(\alpha + \beta)^2 + \omega(\phi + \eta)^2} \tag{12}$$

In the non-cooperative regime the home and foreign governments maximize $\mathcal{U}$ and $\mathcal{U}^*$ respectively, taking as given the actions of the other. This results in the following policy settings:

$$m^N = m^{N^*} = -\frac{\omega\phi s}{\alpha(\alpha + \beta) + \omega\phi(\phi + \eta)} \tag{13}$$

and an expected level of welfare:

$$\tilde{\mathcal{U}}^N(\sigma_S^2) = \tilde{\mathcal{U}}^{N^*}(\sigma_S^2) = -\tfrac{1}{2}\frac{\omega(\alpha + \beta)^2(\alpha^2 + \omega\phi^2)\sigma_S^2}{\{\alpha(\alpha + \beta) + \omega\phi(\phi + \eta)\}^2} \tag{14}$$

From (12) and (14), the expected instantaneous gains from policy coordination are thus:

$$\tilde{\mathcal{G}}^C(\sigma_S^2) = \tilde{\mathcal{G}}^{C^*}(\sigma_S^2)$$

$$= \frac{\omega(\alpha + \beta)^2(\alpha\eta - \beta\phi)^2\sigma_S^2}{2\{(\alpha + \beta)^2 + \omega(\phi + \eta)^2\}\{\alpha(\alpha + \beta) + \omega\phi(\phi + \eta)\}^2} \geq 0$$

$$\tag{15}$$

Suppose that governments are acting cooperatively. If the home government believes that the foreign government will maintain the cooperative monetary policy setting then the home government can raise its own welfare by deviating from the cooperative agreement. Although we adopt the point of view of the home country, by symmetry, of course, the foreign country has the same incentives to abide by or break the cooperative agreement as the home country. Since all cooperative equilibria are Pareto efficient, a deviation by the home government which raises its own welfare must necessarily reduce the welfare of the foreign government. To see how the home government could raise its own welfare we consider the effect on the home country's utility of a perturbation in its instrument at the cooperative equilibrium:

$$\partial \mathcal{U}/\partial m = -\{\alpha(\alpha m + \beta m^*) + \omega\phi(\phi m + \eta m^* + s)\} \tag{16}$$

Evaluating this derivative at the cooperative policy setting (10) yields:

$$\partial \mathcal{U}/\partial m = -(\alpha + \beta)(\beta\phi - \alpha\eta)\omega s \tag{17}$$

For a positive (negative) shock, therefore, the home country can raise its welfare by marginally contracting (expanding) its money supply from the cooperative setting. As long as the foreign government maintains the cooperative monetary policy, the home government can export some its inflation by contracting its money supply. To solve for the maximum instantaneous utility achievable by deviating from the cooperative agreement we solve:

$$\partial \mathcal{U}/\partial m = 0 \Rightarrow m^D = \frac{-\{(\alpha\beta + \omega\phi\eta)m^{C^*} + \omega\phi s\}}{\{\alpha^2 + \omega\phi^2\}} \tag{18}$$

where D denotes the optimal deviation from the cooperative policy setting. Solving for the optimal m^D and substituting into the utility function gives the level of welfare attainable if the home country cheats: $\mathcal{U}^D(s)$.

In period t, a shock to inflation s_t is observed. The home government would choose to break the cooperative agreement if the instantaneous benefit from cheating exceeded the cost of having to play non-cooperatively for the following T periods. Since future realizations of inflation shocks are not known, the government must trade-off the actual benefit of cheating against the expected loss from not being able to coordinate for T periods. If each government can observe the other's money supply next period then *any* deviation from the cooperative policy setting will trigger the reversionary period, regardless of the magnitude of that deviation. Accordingly, if the home government is going to cheat at all, it will choose the monetary policy setting which yields it maximum utility, m^D. More generally, when the probability of detection is an increasing function of the magnitude of the deviation of the policy from the cooperative setting, choosing $m = m^D$ need not be optimal.

The home government breaks the cooperative agreement as long as:

$$\mathcal{G}^D(s) \equiv \mathcal{U}^D(s) - \mathcal{U}^C(s) > \sum_{i=1}^{T} \delta^i \tilde{\mathcal{G}}^C(\sigma_S^2) \tag{21}$$

From (21), the cooperative equilibrium is more likely to be sustained the longer the punishment period T, the higher the discount factor δ, and the lower the current realization of the shock, s, relative to its variance σ_S^2.

Unless the support of the shock s is bounded, there may always be realizations of the inflationary shock which break the cooperative agreement. Quite simply, the temptation to cheat when there has been a sufficiently bad inflationary shock outweighs the *expected* future gains since the latter are bounded. As the rate of discount decreases (i.e. δ increases) and the length of the punishment period, T, increases, the probability of the cooperative regime breaking down becomes arbitrarily small. Nonetheless, there will be periods in which the temptation to cheat becomes too large, both countries will then deviate from the cooperative agreement, and the reversionary period will be triggered.[8]

Despite these limitations, trigger mechanisms appear to provide a reasonably viable way to ensure compliance with coordinated agreements. Their main attraction, of course, is the self-policing nature of these mechanisms: no complicated international agreements need to be negotiated since each government maintains the coordinated regime out of its own self-interest. As shown below, however, once asymmetric information or multiplier uncertainty is introduced, the design and implementation of trigger mechanisms becomes significantly more difficult.

4. Unobservable Policies

In this section we drop the assumption that each government can observe the other's monetary policy, even with a one period lag. As noted in the introduction, it may be unrealistic to suppose that governments cannot observe each other's policy instrument if monetary policy is interpreted narrowly as the money supply, but not if monetary policy consists of several policy instruments being set simultaneously. In fact, some policy instruments, such as daily sterilized intervention in the foreign exchange market, may be very difficult to observe because most central banks guard details of intervention operations jealously, only publishing data on net changes in reserves at monthly frequencies.[9] In the next section, moreover, we show how the main results derived here will still hold if monetary policies must be chosen on the basis of private information (including, for example, each government's forecasts of the shocks to its own economy).

Each country is assumed to be subject to a (common) inflationary shock, s which consists of two components, $\hat{s}$ and ε.

$$s = \hat{s} + \varepsilon \tag{1}$$

The component $\hat{s}$ is observed by both governments before monetary policies must be chosen while ε is not directly observed at all. We can think of $\hat{s}$ as being a (common) forecast of the inflationary shock s, so it is natural to assume that ε is orthogonal to $\hat{s}$. Each component of the shock has mean zero and variance $\sigma_{\hat{s}}^2$ and σ_{ε}^2 respectively. To simplify the exposition, we also assume that the variance of the shock to output, q, is much greater than σ_{ε}^2.

Since the monetary policies cannot be observed, a deviation from the cooperative strategy cannot be detected with certainty. Suppose that the observed component of the inflationary shock, $\hat{s}$, is positive. From (2.17) we know that governments have an incentive to pursue tighter monetary policy than the cooperative policy setting as long as each believes that the other will maintain the cooperative agreement. Therefore, on average, the *ex post* observed inflation rate will be *lower* when governments are cheating than under the cooperative agreement (for positive inflation shocks $\hat{s}$). One possible trigger mechanism would therefore be:[10]

$$\text{Trigger the non-cooperative regime if } \pi < \bar{\pi}(\hat{s}) \text{ or } \pi^* < \bar{\pi}(\hat{s}) \tag{2}$$

where $\bar{\pi}(\hat{s})$ is the agreed trigger level, which depends upon the realized value of $\hat{s}$.

The trick is to choose the constant $\bar{\pi}$ to ensure that neither government has the incentive to deviate from the cooperative equilibrium. We adopt the perspective of the home country, on the understanding that the foreign country has identical incentives. A marginal contraction in the home country's monetary policy from the cooperative policy setting raises the home country's welfare by exporting some of its inflation. However, it also changes the probability that the reversionary period is triggered. The probability that a reversionary period is triggered equals the probability that either the home or the foreign inflation rate (or both) turns out to be lower than expected:

$$z \equiv \{Pr(\pi < \bar{\pi}) + Pr(\pi^* < \bar{\pi}) - Pr(\pi < \bar{\pi}) \times Pr(\pi^* < \bar{\pi})\} \tag{3}$$

Let $\Psi(\cdot)$ denote the cumulative probability distribution function of ε, then:

$$Pr(\pi < \bar{\pi}) = Pr(\phi m + \eta m^* + \hat{s} + \varepsilon < \bar{\pi}) = \Psi(\bar{\pi} - \phi m - \eta m^* - \hat{s}) \tag{4}$$

$$Pr(\pi^* < \bar{\pi}) = Pr(\phi m^* + \eta m + \hat{s} + \varepsilon < \bar{\pi}) = \Psi(\bar{\pi} - \phi m^* - \eta m - \hat{s})$$

$$(5)$$

The effect on the probability of triggering a reversionary period of a marginal increase in the home country's monetary policy is therefore:

$$\partial z / \partial m = -(\phi + \eta)\Psi'(\cdot) + \phi\eta[\Psi'(\cdot)]^2 \tag{6}$$

which is negative.

We can no longer assume that a government which deviates from the cooperative agreement will seek to maximize the instantaneous utility from cheating (i.e. set $m = m^D$). The government will want to trade-off the increasing utility from a large deviation from the cooperative equilibrium against the increased probability of triggering a reversionary period. To simplify the discussion we examine conditions under which governments can be prevented from even a marginal deviation away from the cooperative policy setting. We also assume that the reversionary period lasts for one time period only.

Assuming the world is not in a non-cooperative equilibrium the expected utility of the home government over any two-period horizon is given by:

$$\mathcal{V} = \mathcal{U}_t^C + \delta E\{z\mathcal{U}_{t+1}^N + (1 - z)\mathcal{U}_{t+1}^C\} \tag{7}$$

A perturbation to the home country's money supply changes its instantaneous welfare by $(\partial \mathcal{U}^C / \partial m)$ but also changes the probability, z, of triggering the reversionary period. For the coordinated regime to be sustainable, therefore, requires:

$$(\partial \mathcal{U}^C / \partial m) + (\partial z / \partial m)\delta E\{\mathcal{U}_{t+1}^N - \mathcal{U}_{t+1}^C\} < 0 \tag{8}$$

where all derivatives are evaluated at the cooperative equilibrium. Rewriting (8):

$$\frac{\partial z}{\partial m} < -\frac{(\alpha + \beta)(\beta\phi - \alpha\eta)\omega s}{\delta \mathcal{G}^C(\sigma_S^2)} < 0 \tag{9}$$

From (6), $(\partial z / \partial m)$ is a decreasing function of Ψ'. We let $\bar{\Psi}'$ denote the minimum value of Ψ' which is consistent with (9). The interpretation of condition (9) is straightforward. A monetary contraction raises the home government's welfare so the temptation to break the cooperative agreement can only be resisted if the monetary contraction causes a sufficiently large increase in the probability of triggering the reversionary period.

It remains only to choose the trigger value $\bar{\pi}$. First note that the trigger mechanism $\pi < \bar{\pi}$ can be written equivalently as:

$$Pr(\pi < \bar{\pi}) = Pr(\varepsilon < -\bar{\varepsilon}) = \Psi(-\bar{\varepsilon})$$
$$\text{where} - \bar{\varepsilon} = \bar{\pi} - (\phi + \eta)m^C - \hat{s} \leq 0 \tag{10}$$

and where ε is the difference between the expected inflation rate when governments act cooperatively and the actual inflation rate:

$$\varepsilon = \pi - (\phi + \eta)m^C - \hat{s} \tag{11}$$

Since Ψ is a cumulative distribution function, its derivative is the probability density function, $\psi(\cdot)$. Unless ε is uniformly distributed, therefore, the density function $\psi(\cdot)$ will depend upon the trigger point $\bar{\varepsilon}$. Figure 8.2 shows how $\bar{\varepsilon}$ can be chosen to increase the likelihood that the

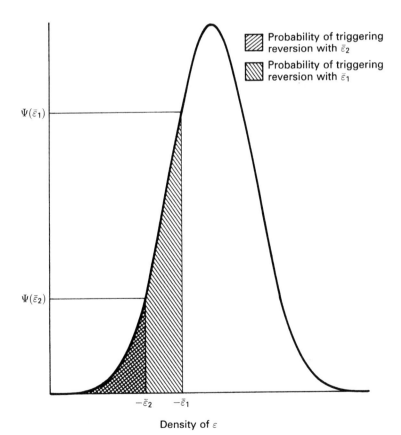

Figure 8.2 Tight vs. loose trigger

incentive compatibility constraint (9) is fulfilled when ε follows a Normal distribution. Notice that the density is at a maximum at the mean of ε, which is zero. By choosing $\bar{\varepsilon} = 0$, therefore, the governments maximize the probability that the incentive compatibility condition (9) is satisfied. Choosing $\bar{\varepsilon}$ is the same as setting the trigger inflation rate, $\bar{\pi}$, close to the rate of inflation which would be expected given the observed shock $\hat{s}$ and given the cooperative monetary policies. This ensures that even a small deviation from the cooperative policy setting results in a large increase in the probability of triggering a reversionary period.

There is an important cost, however, to choosing $\bar{\varepsilon}$ too close to zero because this increases the probability that the reversionary period is triggered *even though neither government is cheating*. Since welfare during reversionary periods is lower than the welfare level when countries coordinate, the higher probability of triggering the non-cooperative regime lowers the expected level of welfare. Thus $\bar{\varepsilon}$ should be the smallest number which satisfies $\psi(\bar{\varepsilon}) > \underline{\psi}$. As above, the current realization of $\hat{s}$ may be so large that there exists no trigger value $\bar{\varepsilon}$ which sustains the cooperative equilibrium.

Figure 8.3 shows what happens as the variance of ε increases: the distribution becomes flatter with greater mass in the tails. Accordingly, a larger value of $\bar{\varepsilon}$ is required to satisfy $\psi(\bar{\varepsilon}) > \underline{\psi}$. A larger value of $\bar{\varepsilon}$ implies a higher probability of triggering the non-cooperative equilibrium and therefore a lower level of welfare. Intuitively, a large variance of ε makes it difficult to infer whether governments have been cheating so a very tight trigger criterion must be adopted to make the cooperative equilibrium incentive compatible. A tight triggering criterion, in turn, results in a high frequency of reversionary periods and thus a lower level of welfare. Notice that if the required level of ψ is too large, say $\overline{\psi}$, then there may be *no* trigger level which supports the cooperative equilibrium. As drawn in Figure 8.3, $\overline{\psi}$ can be supported when ε has a low variance but not when it has a high variance.

It is worth emphasizing that once macroeconomic policies cannot be observed the non-cooperative equilibrium may be triggered for two distinct reasons. First, as in section 3, a sufficiently bad realization of the current inflation shock will tempt governments to cheat and break the cooperative agreement. Second, when a positive (negative) inflation shock is observed, a sufficiently large negative (positive) realization ε may trigger the non-cooperative equilibrium *even when both governments were abiding by the cooperative agreement*.

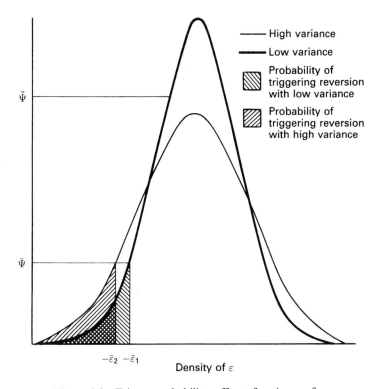

Figure 8.3 Trigger probability: effect of variance of ε

5. Unobservable Shocks

In this section we show that even if the policy instruments being coordinated are contemporaneously observed there may be problems in sustaining the cooperative equilibrium. Specifically we assume that while instrument settings can be instantaneously verified by both countries, the shocks $\hat{s}$ and $\hat{s}^*$ are country specific and cannot be observed by the other government. Thus the home government observes $\hat{s}$ before choosing its monetary policy and the foreign government observes $\hat{s}^*$ before choosing its monetary policy. Governments report the values of these shocks to each other and choose their monetary policies cooperatively. There is then a common shock, ε, to both countries' inflation rates.[11] At the beginning of the next period the realizations of the inflation rates are observed and a reversionary period is triggered if either government is suspected of having reported a false value for its inflationary shock $\hat{s}$ or $\hat{s}^*$.

We begin by deriving the cooperative equilibrium when there are asymmetric shocks to countries. At the cooperative equilibrium each government maximizes:

$$\mathcal{U}^G = \text{Max} - \tfrac{1}{4}E\{y^2 + \omega\pi^2 + y^{*2} + \omega\pi^{*2}\} \tag{1}$$

subject to the reduced-form model of the world economy:

$$y = \alpha m + \beta m^* + q \tag{3}$$

$$y^* = \alpha m^* + \beta m + q^* \tag{3}$$

$$\pi = \phi m + \eta m^* + s \tag{4}$$

$$\pi^* = \phi m^* + \eta m + s^* \tag{5}$$

The first-order conditions for the optimal policies imply the following reaction functions:

$$m = \frac{-\{\omega(\phi\hat{s} + \eta\hat{s}^*) + 2(\alpha\beta + \omega\phi\eta)m^*\}}{\alpha^2 + \beta^2 + \omega(\phi^2 + \eta^2)} \tag{6}$$

$$m^* = \frac{-\{\omega(\phi\hat{s}^* + \eta\hat{s}) + 2(\alpha\beta + \omega\phi\eta)m\}}{\alpha^2 + \beta^2 + \omega(\phi^2 + \eta^2)} \tag{7}$$

Solving the two reaction functions simultaneously gives the cooperative policy setting:

$$m^C = \frac{\omega\{[2\eta - \phi(\alpha^2 + \beta^2 + \omega(\phi^2 + \eta^2))]\hat{s} + [2\phi - \eta(\alpha^2 + \beta^2 + \omega(\phi^2 + \eta^2))]\hat{s}^*\}}{[(\alpha + \beta)^2 + \omega(\phi + \eta)^2][(\alpha - \beta)^2 + \omega(\phi - \eta)^2]} \tag{8}$$

$$m^{C*} = \frac{\omega\{[2\eta - \phi(\alpha^2 + \beta^2 + \omega(\phi^2 + \eta^2))]\hat{s}^* + [2\phi - \eta(\alpha^2 + \beta^2 + \omega(\phi^2 + \eta^2))]\hat{s}\}}{[(\alpha + \beta)^2 + \omega(\phi + \eta)^2][(\alpha - \beta)^2 + \omega(\phi - \eta)^2]} \tag{9}$$

To see how misrepresenting the values of the observed shocks can raise the home country's welfare suppose that the actual realized values of $\hat{s}$ and $\hat{s}^*$ happen to be equal and positive. In that case, the cooperative equilibrium would have $m^C = m^{C*} < 0$. Consider the welfare effect on the home country of a perturbation to the home country's money supply:

$$\partial\mathcal{U}/\partial m = -\{\alpha(\alpha m^C + \beta m^{C*}) + \omega\phi(\phi m^C + \eta m^{C*} + \hat{s})\} \tag{10}$$

Substituting (8) and (9) into (10), and simplifying, shows:

$$\partial\mathcal{U}/\partial m \propto -(\alpha + \beta)(\phi\beta - \alpha\eta)\omega\hat{s} < 0 \tag{11}$$

Therefore, a monetary contraction by the home country would raise its welfare (when $\hat{s}$ is positive). Conversely, an expansion in the foreign country's money supply raises the home country's welfare.

$$\partial\mathcal{U}/\partial m^* = -\{\beta(\alpha m^C + \beta m^{C^*}) + \omega\eta(\phi m^C + \eta m^{C^*} + \hat{s})\}$$
$$\propto (\alpha + \beta)(\phi\beta - \alpha\eta)\omega\hat{s} > 0 \tag{12}$$

A monetary contraction at home and a monetary expansion abroad leads to an appreciation of the home country's exchange rate and thereby enables it to export some of its inflation to the foreign country.

From (8) and (9), the higher the reported value of the shock to the home country the more contractionary (expansionary) is the home (foreign) country's monetary policy setting:

$$\partial m/\partial\hat{s} \propto [2\eta - \phi(\alpha^2 + \beta^2 + \omega(\phi^2 + \eta^2)] < 0;$$
$$\partial m^*/\partial\hat{s} \propto [2\phi - \eta(\alpha^2 + \beta^2 + \omega(\phi^2 + \eta^2)] > 0 \tag{13}$$

Thus, when $\hat{s}$ is positive, the home country can raise its welfare relative to the cooperative equilibrium by reporting a larger positive inflationary shock than it has actually observed.

If the reported values of the inflationary shocks are positive then governments are suspected of having cheated if the realized rate of inflation turns out to be too low. Let the reported values of $\hat{s}$ and $\hat{s}^*$ be $\hat{s}_R$ and $\hat{s}_R^*$, then the probability of triggering a reversionary period is:

$$z = Pr(\varepsilon < \hat{s}_R - \hat{s} - \bar{\varepsilon}) + Pr(\varepsilon < \hat{s}_R^* - \hat{s}^* - \bar{\varepsilon})$$
$$- (Pr(\varepsilon < \hat{s}_R - \hat{s} - \bar{\varepsilon}) \times Pr(\varepsilon < \hat{s}_R^* - \hat{s}^* - \bar{\varepsilon})) \tag{14}$$

where $\bar{\varepsilon}$ is the trigger value. A marginal increase in the reported value of the shock by the home country therefore raises the probability of triggering a reversionary period by:

$$\partial z/\partial\hat{s}_R = \Psi'(\bar{\varepsilon})[1 - \Psi(\bar{\varepsilon})] > 0 \tag{15}$$

The condition for sustainability of the coordinated equilibrium is therefore:

$$\frac{\partial z}{\partial\hat{s}_R} > \frac{(\partial\mathcal{U}^C/\partial m)(\partial m^C/\partial\hat{s}_R) + (\partial\mathcal{U}^C/\partial m^*)(\partial m^{C^*}/\partial\hat{s}_R)}{\delta E\{\mathcal{U}_{t+1}^C - \mathcal{U}_{t+1}^N\}} \tag{16}$$

which is a similar trigger strategy to (2.9). Again, we will want the largest value of $\bar{\varepsilon}$ (i.e. the smallest value of $\psi(\bar{\varepsilon})$) which is consistent with this incentive compatibility condition being fulfilled. As above, sufficiently large realizations of ε will trigger the non-cooperative equilibrium even when neither government has cheated on the cooperative equilibrium. Thus observability of macroeconomic policies in itself is insufficient to make the simple deterministic trigger strategy considered in section 2 feasible. As long as there is some private information being used in setting the cooperative monetary policies there will be an incentive to cheat which cannot be detected with certainty.

6. Multiplier Uncertainty

In sections 4 and 5 we showed how the introduction of additive uncertainty, together with the assumption that policies cannot be observed directly (or that there is asymmetric information about the shocks), makes the design and the implementation of trigger strategies more difficult. In this section we consider the effects of multiplier uncertainty on the incentive to coordinate; the incentive to cheat; and the viability of trigger mechanisms as means of sustaining cooperative agreements. We show three results: the incentive to coordinate is an increasing function of the degree of uncertainty (as was shown in Chapter 3); the instantaneous benefit from defecting from the cooperative agreement is also an increasing function of multiplier uncertainty; and the set of sustainable cooperative equilibria is significantly diminished by the presence of multiplier uncertainty.

We write the home country's objective function in the form:

$$\mathcal{U} = -\tfrac{1}{2}\{\mu_y^2 + \sigma_y^2 + \omega(\mu_\pi^2 + \sigma_\pi^2)\} \qquad (17)$$

where:

$$\mu_y = \mu_\alpha m + \mu_\beta m^* \qquad (18)$$

$$\sigma_y^2 = \sigma_\alpha^2 m^2 + \sigma_\beta^2 m^{*2} \qquad (19)$$

$$\mu_\pi = \mu_\phi m + \mu_\eta m^* + s \qquad (20)$$

$$\sigma_\pi^2 = \sigma_\phi^2 m^2 + \sigma_\eta^2 m^{*2} \qquad (21)$$

An analogous objective function and structural model describe the foreign country, of course.

As shown in Chapter 3 (section 6), the cooperative policy is given by:

$$m^C = m^C = \frac{-\omega(\mu_\phi + \mu_\eta)\hat{s}}{(\mu_\alpha + \mu_\beta)^2 + \omega(\mu_\phi + \mu_\eta)^2 + \sigma_\alpha^2 + \sigma_\beta^2 + \omega(\sigma_\phi^2 + \sigma_\eta^2)}$$

$$(22)$$

and the non-cooperative policy setting is:

$$m^N = m^{N^*} = \frac{-\omega\mu_\phi\hat{s}}{\mu_\alpha^2 + \sigma_\alpha^2 + \mu_\alpha\mu_\beta + \omega(\mu_\phi^2 + \sigma_\phi^2) + \omega(\mu_\phi\mu_\eta)} \qquad (23)$$

In order to determine the effects of multiplier uncertainty on the sustainability of the coordinated regime we need to determine three expressions: the effect on the gains from coordination; the effect on the incentive to deviate from the cooperative agreement; and the effect on the probability that the non-cooperative equilibrium is triggered.

We have already done the first of these in Chapter 3. To recap, we can infer the effect of multiplier uncertainty on the gains from coordination by examining its effect on the welfare benefit to the home country of a marginal change in the foreign country's instrument at the non-cooperative equilibrium. For a positive inflationary shock we know that an expansion in the foreign country's money supply will raise the home country's welfare since the Nash equilibrium is too contractionary: $\partial\mathcal{U}/\partial m^* > 0$. If multiplier uncertainty makes this derivative more positive then it increases the gains from coordination. Let $\Xi_N^* \equiv \partial\mathcal{U}/\partial m^*$, where the derivative is evaluated at the non-cooperative regime, then we want $\partial\Xi^*/\partial\sigma_i^2\{i = \alpha, \beta, \phi, \eta\}$. Differentiating (17) with respect to m^*, and setting $m = m^*$ yields:

$$\Xi_N^* = \partial\mathcal{U}/\partial m^* = -\{\mu_\beta(\mu_\eta + \mu_\beta)m + \sigma_\beta^2\mu$$
$$+ \omega\mu_\eta((\mu_\phi + \mu_\eta)m + s) + \omega\sigma_\eta^2 m\} \qquad (24)$$

Evaluating this derivative at the non-cooperative equilibrium (23) gives:

$$\Xi_N^* = \frac{-\omega\hat{s}\{(\mu_\alpha + \mu_\beta)(\mu_\alpha\mu_\eta - \mu_\phi\mu_\beta) + \mu_\eta\sigma_\alpha^2 + \omega\mu_\eta\sigma_\phi^2 - \mu_\phi(\sigma_\beta^2 + \omega\sigma_\eta^2)\}}{\mu_\alpha(\mu_\alpha + \mu_\beta) + \omega\mu_\phi(\mu_\phi + \mu_\eta) + \sigma_\alpha^2 + \omega\sigma_\phi^2}$$

$$(25)$$

Therefore, the effect of a marginal increase in domestic multiplier uncertainty, starting from zero, is given by:

$$\partial\Xi_N^*/\partial\sigma_\alpha^2 = \frac{-\omega\hat{s}\{\mu_\phi[\mu_\beta(\mu_\alpha + \mu_\beta) + \omega\mu_\eta(\mu_\phi + \mu_\eta)]\}}{\{\mu_\alpha(\mu_\alpha + \mu_\beta) + \omega\mu_\phi(\mu_\phi + \mu_\eta)\}^2} \qquad (26)$$

Therefore, $sgn(\partial\Xi_N^*/\partial\sigma_\alpha^2) = sgn(\Xi_N^*)$ and domestic multiplier uncertainty raises the gains from coordination, if and only if $([\mu_\beta(\mu_\alpha + \mu_\beta) + \omega\mu_\eta(\mu_\phi + \mu_\eta)])$ is negative. The assumption of negative transmission multipliers is sufficient to ensure that an increase in uncertainty raises the incentive to coordinate. As shown in Chapter 3, an increase in transmission uncertainty necessarily raises the gains from coordination since $sgn(\partial\Xi_N^*/\partial\sigma_\beta^2) = sgn(\Xi_N^*)$.[12]

Consider, next, the effect of multiplier uncertainty on the incentive to deviate from the cooperative equilibrium. This incentive is measured by the welfare effect on the home country of a perturbation to its own instrument at the cooperative equilibrium, Ξ_C. We first note that a perturbation to the home country's policy changes its welfare by:

$$\partial \mathcal{U}/\partial m = - \{\mu_\alpha(\mu_\alpha m + \mu_\beta m^*) + \sigma_\alpha^2 m$$
$$+ \omega(\mu_\phi(\mu_\phi m + \mu_\eta m^* + \hat{s}) + \sigma_\phi^2 m)\} \tag{27}$$

Evaluating this derivative at the cooperative equilibrium gives:

$$\Xi_C = \partial \mathcal{U}/\partial m = \frac{-\omega\hat{s}\{(\mu_\alpha + \mu_\beta)(\mu_\phi\mu_\beta - \mu_\alpha\mu_\eta) - \mu_\eta(\sigma_\alpha^2 + \omega\sigma_\phi^2) + \mu_\phi(\sigma_\beta^2 + \omega\sigma_\eta^2)\}}{(\mu_\alpha + \mu_\beta)^2 + \omega(\mu_\phi + \mu_\eta)^2 + \sigma_\alpha^2 + \sigma_\beta^2 + \omega(\sigma_\phi^2 + \sigma_\eta^2)}$$

$$\tag{28}$$

which is negative if the inflationary shock is positive; thus the home country would like to contract its money supply in response to an inflationary shock. An increase in multiplier uncertainty will raise the incentive to cheat if $sgn(\partial \Xi_C/\partial \sigma_i^2) = sgn(\Xi_C)$. Differentiating Ξ_C with respect to σ_α^2 gives the effect of an increase in domestic multiplier uncertainty:

$$\partial \Xi_C/\partial \sigma_\alpha^2 = \frac{\omega\hat{s}\{(\mu_\phi + \mu_\eta)[\mu_\beta(\mu_\alpha + \mu_\beta) + \omega\mu_\eta(\mu_\phi + \mu_\eta)]\}}{\{(\mu_\alpha + \mu_\beta)^2 + \omega(\mu_\phi + \mu_\eta)^2\}^2} \tag{29}$$

Whether $sgn(\partial \Xi_C/\partial \sigma_\alpha^2)$ equals $sgn(\Xi_C)$ depends upon whether $[\mu_\beta(\mu_\alpha + \mu_\beta) + \omega\mu_\eta(\mu_\phi + \mu_\eta)]$ is negative so that the condition is exactly the same as the condition for an increase in domestic multiplier uncertainty to raise the gains from coordination. Again, assuming both transmission multipliers are negative is sufficient for a marginal increase in domestic multiplier uncertainty to increase the incentive to cheat. Likewise, differentiating Ξ_C with respect to the transmission multiplier shows:

$$\partial \Xi_C/\partial \sigma_\beta^2 = \frac{-\omega\hat{s}\{(\mu_\phi + \mu_\eta)[\mu_\alpha(\mu_\alpha + \mu_\beta) + \omega\mu_\phi(\mu_\phi + \mu_\eta)]\}}{\{(\mu_\alpha + \mu_\beta)^2 + \omega(\mu_\phi + \mu_\eta)^2\}^2} \tag{30}$$

so that $sgn(\partial \Xi_C/\partial \sigma_\beta^2) = sgn(\Xi_C)$. Therefore, both domestic and multiplier uncertainty raise the incentive to deviate from the cooperative agreement.

We can understand why multiplier uncertainty raises the incentive to deviate from the cooperative equilibrium more easily by returning to the case in which policymakers care exclusively about inflation, and do not care about output:

$$\mathcal{U} = -\tfrac{1}{2}\{\mu_\pi^2 + \sigma_\pi^2\} \tag{31}$$

It is readily verified that the cooperative policy setting in this case is:

$$m^C = m^{C^*} = \frac{-\hat{s}\{\mu_\phi + \mu_\eta\}}{(\mu_\phi + \mu_\eta)^2 + \sigma_\phi^2 + \sigma_\eta^2} \tag{32}$$

A monetary contraction by the home country, starting from the cooperative equilibrium, will raise the home country's welfare as long as $\partial\mathcal{U}/\partial m < 0$. Differentiating (31) with respect to m gives:

$$\partial\mathcal{U}/\partial m = \frac{\{\mu_\phi(\sigma_\phi^2 + \sigma_\eta^2) - \sigma_\phi^2(\mu_\phi + \mu_\eta)\}\hat{s}}{(\mu_\phi + \mu_\eta)^2 + \sigma_\phi^2 + \sigma_\eta^2} \tag{33}$$

Or,

$$\partial\mathcal{U}/\partial m = \frac{\{\sigma_\phi^2\mu_\eta - \mu_\phi\sigma_\eta^2\}\hat{s}}{(\mu_\phi + \mu_\eta)^2 + \sigma_\phi^2 + \sigma_\eta^2} < 0 \tag{34}$$

Comparing (34) with equation (5.14) of Chapter 3, we see immediately that the condition for a contraction in the home country's money supply from its cooperative setting to benefit the home country is precisely the same as the condition for a monetary expansion by the foreign country, from the non-cooperative setting, to benefit the home country. Recall that a monetary expansion by the foreign country at the non-cooperative equilibrium lowers the home country's mean level of inflation (assuming the transmission effect μ_η is negative) and lowers the variance of the home country's inflation rate. Here a contraction of the home country's money supply lowers its mean inflation rate but raises the variance. The first term of (33) is the benefit from offsetting more of the inflationary shock by deviating from the cooperative equilibrium. Notice that this is increasing in σ_ϕ^2 and σ_η^2 since the greater the multiplier uncertainty, the less of the inflationary shock will be offset in the cooperative equilibrium, and therefore the higher the marginal utility from lowering the mean level of inflation. The second term is the welfare loss from inducing a higher variance in the inflation rate: it is increasing in $(\mu_\phi + \mu_\eta)$ because the greater the degree of activism, the higher the variance of inflation at the cooperative equilibrium, and therefore the greater the disutility from raising the variance further. The first effect is unambiguously larger so that a monetary contraction from the cooperative equilibrium necessarily raises welfare.

For the two-target case the same basic intuition holds, although the expressions are somewhat more complicated since the non-cooperative equilibrium now has a disinflationary bias even when there is no multiplier uncertainty. Again, the incentive to deviate from the cooperative equilibrium exists precisely whenever there is an incentive to coordinate macroeconomic policies since $sgn(\Xi_N^*) = -sgn(\Xi_C)$.

To summarize, an increase in transmission uncertainty necessarily raises both the incentive to coordinate and the incentive to defect from the cooperative equilibrium. An increase in domestic multiplier uncertainty either increases both the incentive to coordinate and to cheat, or reduces both of them.

The cooperative regime will be sustainable if a perturbation lowers the defecting government's expected welfare:

$$(\partial \mathcal{U}^C/\partial m) - (\partial z/\partial m)\delta \tilde{\mathcal{G}}^C < 0 \tag{35}$$

We have shown that an increase in multiplier uncertainty has similar effects on the terms $(\partial \mathcal{U}^C/\partial m)$ and $\tilde{\mathcal{G}}^C$ so that it has little *net* effect on the sustainability of the coordinated regime (through these two terms).

Multiplier uncertainty *does* however affect the sustainability of the coordinated regime by making *detection* of cheating much more difficult. More precisely, the trigger criterion under multiplier uncertainty has to be so tight that, in equilibrium, the reversionary period of non-cooperation will be frequently triggered.[13] Suppose, as in section 4, monetary policies are not observable. To see how multiplier uncertainty makes cheating more difficult to detect we compare two situations. In the first, there is a single reduced-form for inflation given by:

$$\pi = \bar{\phi}m + \eta m^* + \hat{s} + \varepsilon \tag{36}$$

To make the cooperative equilibrium incentive compatible we will want to choose a cut-off value for the implied value of the unobserved component of the inflationary shock, $\varepsilon = \pi - \bar{\phi}m - \eta m^* - \hat{s}$. If the implied value of ε is too small then the reversionary period is triggered since the governments will be suspected of having cheated. Recall from section 4 that we need the density of ε to be sufficiently large at the cut-off point for the cooperative equilibrium to be sustained.

Figure 8.4 shows the density of $\varepsilon, \psi(\varepsilon)$, which is a Normal density with mean zero. To achieve a given level of $\psi(\cdot)$, say $\bar{\psi}(\cdot)$, requires a trigger point $-\bar{\varepsilon}$, so that the probability of triggering the non-cooperative equilibrium is given by the area A.

Next suppose that there is multiplier uncertainty of the simplest form: with two possible reduced-form expressions for inflation, each of which holds with probability of one-half:

$$\pi = (\bar{\phi} - \nu_\phi)m + \eta m^* + s \tag{37}$$

$$\pi = (\bar{\phi} + \nu_\phi)m + \eta m^* + s \tag{38}$$

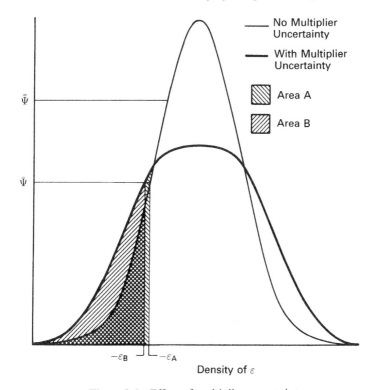

Figure 8.4   Effect of multiplier uncertainty

This formulation has the property that the mean value of the multiplier ϕ is constant at $\bar{\phi}$, and the degree of multiplier uncertainty is increasing in ν_ϕ. Figure 8.4 also shows the density function of ε, the implied value of the shock, under multiplier uncertainty. Given the simple form of multiplier uncertainty assumed here, this is just the average of two Normal density functions, whose means are given by $(-\nu_\phi m^C)$ and $(+\nu_\phi m^C)$ respectively.

As long as $\nu_\phi m^C$ is sufficiently small the density function remains uni-modal and the simple trigger strategy remains optimal.[14] In order to achieve the same level of $\bar{\psi}$ as above now requires a larger value of $\bar{\varepsilon}$, and correspondingly a higher probability of triggering the non-cooperative equilibrium (given by area B). Of course, it is possible that no trigger level supports the cooperative equilibrium, or, it may be possible to support the cooperative equilibrium when there is no multiplier uncertainty but not with multiplier uncertainty. Such a case is depicted in Figure 8.4 when the required level of ψ is $\bar{\bar{\psi}}$.

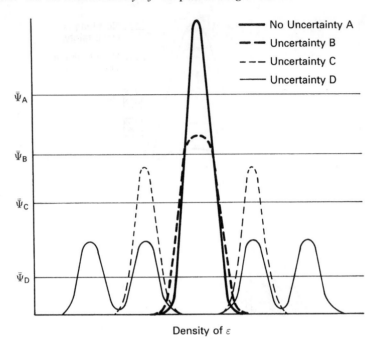

Figure 8.5   Effect of multiplier uncertainty on maximum trigger probability

Note: Increasing multiplier uncertainty: A to D

Figure 8.5 shows the effect of increasing multiplier uncertainty. As the degree of multiplier uncertainty increases (going from density A to D), the maximum height of the density function decreases and therefore the set of sustainable cooperative equilibria shrinks. If, for example, the required level of ψ to sustain the cooperative equilibrium is $\bar{\psi}_A$ then it can only be supported if there is no multiplier uncertainty; if $\bar{\psi}_C$ is required then the cooperative equilibrium cannot be sustained with level of multiplier uncertainty embodied in the distribution labelled D.

Thus increasing multiplier uncertainty either makes the cooperative equilibrium unsustainable or it increases the required probability of triggering the reversionary period; in either case it reduces the expected level of welfare attained by both countries.

7. Summary and Conclusions

An important obstacle to international coordination is the problem of verifiability. This chapter has shown that verifiability, and hence the task of reaching and sustaining cooperative agreements, is made more difficult by unobservable policies or shocks to the economy, and by the existence of uncertainty about the effects of policies. While it may be relatively simple to verify whether policy instruments under the direct control of the authorities take on agreed settings, verifiability remains a problem if policy settings must be based on governments' private forecasts of future developments. In addition, rules that do not specify instrument settings but instead mandate "appropriate responses" to unforeseen circumstances require agreement about an analytical framework for understanding the economy.[15]

In these circumstances, there is a role for international organizations to provide consistent data, monitor developments, and to provide analysis of appropriate policy responses. As Crockett (1989, p. 349) argues, "The need for consultation procedures and policy guidelines is the fundamental justification for assigning a central role to an international institution . . . with a staff that is independent of national capitals. . . . [I]ts staff can provide a common data set as a basis for discussions . . . [and] there is an important role for disinterested analysis from a source that is clearly impartial."

Of course, the importance of such an informational and analytical function depends on the "rules of the game" of the international monetary and trading system. The gold standard did not require discretionary policy coordination, or knowledge of the intentions of other countries, to the same extent that is the case today. The Bretton Woods system also did not operate automatically, and it was realized that mechanisms for monitoring and coordinating policies were necessary. Likewise the European Payments Union in the 1950s was instrumental in influencing the macroeconomic policies of its members and in dismantling restrictions (see the Appendix). Andrew Crockett argues that Working Party 3 of the OECD, established in 1961, had a key role subsequently in providing a forum for consultation and guidelines for policy. Instead of formal rules that would govern the behavior of countries in the international monetary arena, what developed were what Crockett terms "presumptive rules," which constitute an analytical environment in which coordination takes place. However, the policy response is not automatic, but rather "suggested" by the guidelines (Crockett, 1989, p. 346).

Another example of such a coordinating mechanism has been the development, since the move to generalized floating, of guidelines for floating exchange rates embodied in the International Monetary Fund's amended Articles of Agreement. These guidelines attempt to prevent manipulation of exchange rates, but more importantly, mandate the Fund to exercise surveillance over member-country policies. Surveillance procedures have evolved into twice-yearly discussions by the Executive Board of the World Economic Outlook (and subsequent publication of that document), regular "Article IV" consultations, and various other occasions to assess member-country policies. By providing an impartial source of information and policy analysis, the IMF helps to provide a basis for policy coordination, but there is no actual mechanism for achieving policy changes in the major industrial countries.

The recent development of policy coordination among the Group of Five and the Group of Seven has also served to narrow areas of uncertainty by leading governments to agree to assess economic developments using a common set of variables. The Tokyo Economic Declaration of June 1986 established a set of indicator variables (including such variables as GNP growth rates, inflation rates, interest rates, fiscal deficit ratios, among others) that would be monitored with the assistance of the IMF, and, starting in 1987, the G-7 governments agreed to submit individual short-term forecasts and to compare outcomes later in the year to ensure that economic performance was on the intended track (Crockett, 1989, p. 358).

Even if considerable progress has been made in resolving uncertainty concerning economic developments in other countries, thanks to an agreed set of data and policy discussions based on a common starting point, it seems clear that more remains to be done in developing an agreed analytical framework for policy setting. A number of major issues are subject to disagreement. Examples include the following: when are current account imbalances bad, and in need of correction? How can one calculate equilibrium exchange rates, and is this a meaningful concept, different from market exchange rates? What are the criteria for judging the appropriate degree of government intervention, and for evaluating the sustainability of fiscal policy? Uncertainty about how to answer these questions undoubtedly gets in the way of making coordinated policy changes.

Notes

1   Putnam and Henning (1986) point out that at the London Summit agreements were reached in terms of economic outcomes and both Japan and Germany failed to deliver on their promised growth targets. As a result, by the time of the 1978 Bonn Summit, it was agreed that the agreement should be specified in terms of policies.
2   Bisin and Tedeschi (1991) provide an example in which a cooperative equilibrium is sustained via trigger mechanisms; see also Levine and Currie

(1987). Hughes Hallett (1987) examines issues of sustainability in an empirical model.

3 See, for example, Hirschman (1945); Wagner (1988) discusses the validity of this approach.

4 Both Schools were originally more concerned with international security issues, though in recent years their ideas have increasingly been applied to issues in economic interdependence. Classic references in the Realist School include Carr (1964), and Morgenthau (1973); more recent work includes Gilpin (1981). Liberal Institutionalism consists of several sub-Schools such as functionalist integration theory (e.g. Mitrany, 1966), neofunctionalist integration theory (e.g. Nye (1968)) and interdependence theory (e.g. Cooper, 1972). See also the references in Grieco (1988), from whose analysis the discussion here draws heavily.

5 For the clearest articulation of these views see Axelrod (1984), Axelrod and Keohane (1985), Keohane (1984) and Stein (1983).

6 Choosing a very "tight" trigger, whereby even a slightly lower inflation rate than expected triggers the punishment period, is not *necessarily* optimal because there is an exogenous unobserved shock to inflation. A very tight trigger level would therefore trip the punishment period frequently, even when neither government is cheating. Indeed, the effect would probably be exactly the opposite to that intended because when the punishment period is going to be triggered by the exogenous shock anyway, one might as well cheat and get the short-term benefit.

7 Green and Porter discuss how the punishment period, T, can be chosen optimally. We believe that it is more realistic to think of the reversionary period as being set exogenously, possibly because of domestic political pressure not to coordinate in the future if the other government is thought to have reneged on the agreement.

8 Levine and Currie (1987) and Currie, Levine, and Vidalis (1987) also examine the sustainability of the cooperative regime. The criterion they use, however, is somewhat different from our criterion. They do not consider a unilateral defection from the cooperative regime by one country while the other country continues to abide by the cooperative agreement; rather, their concern is a shift from the cooperative to the non-cooperative regime. Moreover, Currie *et al.* do not consider explicit trigger strategies so that their criterion for sustainability is that cooperation must yield higher welfare than non-cooperation for each country at each instant of time.

9 Since these are figures on the *net* change in reserves they reveal almost nothing about the amount of intervention undertaken.

10 In principle, the trigger can also be made a function of the realized level of output. Our assumption that the variance of q is significantly larger than the variance of ε means that, in practice, the additional information from observing y and y^* would be negligible.

11 The assumption of a common shock, ε, simplifies the exposition but is otherwise unimportant.

12   The effects of the other multipliers, ϕ and η, are, of course, identical to α and β respectively.

13   Even though governments are not necessarily cheating; i.e. the reversionary period is triggered by unfavorable realizations of the exogenous shock, ε.

14   If the values of the parameters are very different across models then simple trigger strategies will no longer be optimal. Even in the two model case, if v_ϕ is sufficiently large then the distribution of the implied value of ε will be bi-modal and a compound trigger mechanism will be required.

15   One can also take the results of this chapter as an argument for simple rules, although even then there are likely to be problems of verifiability.

9

Issues in Bargaining

1. Introduction

A crucial issue in reaching cooperative agreements, and one which we have largely ignored thus far, is the bargaining between governments in choosing the cooperative policies. Recall that in the cooperative equilibrium monetary policies are chosen in order to maximize a weighted sum of each country's objective function: $V^G = \chi V + (1 - \chi)V^*$. Once χ has been chosen, the optimal cooperative policies follow mechanically from maximizing V^G; therefore, we can think of governments bargaining over the appropriate value of χ rather than over the monetary policies themselves.

Most of the academic literature on international coordination either imposes symmetry by setting χ to equal one-half (as we have done in previous chapters) or assigns an *ad hoc* weighting scheme such as the relative GDP magnitudes, the justification being that the larger country will have more "bargaining power."[1] At some level, economics has very little to say about the bargaining process surrounding international agreements on macroeconomic policies. In part, this is because governments will be negotiating many other issues – in the areas of international trade, defense, environmental regulations, and so forth – at the same time as their macroeconomic policy agreements. This is particularly true when international coordination is episodic: if coordination is continuous, then external factors may become less important. A second difficulty in applying formal bargaining theories to actual episodes of international cooperation is that negotiators at international meetings represent diverse domestic interests, whose preferences may be difficult to capture in a single objective function. Putnam (1988), for example, argues that the negotiations in the Bonn summit need to be analyzed as a two-level game; that is, a game between negotiators from each country, and a game between various interest groups within the country. According to Putnam, the Bonn negotiations were only successful because there were groups within each country which advocated the proposed coordinated policies:

> In fact, officials in the Chancellor's Office and Economics Ministry, as well as in the Social Democratic Party and the trade unions, had argued privately in early 1978 that further stimulus was domestically desirable . . . However, they had little hope of overcoming the opposition of the Finance Ministry, the Free Democratic party (part of the government coalition), and the business and banking community, especially the leadership of the Bundesbank. Publicly, Helmut Schmidt posed as reluctant to the end. Only his closest advisors suspected the truth: that the chancellor "let himself be pushed" into a policy that he privately favored, but would have found costly and perhaps impossible to enact without the summit's package deal.
>
> Analogously, in Japan a coalition of business interests, the Ministry of Trade and Industry (MITI), the Economic Planning Agency . . . pushed for domestic stimulus, using U.S. pressure as one of their prime arguments against the stubborn resistance of the Ministry of Finance (MOF). (Putnam, 1988, pp. 428-429).

This episode is particularly interesting since it raises the possibility that Chancellor Schmidt's public reluctance at expansion was mere posturing in order to improve his negotiating position. We examine this issue in general form below.

The purpose of this chapter is to survey theoretical models of negotiations and bargaining to see what insights these theories can offer into both the normative aspects of bargaining (what is an equitable outcome?) and its positive aspects (what is a likely outcome?). Undoubtedly, models of negotiation and bargaining, whether taken from the political science literature or from the economics literature, are still at a rudimentary stage. These models seem to suffer from one of two problems: either their predictions are unrealistically sharp (but highly dependent on the exact game structure assumed), or their predictions are too vague to be of much use. Nonetheless, problems about bargaining over cooperative outcomes undoubtedly present a serious impediment to achieving international coordination, particularly when there is uncertainty, so examining these models may be worthwhile.

Some political scientists have also emphasized the obstacles to coordination, or cooperation in general, arising from disagreements about the distribution of the welfare gains. Indeed the Realist School claims that states may not be interested in the absolute level of welfare gains from cooperative agreements but rather the gains *relative* to other participants in the agreement. Grieco (1988, p. 499), for example, writes:

That is, a state will decline to join, will leave, or will sharply limit its commitment to a cooperative arrangement if it believes that partners are achieving, or are likely to achieve, relatively larger gains. It will eschew cooperation even though participation in the arrangement was providing it, or would have provided it, with large absolute gains.

The *distribution* of the gains from coordination may thus be a crucial determinant of the viability of the coordinated regime.

The remainder of this chapter is organized as follows. In section 2 we review the two most popular models of bargaining from the economics literature: the Nash bargaining solution, and the Rubinstein bargaining model. In section 3 we discuss the problems for attaining a cooperative regime when there is asymmetric information concerning either the preferences of the two governments, or their beliefs about the true model of the world economy. Section 4 provides some brief concluding remarks.

2. Bargaining Models

John Nash developed the basic framework for analyzing bargaining situations in his seminal paper, "The Bargaining Problem" (Nash, 1950). Nash envisioned a set of players, say two, who are bargaining over some outcome. If no agreement is reached, each player receives utility levels V^N and V^{N^*} where the N superscript refers to the "no-agreement" outcome. Rather than model the actual process of bargaining, Nash laid out certain properties which any bargaining outcome should possess. This has the advantage that the theory can be completely general about the exact bargaining mechanism but the disadvantage that the plausibility of the axioms is hard to assess without a particular bargaining mechanism in mind. Nash assumed four axioms: (i) Invariance to Equivalent Utility Representations; (ii) Symmetry; (iii) Independence from Irrelevant Alternatives; and (iv) Pareto efficiency.

The first two axioms are very simple and largely non-controversial. Invariance to equivalent utility representations requires that linear transformations of utility functions yield the same bargaining outcomes as the original utility functions.[2] Symmetry requires that there be no inherent bias of the bargaining outcome towards one player. The other two axioms are more controversial.

Independence of Irrelevant Alternatives requires that if players are choosing an outcome (an "agreement", A) within a set S of possible outcomes when a larger set is available, then they should choose the same agreement, A, when only the set S is available. Yet there are situations in which the possibility of another outcome affects the agreement reached even though that outcome is not the one chosen (Osborne and Rubinstein, 1990).

Pareto efficiency states that an agreement $\mathcal{A}$ will not be an equilibrium if there is some other agreement $\mathcal{A}'$ which leaves both players better-off (or at least one of them better-off and the other one indifferent). As we shall see in section 3 below, it is possible that the cooperative equilibrium is not Pareto-efficient in the sense that an omnipotent and *omniscient* global social planner could raise both countries' welfare (the coordinated regime will still be the most efficient possible given the informational constraints of the problem).

A convenient way to specify a bargaining solution is to try to find a utility function for a fictitious global social *arbitrator*. The solution to this fictitious arbitrator's maximization problem is then defined to be the bargaining solution. In his 1950 paper John Nash showed that the unique global arbitrator's utility function which satisfied his four axioms was given by:[3]

$$\mathcal{V}^A = \text{Max}_{m^C, m^{C*}} \quad \{[(\mathcal{V}^C(m^C, m^{C*}) - \mathcal{V}^N)][(\mathcal{V}^{C*}(m^C, m^{C*}) - \mathcal{V}^{N*})]\} \tag{1}$$

where $\mathcal{V}^C$ is the welfare attained under the cooperative bargaining outcome associated with monetary policies m^C and m^{C*}, and $\mathcal{V}^A$ is the arbitrator's objective function. Thus the Nash bargaining solution states that the outcome of a bilateral bargain would yield cooperative monetary policies which would be equivalent to the monetary policies which would be chosen by a global arbitrator trying to maximize the *product* of each country's welfare gain over the non-cooperative equilibrium.

In our discussions above we wrote the global welfare function $\mathcal{V}^G$ in terms of a bargaining parameter χ, rather than specifying that the cooperative monetary policies are those which maximize (1). Moreover, since we assumed that the two countries were symmetric (and when there was uncertainty, the relevant distributions of the stochastic shocks were also assumed to be symmetric) we simply asserted that the most natural value of χ is one-half. It is easy to show that this outcome is also the Nash bargaining solution given the symmetry assumptions.

Suppose that the two governments bargain over the relative weight each country should obtain in the world welfare function:

$$\mathcal{V}^G = \chi \mathcal{V} + (1 - \chi)\mathcal{V}^* \tag{2}$$

Notice that once a welfare weight χ has been chosen, the global planner's optimization problem yields the cooperative monetary policies $m^C(\chi)$ and $m^{C*}(\chi)$, which can be substituted into the individual countries' welfare functions to obtain $\mathcal{V}^C(m^C(\chi), m^{C*}(\chi))$ and $\mathcal{V}^{C*}(m^C(\chi), m^{C*}(\chi))$.

As shown in Chapter 3 (section 3), for a given value of χ, the monetary policies in the coordinated equilibrium will satisfy:

$$\partial \mathcal{V}^G / \partial m = \chi \partial \mathcal{V} / \partial m + (1 - \chi) \partial \mathcal{V}^* / \partial m = 0 \tag{3}$$

$$\partial \mathcal{V}^G / \partial m^* = \chi \partial \mathcal{V} / \partial m^* + (1 - \chi) \partial \mathcal{V}^* / \partial m^* = 0 \tag{4}$$

These optimality conditions imply:

$$\partial \mathcal{V} / \partial m = -\frac{(1 - \chi)}{\chi} \partial \mathcal{V}^* / \partial m \tag{5}$$

$$\partial \mathcal{V} / \partial m^* = -\frac{(1 - \chi)}{\chi} \partial \mathcal{V}^* / \partial m^* \tag{6}$$

In order to choose the value of χ we consider the Nash bargaining solution.

$$\underset{\chi}{\text{Max}}\{[(\mathcal{V}^C(m^C(\chi), m^{C^*}(\chi)) - \mathcal{V}^N)][(\mathcal{V}^{C^*}(m^C(\chi), m^{C^*}(\chi)) - \mathcal{V}^{N^*})]\} \tag{7}$$

The first-order condition for this "social arbitrator's" problem is given by:

$$\left\{ \frac{\partial \mathcal{V}^C}{\partial m^C} \frac{\partial m^C}{\partial \chi} + \frac{\partial \mathcal{V}^C}{\partial m^{C^*}} \frac{\partial m^{C^*}}{\partial \chi} \right\} (\mathcal{V}^{C^*} - \mathcal{V}^{N^*})$$

$$+ \left\{ \frac{\partial \mathcal{V}^{C^*}}{\partial m^C} \frac{\partial m^C}{\partial \chi} + \frac{\partial \mathcal{V}^{C^*}}{\partial m^{C^*}} \frac{\partial m^{C^*}}{\partial \chi} \right\} (\mathcal{V}^C - \mathcal{V}^N) \tag{8}$$

Substituting (5) and (6) gives:

$$\left\{ \frac{\partial \mathcal{V}^C}{\partial m^C} \frac{\partial m^C}{\partial \chi} + \frac{\partial \mathcal{V}^C}{\partial m^{C^*}} \frac{\partial m^{C^*}}{\partial \chi} \right\} \left\{ (\mathcal{V}^{C^*} - \mathcal{V}^{N^*}) - \frac{\chi}{(1 - \chi)} (\mathcal{V}^C - \mathcal{V}^N) \right\} = 0 \tag{9}$$

Since the term in the first set of brackets is positive, the Nash bargaining solution requires:

$$\chi(\mathcal{V}^C(m^C(\chi), m^{C^*}(\chi)) - \mathcal{V}^N) = (1 - \chi)(\mathcal{V}^{C^*}(m^C(\chi), m^{C^*}(\chi)) - \mathcal{V}^{N^*}) \tag{10}$$

Or, more compactly,

$$\chi(\mathcal{V}^C(\chi) - \mathcal{V}^N) = (1 - \chi)(\mathcal{V}^{C^*}(\chi) - \mathcal{V}^{N^*}) \tag{11}$$

If both countries are identical then $\mathcal{V}^N = \mathcal{V}^{N^*}$, and the function $\mathcal{V}^{C^*}(\bar{\chi})$ equals the function $\mathcal{V}^C(1 - \bar{\chi})$; that is, the foreign country's welfare when $\chi = \bar{\chi}$ is equal to the home country's welfare when $\chi = 1 - \bar{\chi}$, for any $\bar{\chi}$. Thus in this perfectly symmetric case the Nash bargaining solution reduces to:

$$\chi(\mathcal{V}^C(\chi) - \mathcal{V}^N) = (1 - \chi)(\mathcal{V}^C(1 - \chi) - \mathcal{V}^N) \tag{12}$$

From (12), $\chi = 1 - \chi$ so $\chi = (1/2)$. Thus the welfare weight which we argued was natural in the context of symmetric countries, turns out to be the Nash bargaining solution as well.

More generally, when countries are not symmetric, (11) describes the Nash bargaining solution (this is a non-linear equation but since the LHS is strictly increasing in χ and the RHS strictly decreasing in χ there is a unique solution). Notice that the larger the welfare gain (i.e. the difference in utility between the coordinated and uncoordinated regimes) to one government, the lower the welfare weight it receives in the social planner's problem. In fact, the weighted gains must be equalized under the Nash bargaining solution. Since the Nash bargaining solution is derived from an axiomatic approach there is no particular "story," or intuition, which explains this result. One can think of the government which gains more as being more willing to accept a smaller welfare weight. Alternatively, the government which gains less may demand a higher welfare weight by threatening not to coordinate, knowing that the potential loss from no agreement is greater to the other government.

One problem with Nash's axiomatic approach is that without a specific model of bargaining it is difficult to judge whether his axioms are very plausible. The axiom of Pareto efficiency, for example, appears to be violated quite often in practice. Both players may be clearly better-off by coming to some agreement yet fail to do so.[4] If bargaining outcomes really are Pareto efficient, it is not clear why there are often costly strikes. Some of Nash's Axioms can be replaced while keeping the general nature of the solution the same. Kalai and Smorodinski (1975) and Kalai (1977) have derived the bargaining solutions under alternative axioms. Numerical exercises by Hughes Hallett (1986b), however, suggest that these alternative solution concepts yield very similar results, at least in the context of international policy coordination.

Ariel Rubinstein has proposed a quite different framework for analyzing bargaining; rather than take an axiomatic approach he begins with an explicit model of bargaining. Players are assumed to be bargaining over shares of a dollar; if they cannot agree on an allocation of shares then neither player gets anything (which is clearly Pareto inefficient); otherwise each player gets the agreed share of the dollar. Player one starts the bargaining by proposing a particular allocation.

Player two can then either accept this outcome or, in the next period, make a counter-offer. Both players discount the future so that delaying an agreement is costly.

The way in which the bargaining is modeled potentially gives player one an unfair advantage simply because he gets to make the first offer. It can be shown, however, that this asymmetry can be eliminated by letting the waiting period between offers and counter-offers tend towards zero. One interesting feature of the Rubinstein model is that it yields equivalent results to the Nash bargaining solution as the length of the waiting period tends towards zero (see, for example, Osborne and Rubinstein, 1990).

Again, we can think of governments bargaining over the welfare weight in the global welfare function, χ. Let each country's welfare gains be given by:

$$\mathcal{G}(\chi) = [\mathcal{V}^C(\chi) - \mathcal{V}^N] \quad \text{and} \quad \mathcal{G}^*(\chi) = [\mathcal{V}^{C^*}(\chi) - \mathcal{V}^{N^*}] \tag{10}$$

where χ is the welfare weight assigned to the home country. To make the problem tractable we linearize the welfare gains functions $\mathcal{G}$ and $\mathcal{G}^*$. We begin by defining the following quantities:

$$\bar{\mathcal{G}} = \mathcal{G}(1) \quad \text{and} \quad \underline{\mathcal{G}} = \mathcal{G}(0) \tag{11}$$

Thus $\bar{\mathcal{G}}$ is the home country's welfare gain in the coordinated regime when it receives a weight of unity in the global welfare function. Likewise, we define:

$$\bar{\mathcal{G}}^* = \mathcal{G}^*(0) \quad \text{and} \quad \underline{\mathcal{G}}^* = \mathcal{G}^*(1) \tag{12}$$

Therefore $\bar{\mathcal{G}} > \underline{\mathcal{G}}$ and $\bar{\mathcal{G}}^* > \underline{\mathcal{G}}^*$. The welfare gains under coordination can then be approximated by:

$$\mathcal{G}(\chi) = \bar{\mathcal{G}}\chi + \underline{\mathcal{G}}(1 - \chi) \tag{13}$$

$$\mathcal{G}^*(\chi) = \bar{\mathcal{G}}^*(1 - \chi) + \underline{\mathcal{G}}^*\chi \tag{14}$$

Consider two possible values of the welfare weights, χ and χ'. Given that once an offer has been rejected re-negotiation is not possible for a period of length h, the home country will be indifferent between accepting χ or waiting an additional period for χ' (where $\chi' > \chi$) if:

$$\bar{\mathcal{G}}\chi + \underline{\mathcal{G}}(1 - \chi) = \frac{\bar{\mathcal{G}}\chi' + \underline{\mathcal{G}}(1 - \chi')}{1 + \rho h} \tag{15}$$

where ρ is the home country's discount rate. The foreign country will be indifferent between accepting χ' or waiting for one negotiation period and accepting χ if:

$$\underline{\mathcal{G}}^*\chi' + \bar{\mathcal{G}}^*(1 - \chi') = \frac{\underline{\mathcal{G}}^*\chi + \bar{\mathcal{G}}^*(1 - \chi)}{1 + \rho^*h} \qquad (16)$$

Conditions (15) and (16) define the Rubinstein bargaining solution, χ. How does the bargaining outcome depend upon the data of the problem? Suppose that both countries are identical except for their discount rates. Then the following symmetry conditions must hold:

$$\bar{\mathcal{G}} = \bar{\mathcal{G}}^* \quad \text{and} \quad \underline{\mathcal{G}} = \underline{\mathcal{G}}^* \qquad (17)$$

Solving for χ' from (16) yields:

$$\chi'(\underline{\mathcal{G}} - \bar{\mathcal{G}}) = \bar{\mathcal{G}} + \frac{(\underline{\mathcal{G}} - \bar{\mathcal{G}})\chi + \bar{\mathcal{G}}}{1 + \rho^*h} \qquad (18)$$

From (15):

$$(\bar{\mathcal{G}} - \underline{\mathcal{G}})\chi = \frac{-\underline{\mathcal{G}}\rho h}{1 + \rho h} + \frac{(\bar{\mathcal{G}} - \underline{\mathcal{G}})\chi'}{1 + \rho h} \qquad (19)$$

substituting (18):

$$\chi = \frac{(\rho^*h\bar{\mathcal{G}} - \rho h\underline{\mathcal{G}}) - \rho h\rho^*h\underline{\mathcal{G}}}{[(\bar{\mathcal{G}} - \underline{\mathcal{G}})(\rho h + \rho^*h)]} \qquad (20)$$

Notice that when $\rho = \rho^*$, the expression for χ collapses to:

$$\chi = \frac{1}{2} - \frac{\rho h\underline{\mathcal{G}}}{(\bar{\mathcal{G}} - \underline{\mathcal{G}})} \qquad (21)$$

Taking the limit $h \Rightarrow 0$, then gives,

$$\chi = \frac{1}{2} \qquad (22)$$

which is again natural, given our assumption of complete symmetry. When $\rho \neq \rho^*$, we first write the expression for χ as:

$$\chi = \frac{h(\rho^*\bar{\mathcal{G}} - \rho\underline{\mathcal{G}}) - h^2\rho\rho^*\underline{\mathcal{G}}}{(\bar{\mathcal{G}} - \underline{\mathcal{G}})(\rho + \rho^*)h} \qquad (23)$$

Using L'Hopital's rule, we take the limit $h \Rightarrow 0$ to obtain:

$$\chi = \frac{(\rho^*\bar{\mathcal{G}} - \rho\underline{\mathcal{G}})}{(\bar{\mathcal{G}} - \underline{\mathcal{G}})(\rho + \rho^*)} \qquad (24)$$

It is straightforward to show from (24) that $\chi > (1/2)$ if and only if $\rho^* > \rho$. Thus we get the intuitively plausible result that the home government gets a larger (smaller) share of the welfare gains if it is more (less) patient than the foreign government. Other variants of the Rubinstein model – some with rather surprising results – are discussed in Kreps (1990).

3. Bargaining Under Incomplete Information

The bargaining models surveyed above make the crucial assumption that there is no asymmetry of information. Uncertainty itself presents no problems, since we can simply think of V^C and V^N as representing *expected* welfare. (But we would need to be clear on whether bargains are struck before the uncertainty is resolved – presumably the relevant case in our context – or afterwards and whether there is any possibility of renegotiation.) Once asymmetry of information is introduced, however, the bargaining problem is qualitatively different. Suppose, for example, the policy preferences of the governments are not common knowledge (although they are known to the governments themselves). As the passage from Putnam (1988) quoted in the introduction suggests, governments may try to misrepresent their preferences in order to achieve better bargains. Alternatively, each government's true beliefs over the possible models of the world economy may be unknown to other governments. Again, there may be an incentive to misrepresent beliefs over macroeconomic models in order to influence negotiations. In this section we examine some of the implications of this type of uncertainty. The results are somewhat disturbing: drawing directly from recent game theory literature on bargaining we find that there may be instances in which bargaining difficulties prevent a cooperative agreement being reached even though this agreement would benefit both parties.

As in the Nash bargaining solution, we can model the bargaining behavior by asking what a global social arbitrator would do. Not only must the social arbitrator choose a solution which is equitable, he or she must also ensure that neither government has the incentive to misrepresent its preferences in order to improve its outcome. The bargaining solution must be *incentive compatible*. The requirement for incentive compatibility, we shall see, severely limits the solutions available to the global social planner; so much so, that the Pareto frontier may not be attainable. If one is willing to forego equity of the outcome then it is always possible to attain the Pareto frontier. Thus a "dictatorship" outcome (in which one party gets all of the welfare *gains* of the agreement) is always feasible but is rather uninteresting as a theory of bargaining. From a normative perspective, a dictatorship outcome is obviously unsatisfactory, but even as a positive theory it is probably of little relevance. Although the other country does not actually lose from the agreement, it is unlikely that domestic political pressures would let a government enter into an agreement in which the other country captures all (or even most) of the welfare gains. So we shall need to focus on bargaining solutions which are both equitable and incentive compatible. The bargaining solution we use is an extension of the Nash bargaining solution, due to Myerson (1979).[5]

The easiest way to model the possibility of different preferences is to think of distinct players, each with a fixed preference. So if the home government can be either strongly anti-inflationary or a weakly anti-inflationary we say that there are two *types* of home government. More generally, we assume that there are n types of home government and n^* types of foreign government. We further assume that there is a known probability distribution of the various types of each government, given by ρ_i, $i = 1, ..., n$ and ρ_i^*, $i = 1, ..., n^*$. Negotiators for the two governments report the type of the government they are representing to the global social arbitrator. In equilibrium, the social arbitrator must try to choose an outcome in which neither party will have the incentive to misrepresent its type.

We follow Myerson (1979) in assuming a global social arbitrator who maximizes the *generalized Nash product:*

$$V^A = \text{Max} \left\{ \prod_{i=1}^{n} (\mathcal{G}_i)^{\rho_i} \right\} \left\{ \prod_{i=1}^{n*} (\mathcal{G}_i^*)^{\rho_i^*} \right\} \tag{1}$$

where the maximization is over the cooperative policies, m^C and m^{C^*}, which will be contingent upon the types reported by the two negotiators. $\mathcal{G}_i$ is the expected utility (relative to the no-agreement outcome) of a home government of type i, where expectation is taken over the set of possible types of the foreign government. $\mathcal{G}_i^*$ is the expected utility of a foreign government of type i, where expectation is taken over the possible types of home government.

Bayesian incentive compatibility requires that neither the home nor the foreign government has the incentive to misrepresent its true type in order to maximize its expected utility, when the other player reports its type honestly. Therefore, if the agreement is Bayesian incentive compatible all agents will be reporting their preferences truthfully.

It is convenient to first express the optimal monetary policies m^C and m^{C^*} as functions of the welfare weight χ_{jj^*}, where j indexes the set of types of the home government and j^* indexes the type of the foreign government. Then, as above, we linearize the welfare gains functions $\mathcal{G}$ and $\mathcal{G}^*$. Define

$$\bar{\mathcal{G}}_i = \mathcal{G}_i(1) \quad \text{and} \quad \underline{\mathcal{G}}_i = \mathcal{G}_i(0) \tag{2}$$

so that $\bar{\mathcal{G}}_i$ ($\underline{\mathcal{G}}_i$) is the welfare attained by the home country when its type is i, and it receives all (none of) the welfare weight in the social planner's objective function. Likewise, let:

$$\bar{\mathcal{G}}_i^* = \mathcal{G}_i^*(0) \quad \text{and} \quad \underline{\mathcal{G}}_i^* = \mathcal{G}_i^*(1) \tag{3}$$

Finally, we define $\bar{\mathcal{G}}_{ij}(\chi)$ and $\underline{\mathcal{G}}_{ij}(\chi)$ as the levels of welfare attained by a government of type i but which claims to be of type j. (Similarly, $\bar{\mathcal{G}}_{ij}^*(\chi)$ and $\underline{\mathcal{G}}_{ij}^*(\chi)$ are the linearized welfare limits of a foreign government of type i but which claims to be of type j.) The advantage of using these linearized welfare functions is that we can very easily parameterize the set of all possible outcomes using just a few choice variables.

With these linearized functions, we can, without loss of generality, write any outcome in the form:

$$\Pi^{jj^*} = \{\pi_N^{jj^*}, \pi_1^{jj^*}, \pi_0^{jj^*}\}, j = 1, ..., n \quad \text{and} \quad j^* = 1, ..., n^* \tag{4}$$

where π_N is the probability weight on no agreement being reached, π_1 is the probability weight on $\chi = 1$, and π_0 is the probability weight on $\chi = 0$. A bargaining outcome is a set of probability weights Π^{jj^*} for each possible *reported* type of government. Given Π^{jj^*} we can determine the welfare levels of all players. For example, if an agreement $\{\hat{\pi}_N^{jj^*}, \hat{\pi}_1^{jj^*}, \hat{\pi}_0^{jj^*}\}$ is reached, then, given that the home government is of type j and the foreign government is of type j^*, the welfare of the home government is:

$$\hat{\pi}_N^{jj^*} \times 0 + \hat{\pi}_1^{jj^*} \times \bar{\mathcal{G}} + \hat{\pi}_0^{jj^*} \times \underline{\mathcal{G}} \tag{5}$$

where 0 is the welfare gain under no agreement, and $\underline{\mathcal{G}}$ and $\bar{\mathcal{G}}$ have been defined above. Notice that an agreement specifies the probability weights as a function of the reported types (in equilibrium the reported types will be truthful since, by design, the equilibrium is incentive compatible). It bears emphasizing that the linearization of the welfare gain functions, and the interpretation of the agreement in terms of probabilities is only made for technical convenience.[6]

If j and j^* are the true types of home and foreign government then the incentive compatibility constraint on the home government is:

$$\hat{\pi}_1^{ij^*} \times \bar{\mathcal{G}}_{ji} + \hat{\pi}_0^{ij^*} \times \underline{\mathcal{G}}_{ji} \leq \hat{\pi}_1^{jj^*} \times \bar{\mathcal{G}} + \hat{\pi}_0^{jj^*} \times \underline{\mathcal{G}} \text{ for all } i \neq j \tag{6}$$

Thus, in equilibrium, the home government should not have an incentive to misrepresent its type (an analogous condition holds for the foreign government as well). Since $\underline{\mathcal{G}}$ and $\underline{\mathcal{G}}^*$ may be negative, an agreement will only be individually rational for each government if:

$$\hat{\pi}_N^{ij^*} \times 0 + \hat{\pi}_1^{ij^*} \times \bar{\mathcal{G}} + \hat{\pi}_0^{ij^*} \times \underline{\mathcal{G}} \geq 0 \tag{7}$$

$$\hat{\pi}_N^{ij^*} \times 0 + \hat{\pi}_1^{ij^*} \times \underline{\mathcal{G}}^* + \hat{\pi}_0^{ij^*} \times \bar{\mathcal{G}}^* \geq 0 \tag{8}$$

The global arbitrator's optimization problem, therefore, is to maximize (1) subject to the incentive compatibility constraints (6) (together with its foreign analog) and the individual rationality constraints (7)–(8). This is a non-linear programming problem subject to inequality constraints; while an analytic solution is not particularly enlightening, it is simple to solve numerically.

The main insight of this section can be obtained by considering the following example. Suppose that both the home and foreign governments target output and inflation, but while the relative weight on the anti-inflation objective in the home country's utility function is known to be ω, the weight in the foreign country's welfare function may be either ω_1^* or ω_2^*:

$$\mathcal{V} = E\{(1 - \omega)y^2 + \omega(\pi^2)\}, \quad 0 \leq \omega \leq 1 \tag{9}$$

$$\mathcal{V}_1^* = E\{(1 - \omega_1^*)y^2 + \omega_1^*(\pi^2)\}, \quad 0 \leq \omega_1^* \leq 1 \tag{10}$$

$$\mathcal{V}_2^* = E\{(1 - \omega_2^*)y^2 + \omega_2^*(\pi^2)\}, \quad 0 \leq \omega_2^* \leq 1 \tag{11}$$

There is thus one type of home government and two types of foreign government. The structural model is given by:

$$y = \alpha m + \beta m^* \tag{12}$$

$$\pi = \phi m + \eta m^* + s \tag{13}$$

(together with its symmetric foreign analogs). For the parameters α, β, ϕ and η we use the mean values of the reduced-form U.S. multipliers from the Brookings survey (see Table 2.1 above) for both the home and the foreign countries ($\alpha = 0.29$, $\beta = 0.070$, $\phi = 0.22$, $\eta = -0.134$). The first type of foreign government is assumed to be identical to the home government with $\omega_1^* = \omega = 0.9$, while the second type of foreign government's anti-inflation weight is given by $\omega_2 = 0.6$. Using these parameter values, we can easily calculate the welfare gains to the home and foreign country as a function of the welfare weight, χ, and the type of foreign government. The limits $\underline{G}$ and $\bar{G}$ are then:

(Type 1 foreign government) $\underline{G} = -5.6$ $\bar{G} = 10.9,$
$$\underline{G}^* = -5.6 \quad \bar{G}^* = 10.9$$

(Type 2 foreign government) $\underline{G} = -5.8$ $\bar{G} = 12.5,$
$$\underline{G}^* = -5.5 \quad \bar{G}^* = 3.1$$

(Type 1 foreign government mimicking Type 2)
$$\underline{\underline{G}}^*_{1,2} = -13.5 \quad \bar{\bar{G}}^*_{1,2} = 8.3$$

Figures 9.1 and 9.2 plot the welfare gains under each type of foreign government. Suppose that the foreign government were *known* to be of type 1 (by all parties) then, given the symmetry of the problem, the natural bargaining solution would be $\chi_1 = 0.5$. If the foreign government were of type 2, however, it would not agree to a solution in which χ_2 equals one-half since, from Figure 9.2, $G^*(0.5) < 0$. For the second type of foreign government to agree to coordinate its policies requires $\chi_2 \leq 0.35$ (for the home government not to suffer a net welfare loss requires $\chi_2 \geq 0.32$). From the figures it is clear that coordination is always feasible if the type of foreign government is known with certainty since, for example, at $\chi = 0.33$ both the home and the foreign government receive net welfare gains from coordination.

Once the type of foreign government is uncertain, however, reaching an agreement becomes more difficult. A bargaining agreement which specifies that χ will be (1/2) if the foreign government is of type 1 but χ be

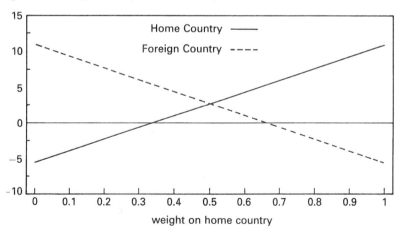

Figure 9.1 Welfare gains from coordination – when foreign government is of type 1

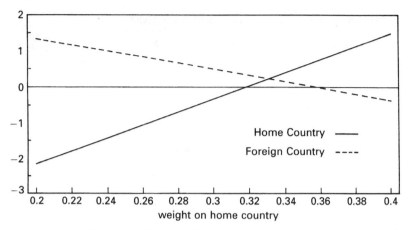

Figure 9.2   Welfare gains from coordination – when foreign government is of type 2

0.33 if the foreign government is of type 2 may not be incentive compatible because a type 1 foreign government could claim to be of type 2 in order to improve its bargaining outcome.[7] One possibility is to set both χ_1 and χ_2 equal to 0.33. This would be incentive compatible but it could be rather unfair to the home country. Suppose that there were only a one percent probability that the foreign country was of type 2. In that case such an agreement would be restricting χ to being below 0.35 even though there is only a very small probability that the symmetric outcome, $\chi = 0.5$, would lead to no agreement.

How does the Myerson incentive-compatible bargaining solution resolve this problem ? If $\omega = \omega_1^* = 0.9$ and $\omega_2^* = 0.6$ and $\rho^* = 0.50$ then maximizing the social arbitrator's function (1) subject to the various incentive compatibility constraints yields:

Type of foreign govt.	π_N	π_1	π_0
1	0.00	0.55	0.45
2	0.25	0.20	0.55

Therefore, if the foreign government claims to be of type 1 then the cooperative regime is always sustainable, with a roughly symmetric distribution of the welfare gains (the home country does slightly better). If the foreign government is of type 2, however, there is only a 75 percent probability of any agreement at all. If there is a cooperative regime, then the foreign country gets the lion's share of the welfare gains.

The interesting point is that there is a 12.5 percent (0.50×0.25) probability that there is no cooperative outcome at all. As discussed above, *if* the type of foreign government were known by all players for certain then there would always be a cooperative agreement. The constraints of incentive compatibility, however, imply that either the cooperative agreement will be very unfair to one of the two countries, or there must be at least some probability of no agreement at all.

4. Conclusions

In this chapter, we have examined some formal models of bargaining in order to obtain insights concerning the process of reaching coordination agreements. Though this area of the literature on coordination is relatively undeveloped, some interesting conclusions emerge concerning the difficulty of reaching negotiated agreement and the incentives for a government to misrepresent its position in order to obtain an agreement that is more favorable to itself. These considerations make it less likely that the gains from coordination, which we have argued in earlier chapters are present even in the context of uncertainty, will materialize.

It is clear that in the field of international economic policy, as in daily life, government officials do at times present their positions in a way that helps to influence agreements in the direction they desire. The introduction to this chapter cited the negotiations leading up to the agreement reached at the 1978 Bonn summit, in which Helmut Schmidt did not reveal until late in the game that the German government would be willing to consider fiscal stimulus. It may also pay to threaten not to reach agreement if a particular demand is not granted fully; this is the well-known tactic of stating that such-and-such is "not negotiable," whether or not that is the case. Trade negotiations may be particularly subject to such tactics, for instance in the area of agriculture, because of the strong political clout of farmers in many countries. This makes EC or Japanese governments, for instance, reluctant to concede much in the way of liberalization. It may pay them to take such a position in early stages, even if government officials and politicians realize that some concessions will eventually be necessary.

It is also the case that there are incentives for officials to use selectively the results of economic theory or econometric models in order to buttress their current policy positions in international negotiations, and to change their "views" when it is convenient. Their beliefs concerning how the economy actually works are clearly of secondary importance, and this is widely recognized. Models are seen as convenient tools, if they support the current government position; otherwise they are ignored. For instance, in the late 1970s with the election of Margaret Thatcher the U.K. government put in place a medium-term financial strategy based on monetary control; this led the U.K. Treasury to de-emphasize its macroeconomic model, which was largely based on a Keynesian view of demand management.

In the debate among G-7 governments about the need to reduce budget deficits, which raged during the 1980s and early 1990s, doctrinal disputes have at times played an important role. In the early 1980s, the U.S. Treasury responded to criticism from Europeans that it was exporting its high interest rates driven by expansionary U.S. fiscal policy to the rest of the world by claiming that there was no empirical evidence of a connection between government deficits and interest rates. At times during the 1980s the U.S. government exhorted other countries, in particular West Germany, to stimulate demand, which it was argued would lead to faster growth; the West German response was that expansionary fiscal policy produced few output gains, but just fed inflation. Curiously, in the early 1990s their positions were reversed; some U.S. government officials claimed that high world interest rates (and, in particular, high rates in the EMS), were the result of the German government borrowing associated with unification. The Germans, as well as noting the irony of the U.S. position (since the U.S. fiscal deficit remained high), downplayed the effect of their fiscal position on interest rates and on developments in the rest of the EMS.

Another area of disagreement among countries has been the effects of monetary and fiscal policies on external imbalances. Given the high U.S. current account deficit for most of the 1980s, there was general agreement about the need to reduce it but no consensus on how this was best done. The United States government has at times prodded its allies to stimulate demand in order to reduce their trade surpluses with the United States, while the response of those governments has been to point to the negligible effect of such action on the U.S. position, especially in the case of monetary stimulus, since it would also have the effect of appreciating the dollar. Despite such arguments, U.S. officials have continued to argue that the U.S. current account surplus is as much a foreign problem as a U.S. problem.

In many areas, then, it seems as though there is much scope for using disputes on technical issues as part of the bargaining process. As our theoretical discussion of bargaining has shown, misrepresenting preferences or views of the world may get in the way of Pareto-improving coordination agreements. There is therefore a clear role for an impartial arbiter to narrow the potential range of disagreement on these technical issues, so that governments cannot take such extreme positions purely for the sake of bargaining. A notable example is the study of exchange market intervention, commissioned at the Versailles G-7 summit. This joint study of the countries concerned examined the evidence and found that sterilized intervention did not have a major influence on exchange rates in most circumstances, unless it was concerted and was consistent with economic fundamentals. This conclusion has probably had a major influence in narrowing the various government positions about what intervention can and cannot do, and helped contribute to limited and realistic agreements reached at the Plaza and at the Louvre.

Notes

1 In Oudiz and Sachs (1984) the Nash bargaining solution (discussed below) is used; while Hughes Hallett (1986b) explores a variety of bargaining models and their implications for the distribution of the gains from coordination.
2 See Roemer (1988) for a criticism of Nash's axiomatic approach. He criticizes Nash's axioms because they are defined over utility space. In practice, agents seldom bargain over utility, they bargain over outcomes. Axioms defined over utility space, however, may not have very appealing properties translated to the space of actual outcomes.
3 In our notation!
4 It turns out that the bargaining outcome from the Rubinstein model (discussed below) is also Pareto efficient, but this is a property of the equilibrium, not an axiom or an assumption. In section 3 we analyze a bargaining outcome which does not constitute an unconstrained Pareto efficient outcome.
5 See Myerson (1984) for a further extension of this solution concept.
6 In particular, the probability weight on the possibility of no agreement, $\hat{\pi}_N$, can also represent a *delayed* agreement; as long as governments discount future utility a positive $\hat{\pi}_N$ is still welfare deteriorating and results in an outcome which is not on the Pareto frontier.
7 One needs to be a little careful here. If a type 1 government claims to be a type 2 government it will end up with monetary policies which would be optimal if its preferences were of type 2. The incentive compatibility constraint actually requires that a type 1 government not prefer the agreement χ_2 together with the policies which would be chosen for a type 2 government over its own outcome, χ_1 and $\{m_1^C, m_1^{C*}\}$.

10

Conclusions

Economic and political developments since World War II have led almost inexorably towards greater integration and policy interdependence. The Bretton Woods Agreement started this process by ushering in an era of open, non-discriminatory trade and payments systems. Most industrialized countries have gone much further, however, by allowing the free movement of capital across their borders. This global integration has afforded extraordinary opportunities for growth in world trade and income. At the same time, however, it presents challenges for, and imposes constraints upon, national macroeconomic policies.

Governments pursue diverse, and frequently conflicting, economic goals. These may include low unemployment, rapid economic growth, low inflation, and a current account or balance of payments surplus. Armed with few policy instruments, policymakers cannot achieve all of these goals simultaneously; trade-offs are inevitable. Moreover, the free movement of goods and capital – an objective in itself – severely limits the welfare benefits of macroeconomic policies that are chosen without regard to their international repercussions. With integrated markets for goods and capital, exchange rates and interest rates link national economies so that macroeconomic policies pursued by one country inevitably have repercussions – beneficial or detrimental – abroad. If governments jointly take account of these repercussions when setting policies, they will use their policy instruments more efficiently, in the sense of attaining outcomes that yield higher levels of welfare. This is not to suggest that policy coordination eliminates the trade-offs between macroeconomic targets, but it does allow policymakers to exploit those trade-offs more efficiently. Coordination, in fact, is very similar to engaging in international trade: under trade there is still a trade-off between producing more of one good and less of another, but by exploiting their comparative advantage, both parties gain relative to the autarkic equilibrium.

Yet this textbook case for policy coordination is perhaps too sanguine, for policymaking is fraught with uncertainties. Indeed, such uncertainties are so pervasive that they raise legitimate concerns about the viability and desirability of international macroeconomic policy coordination. Because various macroeconomic data are available at different frequencies, and with widely differing time lags, there will generally be uncertainty about the current state of the economy (what in our analytic framework we termed additive uncertainty). Thus the deviation of macroeconomic variables from their targets will often be unknown at the time that policies must be chosen. Perhaps more important, there is always uncertainty about the effects of policy instruments on macroeconomic targets (multiplier uncertainty). While we are constantly learning more about the dynamics of the world economy, its very structure changes all the while. Some lessons about the effects of monetary and fiscal policy have certainly been learnt; thus we would not expect central banks to tighten monetary policies at the depth of a world depression. But clearly our knowledge of the effects of various policies on macroeconomic targets is imperfect, and there are many competing theoretical paradigms and empirical models. Yet another source of uncertainty is the strategic behavior of foreign governments. Will they honor international agreements? Can they be trusted not to manipulate information available to them in order to improve their bargaining position?

In this book we have tried to make the case that coordinated policies will, at least on average, be better than uncoordinated policies. Indeed, uncertainty, far from reducing the benefits from coordination, actually provides additional incentives to coordinate policies. At a theoretical level, we showed how multiplier uncertainty exacerbates the inefficiency of uncoordinated policies, thus enhancing the argument for coordination. There certainly seem to have been particular episodes – such as the 1987 stock market crash – in which a sense of heightened uncertainty led to greater coordination among the central banks of the major industrialized countries. But our argument for coordination goes beyond mere theory. Using different variants – both classical and Keynesian – of a two-country empirical model, we explored the properties of coordinated and uncoordinated monetary policies in the presence of uncertainty. If policymakers face only parameter uncertainty, so that they know the general structure of the correct model but not the exact values of its parameters, then uncertainty on average increases the benefits from coordination, just as theory suggests. When policymakers have the wrong model entirely then any activist policy – coordinated or not – can be dangerous, and simple fixed policy rules perform much better. If policymakers are assumed to update their beliefs about the correct structure of the world economy, then coordinated policies may once again be superior to uncoordinated policies and to fixed rules even if the exact structural parameters of the model always remain uncertain. This conclusion needs to be qualified, however, when none of the models being used by policymakers is, even on average, a correct representation of reality. In that case, we continue to find that coordination is superior to non-coordination, though little better than some model-independent fixed rules.

It should be stressed that real-world policymaking is a far less ambitious thing than what is usually represented in the literature. Rather than optimization of some objective function, policy changes are made cautiously, precisely because there is no consensus either on the effects of policies or on the appropriate objective function. In addition, despite the favorable effects of rules on expectations, policymakers in practice do not allow themselves to be strictly bound by rules because of a desire to retain flexibility in order to respond to unexpected developments. In these circumstances, policy coordination cannot be characterized as joint optimization, or even as simple, internationally agreed rules; nevertheless, to the extent that policymaking involves taking into account repercussions on foreign countries as well as on the home country, it may be able to realize some of the gains from coordination that we have identified.

It is perhaps ironic that uncertainty, though making coordination more desirable, probably makes it more difficult to achieve and to sustain. In a repeated game context, a cooperative agreement may be sustained without direct enforcement if governments can credibly threaten not to coordinate again should the other government be caught cheating. With macroeconomic uncertainty, however, such mechanisms are unlikely to suffice, because it is difficult to detect whether a government has indeed reneged on the cooperative agreement. Verification is particularly difficult when such agreements are based upon each government's forecast of the state of its economy, since it may be impossible to disentangle genuine forecast errors from deliberate attempts to deviate from the agreement. International organizations can help to alleviate problems of monitoring adherence to cooperative agreements by producing consistent and comparable forecasts and undertaking multilateral surveillance of macroeconomic policies. Likewise, governments may attempt to misrepresent their beliefs over the effects of macroeconomic policies during negotiations with a view to improving their bargaining positions. Again, a strong case can be made for an independent body being charged with undertaking research to resolve controversial technical issues; the commissioning of the Jurgensen Report by the G-7 was an example.

As the world economy grows ever more interdependent, and the postwar hegemony of the United States diminishes, there will be an increasing need for greater coordination of macroeconomic policies. It remains to be seen whether governments of the major industrialized countries will face the political challenges of international policy coordination, and seize the opportunities for sustainable growth and macroeconomic stability.

Appendix: Cooperation and Coordination in Historical Perspective

1. Introduction

In this Appendix, the experience of international macroeconomic policy coordination since World War II is briefly surveyed, with particular focus on how uncertainty has affected attempts at policy coordination. As will be seen below, at a number of points in history, the incentive to cooperate came precisely from the perception that a wide dispersion of outcomes – some of them particularly unfavorable – was possible. In these episodes, governments managed to agree to various policy packages or mechanisms that assisted policy coordination, in the belief that independent policymaking increased the risk of the bad outcomes.

At other times, uncertainty about the current state of the domestic or foreign economy, distrust of the motives of foreign governments, or disagreement about the correct way to view the effects of policies, seems to have got in the way of reaching agreement. For these reasons, perhaps, cooperation in the international monetary arena has often taken the form of specifying rules of the game rather than agreements to change policies in a particular way or to coordinate the implementation of policies. By articulating clearly the responsibilities of each country, a framework for the international monetary system reduces difficulties in negotiating agreements and in verifying adherence to them.

Section 2 provides a brief overview of the history of international monetary cooperation since World War II. Our discussion draws upon four excellent sources: Solomon (1977), Funabashi (1988), Putnam and Bayne (1987), and Volcker and Gyohten (1992), all of which provide much greater detail about the periods they cover. Sections 3 to 9 discuss selected episodes with a view to drawing some conclusions about how cooperation and coordination have worked in practice.

2. An Overview

The first twenty-five years after the World War II were the heyday of international cooperation in monetary relations. Even before hostilities had ended, the Monetary and Financial Conference of the Allied and United Nations, meeting in 1944 at Bretton Woods, New Hampshire, had laid the plans for the post-war monetary system. Two new institutions were created: the International Monetary Fund and the World Bank. Their purpose was to allow governments to pursue national goals of full employment and reconstruction and development while avoiding the competitive beggar-thy-neighbor policies which had been so disastrous for the world trade and payments system in the 1930s. Many other new institutions, such as the Organization for European Economic Cooperation (later the Organization for Economic Cooperation and Development, OECD), the European Payments Union, and the Gold Pool, were established in subsequent years to foster greater cooperation among governments in their monetary relations.

If the 1950s and 1960s were the zenith of international cooperation, the early 1970s were certainly its nadir. In August 1971, the Bretton Woods system of fixed exchange rates collapsed; the Smithsonian Agreement of December 1971, which set new parities and wider margins, lasted a little over a year; and attempts at fundamental reform of the system in the next few years were unsuccessful. A hybrid "non-system" was institutionalized by the 1976 Jamaica agreement to amend the Articles of Agreement of the IMF, in order to permit countries to adopt various degrees of exchange rate flexibility, but subject to guidelines to floating and IMF surveillance over their policies.[1] At the same time, however, the economic summit process was getting under way, growing out of informal meetings among the finance ministers of the United States, the United Kingdom, Germany and France – the so-called Library Group because they initially met at the White House library. International coordination through summitry culminated at the Bonn Summit of 1978 when the United States adjusted its policies to limit its external imbalance and reduce energy consumption, while Japan and Germany tried to act as locomotives for the world economy, pulling it out of recession through expansionary monetary and fiscal policies. Monetary cooperation in Europe during this period also led to the establishment of the European Monetary System, in March 1979, partly in reaction to fluctuations in the dollar that induced volatility in intra-European exchange rates.

The Bonn Summit experiment was subsequently viewed as less than a full success, in large part because the oil crisis of 1979 meant that the expansionary policies envisioned at Bonn were no longer appropriate.

Coordination thus fell into disfavor among the leaders of the largest economies. The early 1980s were a period of "going it alone" with virtually all of the largest industrialized countries unilaterally adopting a strong anti-inflationary stance (though with very different policy mixes).

The pendulum swung back in favor of coordination by the mid-1980s, because the dollar was viewed as increasingly misaligned and divorced from economic fundamentals. New vigor was injected into the coordination process by the Plaza Agreement of 1985 and the Louvre Accord of 1987, where the central bank governors and ministers of finance sought first to depreciate the dollar, and then stabilize its value, through coordinated intervention. Economic policy coordination was once again a favorite buzzword at the Tokyo (1986) and Venice (1987) summits. Since then, however, macroeconomic policy coordination has occurred primarily at meetings of finance ministers, and has lost some of its prominence in summit discussions.

3. The Bretton Woods System

The agreement to create the International Monetary Fund (and its sister institution, the International Bank for Reconstruction and Development) at a conference at Bretton Woods, New Hampshire in July 1944, was to a large extent a response to uncertainties created by the World War II and fears of a return to the instability of the inter-war period. That period had been characterized by a breakdown of the Gold Standard, instability of floating exchange rates, and beggar-thy-neighbor practices that involved attempts to improve employment at home through increased tariffs and exchange rate depreciation. The Great Depression had resulted, and many economists feared that the immediate post-war period would be plagued by inadequate demand and unemployed resources after war-related expenditures were reduced.

The founders of the IMF created a system of stable exchange rate parities and a fund for financing payments imbalances with the goal of avoiding a deflationary bias to the international monetary system that many associated with the Gold Standard. The original Articles of Agreement of the Fund made it clear that the exchange rate system involved elements of both institutionalized and ad hoc coordination. Parity changes in excess of 10 percent could only be taken in consultation with other members. Rules governed the commitment to make a member's currency convertible into other currencies for current account payments (Article VIII), but subject to transitional arrangements specified in Article XIV. More generally, the IMF was to be a forum for consultation and surveillance over member countries' policies, whose first purpose was "To promote international monetary cooperation through a permanent institution which provides the machinery for consultation and collaboration on international monetary problems" (Article I(i)).

At the heart of the Bretton Woods system was the recognition that monetary order could only be sustained if national governments were able to maintain sufficient sovereignty *within* the system. Keynes, with his emphasis on active demand management, foresaw a large fund (some $35bn) which would be able to finance governments that were facing balance of payments difficulties without requiring severe economic adjustment.[2] Fearing that the cost of the Fund would fall mainly on American shoulders, the United States would only agree to a much smaller initial subscription of $8bn. A second proposal of Keynes, that surplus countries should have to pay interest charges on their "excess" reserves, was also vetoed by the Americans who assumed that they would always be the main surplus country. Ironically, some thirty years later, the United States was to propose a similar measure at the Committee of Twenty Reforms, only to have it rejected by the European governments.[3]

4. The Marshall Plan and the European Payments Union

In the immediate post-war years, however, the issue was reviving the war-torn European economies. A number of initiatives were undertaken by the United States to provide aid to Europe, including the Anglo-American Loan Agreement of 1945, an interim aid package for Europe, and finally the Marshall Plan. But European economies were more vulnerable than had been envisaged: as part of the Anglo-American Loan Agreement Britain was supposed to restore convertibility by July 1947. Britain did so, only to suspend convertibility within a month as foreign holders of Sterling balances rushed to convert them into dollars. The years 1946 and 1947 were particularly difficult for Europe; the U.S. continued to enjoy a trade surplus of $10bn while Europe and Japan lost more than $6bn of gold and dollar reserves. But in June 1947 Secretary of State Marshall announced the European Recovery Program – soon dubbed the Marshall Plan – and by June 1948 President Truman had appropriated more than $4bn for European recovery. The United States provided some $12bn between 1948 and 1952. The Organization of European Economic Cooperation (OEEC) was created to administer these funds, part of which were used as an initial kitty for the European Payments Union (EPU).

The EPU was a payments mechanism that allowed European countries to save on their scarce dollars by netting bilateral balances. But the EPU was much more; in fact it represented one of the first instances of institutionalized policy cooperation. The EPU was established in 1950, and lasted until 1958, when most countries achieved de facto convertibility. The EPU instituted monthly settlement, partly in gold or dollars and partly in credit, with prior netting of bilateral imbalances. In this way, it helped alleviate the shortage of foreign exchange, and permitted the reduction of quantitative restrictions that member countries had in place. Credits cumulated from month to month up to some credit ceiling, or quota, which had been fixed on the basis of each country's trade in 1949.

The EPU thus incorporated a mechanism that could operate automatically, and the rules for which were specified precisely and in detail: the timing and form of settlement, the extent of automatic credit facilities, exchange rate guarantees, etc. However, a basic aspect of the EPU that was crucial to its success was uncertain, namely whether credit limits would be quickly reached; if so, and additional credit was not made available, then trade would revert to its earlier form, namely settlement in hard currency or on the basis of bilateral trading agreements. The key to the successful operation of the EPU was therefore for balance of payments adjustment to operate smoothly: deficit countries had to take prompt measures to restrict demand; so the burden would not fall solely on them, chronic surplus countries also had to adjust, in particular by reducing restrictions on imports and stimulating demand.

However, the rules for achieving adjustment by deficit and surplus countries could not be spelled out in detail; the mechanisms involved were complex and uncertain, and prior agreement concerning the steps to be taken also required agreement concerning the effects of the policy actions. Instead, the Managing Board of the EPU evolved into a forum for examining the policies of the member countries, and making recommendations concerning policy changes – particularly by those countries approaching their credit ceilings.

Thus the Managing Board, on which all member countries were represented, became a vehicle for policy coordination. In summarizing the EPU's first two years of operation, Kaplan and Schleiminger (1989, p. 149) conclude:

> Critical situations, well beyond the capacity of the automatic mechanism alone, descended on the Board with unrelenting regularity. . . . In the broadest sense, the Board helped gain acceptability for macroeconomic policy, though the term itself was hardly known at the time. Fiscal and monetary measures then became the principal policy tool for controlling inflation. . . . As one country after another threatened to exhaust its debtor quota, the Board consistently urged readjustment through

restrictive fiscal and monetary policies. . . . Countries that threatened to exhaust their creditor quotas received correspondingly appropriate advice – remove trade restrictions and use fiscal and monetary measures to promote increased demand for imports.

As the European economies enjoyed unprecedented growth, with industrial production rising 40 percent between 1948 and 1952, and a modest surplus for OEEC (Organization for European Economic Cooperation) countries by 1952 (helped by a major devaluation of European currencies in 1949), the dollar shortage began to disappear. At the same time, the Korean War helped Japan's external position and by 1950 the U.S. balance of payments showed a small deficit. By 1958 most European countries were able to achieve current account convertibility, and the Bretton Woods system came into operation as it had originally been envisioned.

5. U.S. Balance of Payments Deficits and Strains on the Bretton Woods System

The linchpin of the Bretton Woods system was gold, which had long been the ultimate reserve asset. As long as there was no danger of devaluation, however, the U.S. dollar was the reserve asset of choice because dollar reserves could more easily be used in international payments and be held in interest-bearing form. At the beginning of the Bretton Woods period, with the United States holding some $20bn of gold or roughly 60 percent of all the gold held by central banks, it seemed inconceivable that the dollar would ever be devalued. By the time that the EPU was disbanded in 1958, however, the "dollar shortage" had been replaced by the "dollar glut." While the U.S. current account remained firmly in the black, large-scale capital outflows, due to higher interest rates available in Europe, resulted in an overall balance of payments deficit of $2.9bn in 1959 and $2.5bn in 1960. The year 1960 saw a marked improvement in the U.S. trade surplus as the recession dampened imports and trade liberalization in Europe helped boost exports. Substantial capital outflows continued, however, and the U.S. balance of payments was in deficit by $3.4bn; almost $2bn of that deficit had to be financed by sales of gold reserves to foreign central banks.

The special position of the dollar in the Bretton Woods system meant that the United States in effect determined international liquidity through its monetary policies. If its monetary policies were too stringent, then the U.S. would run balance of payments surpluses and other countries would run down their dollar holdings and world liquidity would contract. If too expansionary, world holdings of dollars would increase too fast, and there would be inflationary pressures. In addition, foreign holders of dollars (residents of the United States were restricted in their holdings of gold at this time) would try to shift out of dollars into gold, since the United States was committed to convert official holdings of dollars into gold at a fixed price – $35 an ounce. By 1962, U.S. gold reserves had fallen to $16 billion, from $24 billion in 1948, and U.S. official liabilities exceeded $12 billion. There was also a private market for gold; though the United States was not obliged to sell gold for dollars presented by private holders, if the price in the private market exceeded the official price, there would be strong incentives for foreign central banks to arbitrage between the two markets. Moreover, a decline in the value of dollar on the private gold market might trigger a crisis of confidence, leading to a run on the U.S. gold stock.[4]

This risk led to an agreement between the Federal Reserve and leading foreign central banks in November 1961 to jointly intervene with their gold stocks in order to maintain the London gold market price at 35 dollars (Coombs, 1976). The central banks of the United States, Belgium, France, Italy, the Netherlands, Switzerland, West Germany, and the United Kingdom agreed to supply gold in agreed proportions whenever the market price rose above the official price. This arrangement was successful until early in 1968, when the needed gold sales rose markedly. In four days in March 1968, gold sales totaled over 500 million dollars. At this point the Gold Pool members agreed to disband the pool and not to support the private market, creating a two-tier system in which the official price was maintained at $35, the private price was freed, but central banks agreed, at least informally, to limit their requests for the conversion of their dollar holdings into gold.[5]

Robert Triffin (1960) was the first to point out the absurdity of a system in which the growth of global liquidity depended on U.S. balance of payments deficits, but confidence in the U.S. dollar was weakened by those very deficits. This Triffin "dilemma" was ultimately solved by the creation, after protracted negotiations both at the level of Ministers and Deputies of the G-10 and at the level of Fund Executive Directors, of a new international asset, the Special Drawing Right (SDR). By allocating SDRs and thus creating new international liquidity, the IMF could supplement the level of liquidity being created by U.S. balance of payments deficits. The first SDR allocation, of $3.5bn ($9.5bn over three years), was made on 1 January 1970. The allocation had been chosen on the expectation that the U.S. balance of payments deficit would be no more than $1bn per year; in the first quarter of 1973 the U.S. balance of payments had a $3bn deficit.

The Gold Pool was only one of many measures undertaken to stop the U.S. balance of payments deficits from destabilizing the international monetary system; some measures were taken unilaterally, others were taken in cooperation with the central banks of the major nations. For example, Operation Twist was an attempt to raise short-term interest rates in the United States while keeping long-term rates low in the belief that short rates were responsible for the capital outflow while productive investment in the U.S. would be more affected by longer rates. Similarly, the Kennedy administration announced an investment tax credit in 1961 so that interest rates could be raised while stimulating investment. The most direct control on capital flows came in the form of the Interest Equalization Tax (IET) which was first introduced in 1963, becoming progressively tighter, until it was removed in 1970 shortly before the breakdown of the Bretton Woods system. The IET was a tax on capital outflows (initially on the issuance of foreign securities in the U.S. market) which sought to equalize the net of tax return on investment in the U.S. and abroad.

International cooperation was also essential to the continued survival of the system. There were two main forums for this cooperation: Working Party 3 of the OECD (which Japan had joined in 1964) and the monthly meetings of central bankers at the Bank for International Settlements. Charles Coombs (1976) provides a fascinating account of the various "defense" mechanisms set up by the major central banks. Amongst these was an extensive "swap" network which a central bank facing a speculative attack could draw upon. Foreign central banks were also persuaded not to exchange their dollar holdings for gold at the Treasury's gold window by the issuance of Roosa Bonds, which were essentially foreign currency denominated bonds.[6] The Group of Ten (G-10) countries were parties to the General Arrangements to Borrow (GAB). This was a facility which was to be made available to the IMF in the event that a country with a large quota (most notably the United States) borrowed its maximum allowable from the IMF.

6. The Smithsonian Agreement

Strains on the Bretton Woods system could, at least temporarily, be eased by a devaluation of the dollar as an increased surplus on the U.S. trade account would offset outflows of short-term capital. Yet a devaluation of the dollar was very hard to engineer given the dollar's unique position. An adjustment of the official gold price was not sufficient, because of a feature of the dollar exchange standard: since other currencies were pegged to the dollar, not to gold, their dollar exchange rates would not be affected. Nor could countries unilaterally revalue against the dollar without considering what their trading partners would do; some coordinated solution was necessary. Moreover, the Americans were concerned that once a devaluation of the dollar had occurred foreign central banks would never again trust the dollar as a reserve asset (Volcker and Gyohten, 1992). Perhaps more importantly, it was the central banks which had cooperated most closely with the United States in not asking for gold in exchange for dollars – mainly the British and the Germans – which would suffer the largest capital losses. There emerged, therefore, a form of paralysis: even discussions about a dollar devaluation were impossible for fear of triggering a speculative attack.

After a promising balance of payments surplus in 1969, reflecting a modest trade surplus and a capital inflow, the U.S. entered into recession in 1970. While Germany was using tight monetary policy to dampen inflationary pressures, monetary policy was eased in the U.S. to promote economic recovery. As the interest rate differential widened, capital outflows began at an alarming pace; by the end of 1970 the overall U.S. balance of payments deficit had reached $9.8bn. From then, the hemorrhaging of the U.S. balance of payments continued almost unabated.

On 5 May 1971, the Bundesbank, facing massive dollar purchases, suspended intervention operations, and was followed by the central banks of Austria, Belgium, the Netherlands, and Switzerland. Canada had earlier (May 1970) floated its exchange rate, and as the crisis proceeded, one danger feared by some, including Paul Volcker and Paul McCracken, was that the world would move to widespread floating and that this would produce disruption to trade and investment (Solomon, 1977, p. 186). Germany and The Netherlands let their currencies float temporarily with the mark revaluing by 5 percent before the Bundesbank resumed intervention operations; meanwhile Switzerland and Austria revalued by 7.1 percent and 5 percent respectively. Although the pressure on the dollar lessened somewhat in June of that year, by that point Congressman Henry Reuss and Senator Jacob Javits were openly calling for a float for the dollar. Paul Volcker during Congressional testimony argued that the underlying deficit was no more than $2.5bn–$3bn, with the remainder composed of short-term capital flows responding to divergent interest rates. But a Working Party 3 meeting in July argued that, cyclically adjusted, the U.S. balance of payments deficit was significantly larger so that narrowing the interest differential would be insufficient to restore equilibrium as the U.S. emerged from recession. Thus it appeared that a revaluation of European currencies and the yen would be needed. But without a joint revaluation, these governments were unlikely to be willing to agree to any revaluation; even then, there were likely to be free-rider problems as each government tried to limit its own revaluation.

In the second week of August the outflow of dollars became enormous, and foreign central banks, which hitherto had been willing to hold dollars (U.S. liabilities rose by $21bn in 1971 but gold sales only amounted to $840m), began to ask for gold, or at least gold cover. President Nixon responded to the crisis by announcing his New Economic Program. In addition to wage and price controls, the Program also suspended official gold sales ("closed the gold window") and unilaterally imposed a 10 percent import surcharge.

During the lengthy negotiations on the revaluation of the yen and the European currencies which followed, each government sought to minimize its own revaluation in order to protect balance of payments surpluses. Negotiations were complicated by the lack of agreement on the required swing in the U.S. balance of payments. The official U.S. position was that a $13 billion improvement would be necessary, while IMF and OECD staff reportedly estimated the needed swing to be $8 billion (Solomon, 1977). Volcker (in Volcker and Gyohten, 1992) provides a particularly vivid account of how each country tried to limit its own "contribution" to reducing the U.S. deficit; going around the table at a Working Party 3 meeting in October 1971 the sum of the European and Japanese offers came to only $3bn. A series of negotiations eventually led to agreement in Washington for an increase of the price of gold from $35 to $38 an ounce, and exchange rate revaluations of other currencies against the dollar that amounted to about 11 percent, which the Federal Reserve expected would produce an improvement in the U.S. balance of $8 billion (Solomon, 1977, p. 208).

These parity changes agreed to in December 1971 were known as the Smithsonian Agreement, which was termed by President Nixon "the most significant monetary agreement in the history of the world." But by early 1973 pressures developed in exchange markets that were too great for the new set of parities. Despite controls on capital inflows in Germany, the Bundesbank was forced to acquire increasing amounts of U.S. dollars; it and other European central banks closed exchange markets on 12 February. At this point, the U.S. Secretary of the Treasury George Shultz announced a further 10 percent devaluation (defined in terms of the SDR's value, which was at that time linked to gold), but did not commit the U.S. to intervene to defend par values. By that time, several major currencies were floating, however, and in March 1973 generalized floating of exchange rates began.

Discussions on long-term reform of the monetary system had already started in the Committee of Twenty (C-20), formed in 1972. Member countries were those representing IMF Executive Board constituencies. The reforms discussed at C-20 meetings – which included "objective indicators" for monitoring policies and balance of payments developments and some form of penalty on surplus countries which were not adjusting – did not, in the end, come to fruition. In part this was because the specter of floating exchange rates, so feared during the Bretton Woods years, turned out not to be so disastrous or chaotic. But perhaps more importantly, the oil price increase following the Yom Kippur war (with crude oil prices going from $3.01 a barrel before the war to $5.12 in October 1973 and then to $11.65 in December), and the resulting changes in external balances of all countries, would have put unbearable strains on any system of fixed exchange rates. But one outcome of the C-20 meetings was the formation of the Group of Five finance ministers (G-5). George Shultz invited his British, German, and French counterparts to an informal meeting in the White House Library. The following year they met again in France, this time joined by the Japanese finance minister and by Arthur Burns (central bank governors of all five countries joined the G-5 finance ministers the following year).[7] With two of the Library Group finance ministers rising to Head of State – Giscard as President, and Schmidt as Chancellor – the G-5 evolved into Economic Summits, attended by heads of state and their finance ministers though not central bank governors. At the summit level, the five countries were joined by Italy and Canada after the Rambouillet Summit of 1975. However, finance ministers and central bank governors continued to meet in the smaller group of the G-5 until the September 1986 meeting, where they were joined by the Canadians and the Italians.

7. The Group of Seven Economic Summits

Each country had greater freedom to pursue its own macroeconomic policies after generalized floating of exchange rates, but this freedom did not change the underlying reality of increasing interdependence. The economic summits of the major industrial countries were inaugurated at Rambouillet in November 1975, the result of an initiative by the President of France, Valéry Giscard d'Estaing. The summits were intended to be occasions for informal chats among leaders, rather than intensively prepared meetings. Though they might lead to agreement on economic issues, they also served as means of communicating information about objectives, and thereby reducing uncertainty. For instance, Helmut Schmidt, German Chancellor from 1974 to 1982, is quoted as saying "Summit meetings are not only designed to strengthen the readiness for compromise; they also create mutual trust and increase mutual predictability" (Putnam and Bayne, 1987, p. 33).

In the area of international monetary affairs, Rambouillet reached a compromise (prepared in advance by officials) between U.S. and French views on monetary reform, a compromise that would eventually lead to the Jamaica Agreement and the Second Amendment to the IMF's Articles of Agreement. This concerned the new "rules of the game" for floating exchange rates. Though the compromise did not meet the French objective of achieving greater "viscosity" of exchange rates, it did admit that some movements of exchange rates should be avoided.

The Bonn Summit of 1978 was the first significant example of explicit coordination of macroeconomic policies to emerge from a G-7 summit, achieving agreement that had been impossible at London the previous year on a package of measures that involved fiscal expansion in Germany and Japan, measures to restrict oil imports in the United States, and a commitment to proceed with trade liberalization negotiations. Putnam and Bayne (1987, p. 87) characterize the Bonn summit in the following terms: ". . . the agreement announced at Bonn would present the clearest case, by far, of a summit deal that left all participants happier than when they arrived." Because it is often cited as the one major example of macroeconomic policy coordination, it is worth discussing the meeting and the lead-up to it in some detail.

The context of the summit was a concern of the Carter Administration to sustain growth; but this was complicated by a weak dollar associated with lack of confidence in U.S. policies. Stimulus abroad could help the United States; however, the Japanese and especially the Germans feared the inflationary consequences of such stimulus. The idea that all countries could, however, benefit in terms of economic activity by concerted fiscal stimulus, especially in countries with relatively low deficits, came to be known as the "locomotive" or "convoy" principle.

The German response was twofold. First, they protested that their growth rate was already high: their forecast, of German GDP growth in the 4.5–5.5 percent range for 1977, was however considerably above the forecast made by the OECD (Putnam and Bayne 1987, p. 66). Second, they disputed that fiscal stimulus would produce the expected effects on growth, rather than simply exacerbating inflation. The German official preparing the London summit, Karl Otto Poehl, succeeded in inserting in the communique the statement that "inflation does not reduce unemployment. On the contrary, it is one of its major causes" (Putnam and Bayne, 1987, p. 69).

It became clear that Germany would not meet its growth projections for 1977, and a debate was privately engaged among the advisors to Chancellor Schmidt concerning the desirability of fiscal stimulus.

However, in order to ensure that he got something in return for agreeing to stimulate demand, he did not volunteer to do so. Instead, the public German stance was still to oppose fiscal stimulus.

A factor contributing to the success in reaching agreement at Bonn was a switch from framing an accord in terms of objectives to one in terms of policy measures. It was always possible to claim that growth was weaker than expected because of various special factors not under the control of the government. Such an excuse was more difficult for the policy measures themselves. Uncertainty about their effects did not prevent agreement concerning those policies to be reached at the Bonn Summit.

In the end, a fairly wide-ranging agreement was reached cutting across a number of areas. Putnam and Henning (1989, p. 101) conclude that "we have found little evidence that the negotiations were hampered by mutual fear of reneging." Moreover, Putnam and Bayne (1987, p. 87) judge that all the pledges were carried out, even if the policies did not always have their intended effects. In particular, the subsequent second oil price shock exacerbated inflation, and as a result the fiscal stimulus measures were generally judged, especially in Germany, to have been a mistake.

The 1982 Versailles summit, in contrast, was unable to reach broad agreement and was considered a failure at the time. Moreover, in the limited areas of agreement what was thought to have been approved was soon subject to very different interpretations by the summit participants, and as a result agreements fell apart. In two areas, some compromise seemed to have emerged. The first area was the international monetary system – one of the reasons for the first summit at Rambouillet. Once again, the French were intent on producing a mechanism for limiting exchange rate movements and establishing "target zones" for their fluctuation. However, the Americans resisted such an initiative, partly because they were less concerned by the effects of currency movements, and partly because they thought that only policy convergence, not exchange market intervention, could achieve exchange rate stability. A compromise was nevertheless reached to undertake multilateral surveillance by G-5 finance ministers, joined by the Managing Director of the IMF. Moreover, a study of the effects of exchange market intervention was commissioned.

The second area in which there was disagreement between the United States and European governments was on East–West trade. While the United States was primarily concerned not to allow the spread of technology to the Soviet Union, the Europeans had committed themselves to purchases of Soviet gas and the construction of a gas pipeline to Western Europe. Though compromise language in the communique seemed to have emerged, it proved impossible to reach agreement and this left hard feelings among the participants.

Putnam and Bayne (1987, p. 138) conclude that a major reason for the summit debacle was that there was a failure to realize that though ambiguities in wording produced apparent success, they would quickly lead to the unraveling of agreements. Putnam and Bayne also argue that the summit was inadequately prepared. However, they deny that the summit was a failure, because it made some significant procedural advances. It established the principle of G-5 (later G-7) surveillance by finance ministers, and also commissioned the study on exchange market intervention that was to narrow differences concerning the actual mechanisms (and their importance) by which intervention affects exchange rates. That report, the so-called "Jurgensen Report,"[8] was delivered to the Williamsburg summit in the following year. Both advances helped to make possible later policy coordination agreements, in particular the Plaza Agreement (see below).

8. The European Monetary System

The European Monetary System (EMS) began its operations in March 1979. Though they had intellectual precursors (in particular, the authors of the Werner Report commissioned by the EC Summit in December 1969, and which envisaged steps toward economic and monetary union), the immediate architects of the EMS were two former finance ministers who were now President and Chancellor, respectively, of their countries – the Frenchman Valéry Giscard d'Estaing and the German Helmut Schmidt. The EMS also had the example of an existing system linking European currencies in an adjustable peg – the Snake, formed in 1972, which allowed a maximum margin between EC currencies of 2.25 percent. However, this arrangement showed the drawbacks of an arrangement which set exchange rates but did not oblige governments to modify policies in order to defend them. Instead, the Snake by 1978 was reduced to the currencies of only a few countries; France had joined, withdrawn, joined once again, and then finally withdrawn.

The aim of the EMS was to form a "zone of monetary stability in Europe." The international context since the breakdown of the Bretton Woods system was of widespread instability in world markets. The oil price shock of 1973 was followed by several international financial crises, including the failure of the Herstatt Bank in Germany and the U.K. fringe banking crisis. In the late 1970s, the concern in Europe was once again that U.S. monetary policy was too expansionary, as was suggested by the long slide in the U.S. dollar against other major currencies. Because of strengthening trade ties, exchange rate instability among European currencies was viewed as especially costly, and the EMS was set up to shelter those exchange rate relationships from turmoil in international financial markets. In particular, shifts out of the dollar risked inducing volatility in the values of European currencies against the deutsche mark.

Thus, uncertainty about portfolio preferences (see also Chapter 4) was a prime motivation for the establishment of the EMS, as was the Maastricht Treaty, agreed in December 1991, to permit those EC countries that satisfy certain criteria to proceed to full economic and monetary union by 1999 at the latest. However, the turmoil in exchange markets beginning in September 1992, leading to a widening of EMS exchange rate fluctuation bands in August 1993, shows the limits of policy coordination when policy credibility is lacking.

9. The Plaza Agreement and the Louvre Accord: G-5/G-7 Policy Coordination among Finance Ministers and their Deputies

Partly as a result of the procedural changes agreed at the Versailles summit, as well as the replacement of Donald Regan as Treasury Secretary by James Baker, the forum for policy coordination among the major countries shifted from the economic summits to meetings of finance ministers. A significant agreement was reached by finance ministers at the Plaza Hotel in New York, in September 1985, to bring about an orderly decline in the dollar. Indeed, Putnam and Bayne (1987, p. 208) quote one summit participant as saying that "The Bonn summit [of 1985] really took place at the Plaza hotel." In their view, the summit was losing its central place in economic diplomacy.

By early 1985, the U.S. dollar had been rising almost continuously since 1981, and was generally judged to be greatly overvalued. As a result of this appreciation, the United States was running a current account deficit which equaled 4 percent of GNP and was in the process of becoming a debtor country on its international transactions – a sharp reversal from being the world's largest net creditor a few years before. As a result of the widening trade deficit, there were increasingly strident calls in the U.S. Congress and elsewhere for protection of U.S. industry.

Moreover, since the U.S. current account deficit was viewed as being unsustainable, a number of economists predicted a "hard landing" for the dollar. The most vocal of these was probably Stephen Marris, who predicted that the longer the problem persisted, the more likely was a scenario in which financial markets were disrupted, the dollar went into free fall, and interest rates in the United States had to be raised sharply, with disastrous consequences for both output and inflation (Marris, 1985).

The official U.S. position until then was that the strong dollar was not a problem; in fact, it was an indication of the health of the U.S. economy. There was much disagreement, however, both within and outside official circles, concerning the causes of the strength of the dollar. Many pointed the finger at U.S. expansionary fiscal policy (the result of increased defense spending and tax cuts),[9] but the U.S. Treasury disputed that fiscal policy was the cause of either higher interest rates or dollar appreciation. Other explanations of the strong dollar included capital flight from Latin America associated with the debt crisis there, increased U.S. productivity, and speculative bubbles (see Council of Economic Advisors, 1984).

Even accepting the view that the dollar was overvalued and should be pushed down, the effectiveness of the instruments that could be used to achieve a depreciation was in dispute. As mentioned above, the Treasury denied that fiscal expansion was the cause of the strong dollar, hence a more contractionary stance was not the way to bring it down. As for sterilized foreign exchange market intervention, the Jurgensen Report, presented to the leaders of the G-7 at the 1983 Williamsburg summit, concluded from the evidence of econometric models and specific episodes, that intervention had little durable effect if sterilized.[10] The report did, however, argue that coordinated intervention could play a significant short-term role. The U.S. Treasury viewed intervention as generally ineffective, while the positions of other finance ministries were generally more favorable.

Despite wide disagreement and uncertainty about the effects of policy, the finance ministers of the five largest industrial countries (the United States, Japan, Germany, France, and the United Kingdom) reached an agreement on 22 September 1985, at the Plaza Hotel in New York, to use sterilized intervention to bring down the value of the dollar against other major currencies. According to Funabashi (1988), the agreement included target ranges for the dollar as well as specific amounts by which each government would intervene. The total "war chest" for intervention was $18 billion, and by the end of October at least $10 billion had been spent; the decline in the dollar from its levels a week before the Plaza was about 13 percent (Funabashi, 1988, p. 22).

How was the Plaza Agreement possible, given the disputes concerning both the causes of the dollar appreciation and uncertainty about how to correct it? To a large extent, it was uncertainty about the larger consequences of dollar strength that led to the agreement. On the one hand, there was the fear that if its rise was unsustainable, the dollar might crash with effects on international financial markets that were difficult to assess. On the other hand, while the dollar stayed high foreign governments increasingly feared that U.S. protectionism could be rekindled, with possibly sharply negative consequences for international trade and global economic activity. According to Funabashi (1988, p. 4), ". . . the rest of the G-5 participants supported the new policy initiative primarily out of fear of the destructive effects of protectionism and of recession caused by unsustainable imbalances." Thus, though treasury officials and central bankers had reservations about the Agreement, coordination was achievable precisely because the degree of uncertainty associated with the status quo.

Although there was agreement on sterilized intervention operations, there was little coordination of monetary policies themselves at the Plaza. According to Funabashi, there was discussion of interest rates but no agreement on a coordinated interest rate cut. Indeed, when the Bank of Japan suddenly raised the short-term interest rate, Volcker, who had been concerned about a possible free fall of the dollar, was apparently dismayed, feeling that the BOJ's policy had been "unnecessary and unwise" (Funabashi, 1988, p. 33).

At the 1986 Tokyo summit, Secretary Baker proposed a much more ambitious program of international economic policy coordination based, in part, on an "objective indicator" system. The idea of using such indicators was not, of course, new; it had already been proposed in the Committee of Twenty reform plans in the nineteen seventies and, indeed, similar measures were part of Keynes' plan for Bretton Woods. The purpose of these indicators was to put greater structure into G-5 meetings; the U.S. administration complained that the informal nature of those meetings resulted in misunderstandings. Amongst Baker's recommendations was the inclusion of a presentation by the IMF's Managing Director with the institution's view of economic developments in each of the participating countries. It was also proposed that Italy and Canada be included in the G-5 Finance Ministers meeting, thus expanding it to the G-7 (at the summit level all seven countries had been meeting since the second summit). The Tokyo summit communique thus called for two groups: the Group of Seven Finance Ministers who would "work together more closely and more frequently in the periods between the annual summit meetings . . . [and] review their individual economic objectives and forecasts collectively at least once a year, using the indicators . . . with a particular view to examining their mutual compatibility" (Funabashi, 1988, p. 141). The G-5, now referred to by the cumbersome phrase "those countries whose currencies constitute the Special Drawing Rights," were urged to conduct multilateral surveillance and to intervene in exchange markets when "to do so would be helpful."

But both Japan and Germany were suspicious of the automaticity implied by the use of such indicators, which were viewed as an American ploy to force greater stimulus from them. There was, moreover, significant disagreement on which macroeconomic variables should be included and how much weight they should receive. Were exchange rates supposed to be policy instruments? Final targets? Or just intermediate targets? The enthusiasm for multilateral policy coordination began to wane, and Baker shifted towards a more bilateral approach. The result was the Baker–Miyazawa agreement of October 1986 in which Japan agreed to an additional fiscal stimulus, a reduction in the discount rate, and a tax reform plan to stimulate investment. In exchange, Baker promised continued commitment to the Gramm–Rudman–Hollings amendment, resistance to protectionist pressures and, most important to Miyazawa, an announcement that "the exchange rate realignment achieved between the yen and the dollar since the Plaza Agreement is now broadly consistent with the present underlying fundamentals." However, the dollar continue to decline, and on January 19 the dollar fell below the psychologically important 150 Yen rate.

One month later, on 21 February, the G-5 finance ministers and central bank governors met at the Palais du Louvre (they were joined the next day by the Canadians, while the Italian delegation boycotted the meeting). The dollar had depreciated substantially at that point and emphasis shifted towards stabilizing the dollar instead. In the (G-6) communique, both Japan and Germany promised to pursue more expansionary fiscal policies while the United States reaffirmed its commitment to reducing its budget deficit from 3.9 percent of GDP in 1987 to 2.3 percent of GDP in 1988. Ministers agreed to "regularly examine, using performance indicators, whether current economic development and trends are consistent with the medium-term objectives and projections and consider the need for remedial action." Finally, the ministers "agreed to cooperate closely to foster stability of exchange rates around current levels."

In subsequent months however, the U.S. trade balance responded very slowly to the dollar depreciation that had occurred earlier. The figures for the U.S. trade balance released on 14 October 1987 showed a much smaller improvement than the market had expected. As a result, stock prices plunged because investors feared that the Fed would raise interest rates to stave off the inflationary consequences of a dollar free fall. Reflecting more general doubts about the Group of Seven's commitment to coordination the collapse of stock prices was a global phenomenon and by no means limited to the United States. Central banks of the major industrialized countries, acting cooperatively, immediately injected additional liquidity and cut interest rates. (The stock market crash, and the policy response of the G-7 central banks is analyzed in greater detail in Chapter 4.) This coordinated action appears to have been instrumental in reversing the world stock price fall and, more importantly, preventing it from having serious consequences for the financial system.

Notes

1   The term "non-system" has been used by Max Corden, among others. See Corden (1983).
2   To put into perspective the amount requested by Keynes it is worth noting that U.S. GDP at the time was only $280 bn.
3   In the Bretton Woods agreement, the United States only acceded to a "scarce currency clause" which allowed payments discrimination by countries when the IMF itself was short a particular currency (see Solomon, 1977, for a discussion).
4   On 20 October 1960 the London gold price, which usually hovered within one percent of the official $35 per oz., shot up to $40.
5   The most formal agreement was with the Bundesbank; in 1967 Karl Blessing, then president of the Bundesbank, wrote to McChesney Martin promising not to use dollar reserves to buy gold.
6   The original Roosa Bonds were dollar denominated but offered higher interest rates than regulation Q allowed for private investors.
7   Gyohten recounts a delightful story of the Japanese diplomatic coup in being invited to the (then) G-4, thus making it the G-5 (Volcker and Gyohten, 1992, p. 134).
8   Named for its chairman, Philippe Jurgensen, of the French Treasury.
9   See, for instance, Hooper (1984).
10   See Jurgensen (1983) for a summary of the evidence and the conclusions of the studies.

Bibliography

Akerlof, George (1969). "Relative Wages and the Rate of Inflation," *Quarterly Journal of Economics*, vol. 83 (August), pp. 353–74.

Amano, A., E. Kurihara, and L. Samuelson (1980). "Trade Linkage Sub-Models in the EPA World Economic Model," *Economic Bulletin* 19 (Tokyo: Economic Planning Agency, Economic Research Institute).

Argy, Victor, and Jo-Anne Salop. (1979) "Price and Output Effects of Monetary and Fiscal Policy Under Flexible Exchange Rates," *International Monetary Fund Staff Papers*, vol. 26 (June), pp. 224–56.

Arrow, Kenneth (1953). "Le Role des Valeurs Boursieres pour la Repartition la meilleur des risques," *Econometrie,* Colloques Internationaux du Centre National de la Recherche Scientifique, Paris, 40, pp. 41–47 (English translation: *Review of Economic Studies*, 31 (April) 1964, pp. 91–96).

Artis, M. and S. Ostry (1986). *International Economic Policy Coordination*, Chatham House Papers No. 30, Royal Institute of International Affairs (London: Routledge & Kegan Paul).

Axelrod, Robert (1984). *The Evolution of Cooperation* (New York: Basic Books).

Axelrod, Robert and Robert Keohane (1985). "Achieving Cooperation Under Anarchy: Strategies and Institutions," *World Politics*, vol. 38 (October), pp. 226–54.

Ball, R. J. (ed.) (1973). *The International Linkage of National Economic Models.* Amsterdam: North-Holland.

Barro, Robert and David Gordon (1983). "Rules, Discretion and Reputation in a Model of Monetary Policy," *Journal of Monetary Economics*, vol. 12 (July), pp. 101–21.

Bellman, Richard and Robert Kalaba (1964). *Dynamic Programming and Modern Control Theory.* (New York: Academic Press).

Bernanke, Ben (1990). "Clearing and Settlement During the Crash," *Review of Financial Studies*, vol. 3, pp. 133–51.

Bertero, Elisabetta and Colin Mayer (1989). "Structure and Performance: Global Interdependence of Stock Markets Around the Crash of October 1987," Centre for Economic Policy Research (London) Discussion Paper No. 307.

Bhagwati, Jagdish (1983). *Lectures on International Trade* (Cambridge, Mass.: MIT Press).

Bisin, Alberto and Piero Tedeschi (1991). "International Policy Coordination, Imperfect Information and Target Zones," in Carlo Carraro, Didier Laussel, Mark Salmon and Antoine Soubeyran (eds), *International Economic Policy Coordination* (Oxford: Basil Blackwell) pp. 108–26.

Blanchard, Olivier Jean and Charles Kahn (1980). "The Solution of Linear Difference Models under Rational Expectations," *Econometrica*, vol. 48 (July) pp. 114–18.

Blanchard, Olivier Jean and Danny Quah (1989). "The Dynamic Effects of Aggregate Demand and Supply Disturbances," *American Economic Review*, vol. 79 (September), pp. 655–73.

Bloomfield, Arthur (1959). *Monetary Policy Under the International Gold Standard: 1800–1914.* (New York: Federal Reserve Bank of New York).

Bodkin, Ronald., Lawrence Klein, and Kanta Marwah (1991). *A History of Macroeconometric Model-Building* (Aldershot: Edward Elgar).

Boughton, James (1988). "Policy Assignment Strategies with Somewhat Flexible Exchange Rates," International Monetary Fund Working Paper, 88/40 (Washington: International Monetary Fund).

Brainard, William (1967). "Uncertainty and the Effectiveness of Policy," *American Economic Review*, vol. 57 (May), pp. 411–25.

Brandsma, Andries and Andrew Hughes Hallett (1984). "Economic Conflict and the Solution of Dynamic Games," *European Economic Review*, vol. 26, pp. 13–32.

Brandsma, Andries, Andrew Hughes Hallett, and J. Swank (1987). "The Robustness of Economic Policy Selections and the Incentive to Cooperate," *Journal of Economic Dynamics and Control*, vol. 11 (June) pp. 163–70.

Branson, William and Willem Buiter (1983). "Monetary and Fiscal Policy with Flexible Exchange Rates," in J. Bhandari and B. Putnam (eds), *Economic Interdependence and Flexible Exchange Rates* (Cambridge, Mass.: MIT Press).

Brinner, R. (1985). "The 1985 DRI Model: Overview," in *Data Resources Review of the U.S. Economy* (Lexington, Mass.: Data Resources McGraw Hill).

Bryant, Ralph, Dale Henderson, Gerald Holtham, Peter Hooper, and Steven Symansky (eds) (1988). *Empirical Macroeconomics for Interdependent Economies* (Washington, D.C.: Brookings Institution).

Buiter, Willem (1979). "Unemployment-Inflation Trade-Offs with Rational Expectations in an Open Economy," *Journal of Economic Dynamics and Control*, vol. 1, pp. 117–41.

Buiter, Willem and Marcus Miller (1982). "Real Exchange Rate Overshooting and the Output Cost of Bring Down Inflation," *European Economic Review*, vol. 18 (May/June), pp. 85–123.

Buiter, Willem and Richard Marston (1985). *International Economic Policy Coordination* (Cambridge: Cambridge University Press).

Calvo, Guillermo (1983). "Staggered Contracts and Exchange Rate Policy," in Jacob Frenkel (ed.), *Exchange Rates and International Macroeconomics* (Chicago: University of Chicago Press), pp. 235–52.

Calvo, Guillermo (1978). "On the Time Consistency of Optimal Policy in a Monetary Economy," *Econometrica*, vol. 46 (November), pp. 1411–28.

Campbell, John Y. and N. Gregory Mankiw (1987). "Permanent and Transitory Components in Macroeconomic Fluctuations," *American Economic Review*, vol. 77 (May), pp. 111–17.

Canzoneri, Matthew (1985). "Monetary Policy Games and the Role of Private Information," *American Economic Review*, vol. 75 (December), pp. 1056–70.

Canzoneri, Matthew and Jo Anna Gray (1985). "Monetary Policy Games and the Consequences of Non-cooperative Behavior," *International Economic Review*, vol. 26, pp. 547–64.

Canzoneri, Matthew and Dale Henderson (1991). *Monetary Policy in Interdependent Economies: A Game Theoretic Approach* (Cambridge, Mass.: MIT Press).

Canzoneri, Matthew and Patrick Minford (1988). "When International Policy Coordination Matters: An Empirical Analysis," *Applied Economics*, vol. 20 (September), pp. 1137–54.

Carlozzi, Nicholas and John Taylor (1985). "International Capital Mobility and the Coordination of Monetary Rules," in Jagdeep Bhandari (ed.), *Exchange Rate Management Under Uncertainty* (Cambridge, Mass: MIT Press).

Carr, E. (1964). *The Twenty Years Crisis, 1919–1939: An Introduction to the Study of International Relations* (London: Harper Torchbooks).

Carraro, Carlo and Francesco Giavazzi (1991). "Can International Policy Coordination Really be Counterproductive?" in Carlo Carraro, Didier Laussel, Mark Salmon and Antoine Soubeyran (eds), *International Economic Policy Coordination* (Oxford: Basil Blackwell).

Clarke, R. (1983) "Collusion and Incentive for Information Sharing," *Bell Journal of Economics*, vol. 14 (Autumn), pp. 383–94.

Cochrane, John (1991). "A Critique of the Application of Unit Root Tests," *Journal of Economic Dynamics and Control*, vol. 15 (April), pp. 275–84.

Coombs, Charles (1976). *The Arena of International Finance* (Wiley: New York).

Cooper, Richard N. (1968). *The Economics of Interdependence* (New York: McGraw Hill).

Cooper, Richard (1969). "Macroeconomic Policy Adjustment in Interdependent Economies," *Quarterly Journal of Economics*, vol. 83 (February) pp. 1–24.

Cooper, Richard (1972). "Economic Interdependence and Foreign Policies in the 1970s," *World Politics*, vol. 24 (January), pp. 158–81.

Cooper, Richard N. (1985). "Economic Interdependencies and Coordination of Policies," in Ronald Jones and Peter Kenen (eds), *Handbook of International Economics*, vol. 2 (Amsterdam: North-Holland).

Corden, W. Max (1983). "The Logic of the International Monetary Non-system," in Fritz Machlup, Gerhard Fels, and Hubertus Müller-Groeling (eds), *Reflections on a Troubled World Economy* (New York: St. Martin's Press).

Cripps, Martin (1991). "Asymmetric Information and Policy Coordination," in Carlo Carraro, Didier Laussel, Mark Salmon, and Antoine Soubeyran (eds), *International Economic Policy Coordination* (Oxford: Blackwell), pp. 242–51.

Crockett, Andrew (1989). "The Role of International Institutions in Surveillance and Policy Coordination," in Ralph Bryant et. al. (eds), *Macroeconomic*

Policies in an Interdependent World (Washington, D.C.: International Monetary Fund), pp. 343–64.

Crow, John (1990). "Note for Remarks at the Treasury Management Association of Canada's Eighth Annual Cash and Treasury Management Conference," *BIS Review*, no. 231, November 26, pp. 1–6.

Currie, David and Paul Levine (1985). "Simple Macropolicy Rules for the Open Economy," *Economic Journal*, vol. 95 (supplement), pp. 60–70.

Currie, David, Paul Levine, and Nic Vidalis (1987). "International Cooperation and Reputation in an Empirical Two-Bloc Model," in Ralph Bryant and Richard Portes (eds), *Global Macroeconomics* (New York: St. Martin's Press), pp. 75–127.

Currie, David and Simon Wren-Lewis (1989). "An Appraisal of Alternative Blueprints for International Policy Coordination," *European Economic Review*, vol. 33 (December), pp. 1769–85.

Currie, David, Gerald Holtham, and Andrew Hughes Hallett (1989). "The Theory and Practice of International Policy Coordination: Does Coordination Pay," in Ralph Bryant et al. (eds), *Macroeconomic Policies in an Interdependent World* (Washington D.C.: International Monetary Fund).

Davidson, Paul (1991). "Is Probability Theory Relevant for Uncertainty? A Post Keynesian Perspective," *Journal of Economic Perspectives*, vol. 5 (Winter), pp. 129–43.

Debreu, Gerard (1959). *Theory of Value: An Axiomatic Analysis of General Equilibrium* (New Haven: Yale University Press).

Destler, I.M. and C. Randall Henning (1989). *Dollar Politics: Exchange Rate Policymaking in the United States* (Washington D.C.: Institute for International Economics).

Diamond, Peter (1967). "The Role of a Stock Market in a General Equilibrium Model with Technological Uncertainty," *American Economic Review*, vol. 57 (December), pp. 759–76.

Dickey, David and Wayne Fuller (1979). "Distribution of the Estimators for Autoregressive Time Series with a Unit Root," *Journal of the American Statistical Association*, vol. 74 (June), pp. 427–31.

Dickey, David and Wayne Fuller (1981). "Likelihood Ratio Statistics for Autoregressive Time Series with a Unit Root," *Econometrica*, vol. 49 (June), pp. 1057–72.

Dobson, Wendy (1991). *Economic Policy Coordination: Requiem or Prologue?*, Policy Analyses in International Economics No. 30 (Washington, D.C.: Institute for International Economics).

Dornbusch, Rudiger (1976). "Expectations and Exchange Rate Dynamics," *Journal of Political Economy*, vol. 84 (December), pp. 1161–76.

Dramais, A. (1986). "COMPACT-Prototype of a Macro Model for the European Community in the World Economy," Discussion Paper 27 (Brussels: Commission of the European Communities), March, pp. 113–66.

Eichengreen, Barry (1985). "International Policy Coordination in Historical Perspective: A View from the Interwar Years," in Willem Buiter and Richard

Marston (eds), *International Economic Policy Coordination* (Cambridge: Cambridge University Press).

Engle, Robert and Clive Granger (1987). "Co-Integration and Error Correction: Representation, Estimation and Testing," *Econometrica*, vol. 55 (March), pp. 251–76.

Engle, Robert and Byung Sam Yoo (1987). "Forecasting and Testing in Co-Integrated Systems," *Journal of Econometrics*, vol. 35 (May), pp. 143–59.

EPA (1986). "The EPA World Economic Model: An Overview," Discussion Paper 37 (Tokyo: Economic Planning Agency, Economic Research Institute).

Fair, Ray C. (1984). *Specification, Estimation, and Analysis of Macroeconometric Models*, (Cambridge, Mass.: Harvard University Press).

Federal Reserve Bank of New York (FRBNY) (1988). *Quarterly Review*, vol. 13 (Summer).

Feldstein, Martin (1983). "Signs of Recovery," *The Economist*, 11 June, pp. 43–48.

Feldstein, Martin (1988b). *International Economic Cooperation* (University of Chicago Press).

Feldstein, Martin (1988a). "Distinguished Lecture on Economics in Government: Thinking about International Economic Coordination," *Journal of Economic Perspectives*, vol. 2 (Spring), pp. 3–13.

Fischer, Stanley (1977). "Long-term Contracts, Rational Expectations, and the Optimal Money Supply Rule," *Journal of Political Economy*, vol. 85 (February), pp. 191–206.

Flavin, Marjorie (1983). "Excess Volatility in the Financial Markets: A Reassessment of the Empirical Evidence," *Journal of Political Economy*, vol. 91 (December), pp. 929–56.

Fleming, Marcus (1962). "Domestic Financial Policies Under Fixed and Under Floating Exchange Rates," *International Monetary Fund Staff Papers*, vol. 9 (November), pp. 369–79.

Flood, Robert, Jagdeep Bhandari, and Jocelyn Horne (1989). "Evolution of Exchange Rate Regimes," *International Monetary Fund Staff Papers* vol. 36 (December) pp. 810–35.

Flood, Robert and Robert Hodrick (1986). "Asset Price Volatility, Bubbles, and Process Switching," *Journal of Finance*, vol. 41 (September), pp. 831–42.

Frankel, Jeffrey (1988a). *Obstacles to International Macroeconomic Policy Coordination* (Princeton N.J.: International Finance Section, Princeton University).

Frankel, Jeffrey (1988b). "Ambiguous Policy Multipliers in Theory and in Empirical Models," in Ralph Bryant et al. (eds), *Empirical Macroeconomics for Interdependent Economies* (Washington D.C.: Brookings Institution).

Frankel, Jeffrey (1991). "The Obstacles to Macroeconomic Policy Coordination in the 1990s and an Analysis of International Nominal Targeting (INT)," University of California, Berkeley Working Paper 91–160 (March).

Frankel, Jeffrey and Katherine Dominguez (1990). "Does Foreign Exchange Intervention Matter? Disentangling the Portfolio and Expectations Effects for the Mark," *National Bureau of Economic Research Working Paper* 3299 (March).

Frankel, Jeffrey and Katherine Rockett (1988). "International Macroeconomic Policy Coordination when Policymakers Do Not Agree on the True Model," *American Economic Review*, vol. 78 (June), pp. 318–40.

Frenkel, Jacob A., Morris Goldstein, and Paul Masson (1989). "Simulating the Effects of Some Simple Coordinated Versus Uncoordinated Policy Rules," in Ralph Bryant et al. (eds), *Macroeconomic Policies in an Interdependent World* (Washington, D.C.: International Monetary Fund).

Frenkel, Jacob A. and Assaf Razin (1987). "The Mundell–Fleming Model a Quarter Century Later: a Unified Exposition," *International Monetary Fund Staff Papers*, vol. 34 (December), pp. 567–620.

Fried, Dov (1984) "Incentives for Information Production and Disclosure in a Duopolistic Environment," *Quarterly Journal of Economics*, vol. 99 (May), pp. 367-381.

Friedman, James (1971). "A Noncooperative Equilibrium for Supergames," *Review of Economic Studies*, 38 (January), pp. 1–12.

Friedman, James (1986). *Game Theory with Applications to Economics* (New York: Oxford University Press).

Friedman, Milton (1948). "A Monetary and Fiscal Framework for Economic Stability," *American Economic Review*, vol. 38 (June), pp. 245–64.

Friedman, Milton (1968). "The Role of Monetary Policy," *American Economic Review*, vol. 58 (March), pp. 1–17.

Friedman, Milton (1977). "Inflation and Unemployment," *Journal of Political Economy*, vol. 85 (June), pp. 451–72.

Fuller, Wayne A (1976). *Introduction to Statistical Time Series* (New York: Wiley).

Funabashi, Yoichi (1988). *Managing the Dollar: From the Plaza to the Louvre* (Washington D.C.: Institute for International Economics).

Gal-Or, E. (1986). "Information Transmission: Cournot and Bertrand Equilibria," *Review of Economic Studies*, vol. 53.

Gavin, Michael (1986). "Macroeconomic Policy Coordination Under Alternative Exchange Rate Regimes," mimeo (Washington D.C.: Federal Reserve Board).

Ghosh, Atish (1986). "International Policy Coordination in an Uncertain World," *Economics Letters*, vol. 3, pp. 271–76.

Ghosh, Atish (1991a). "Strategic Aspects of Public Finance in a World with High Capital Mobility," *Journal of International Economics*, vol. 30 (May) pp. 229–47.

Ghosh, Atish (1991b). "Information, Cooperation, and Coordination: Can Summit Meetings be Counterproductive?" mimeo, Princeton University.

Ghosh, Atish (1992). "Is It Signalling? Exchange Market Intervention and the Dollar- Deutschemark Rate," *Journal of International Economics*, vol. 32 (May) pp. 201–20.

Ghosh, Atish and Swati Ghosh (1986). "International Policy Coordination When the Model is Unknown," mimeo, Geneva, Switzerland, December 1986.

Ghosh, Atish and Swati Ghosh (1991). "Does Model Uncertainty Really Preclude International Policy Coordination?" *Journal of International Economics*, vol. 31 (November), pp. 325–40.

Ghosh, Atish and Paul Masson (1988). "International Policy Coordination in a World with Model Uncertainty," *International Monetary Fund Staff Papers*, vol. 35 (June), pp. 230–58.

Ghosh, Atish and Paul Masson (1991). "Model Uncertainty, Learning, and the Gains from Coordination," *American Economic Review*, vol. 81 (June), pp. 465–79.

Ghosh, Swati (1987). "International Policy Coordination Under Model Uncertainty," M.Phil. Thesis, Oxford University.

Ghosh, Swati (1992). "International Policy Coordination Under Uncertainty," D.Phil. Thesis, Oxford University.

Gilpin, Robert (1981). *War and Change in World Politics* (Cambridge: Cambridge University Press).

Goldfeld, Stephen (1973). "The Demand for Money Revisited," *Brookings Papers on Economic Activity*, no. 3, pp. 577–637.

Granger, Clive and Paul Newbold (1974). "Spurious Regressions in Econometrics," *Journal of Econometrics*, vol. 2 (July), pp. 111–20.

Green, Edward and Robert Porter (1984). "Noncooperative Collusion under Imperfect Price Information," *Econometrica*, vol. 52 (January) pp. 87–100.

Green, John, and Howard Howe (1987). "Results from the WEFA World Model," *Brookings Discussion Papers in International Economics* 59-B (Washington, D.C.: Brookings Institution, March).

Greenspan, Alan (1988). Testimony at Hearings before the Committee on Banking, Housing, and Urban Affairs of the U.S. Senate, on "'Black Monday,' The Stock Market Crash of October 19, 1987" (Washington, D.C.: U.S. Government Printing Office), pp. 88–100.

Grieco, Joseph (1988). "Anarchy and the Limits of Cooperation: A Realist Critique of the Newest Liberal Institutionalism," *International Organization*, vol. 42 (Summer), pp. 484–507.

Haas, Ernst (1968). "Technology, Pluralism, and the New Europe," in Joseph Nye (ed.) *International Regionalism* (Boston: Little Brown).

Haas, Richard and Paul Masson (1986). "MINIMOD: Specification and Simulation Results," *International Monetary Fund Staff Papers*, vol. 33 (December), pp. 722–67.

Hamada, Koichi (1974). "Alternative Exchange Rate Systems and the Interdependence of Monetary Policies," in Robert Z. Aliber (ed.), *National Monetary Policies and the International Financial System* (Chicago: University of Chicago Press).

Hamada, Koichi (1976). "A Strategic Analysis of Monetary Interdependence," *Journal of Political Economy*, vol. 84 (August), pp. 677–700.

Hamada, Koichi (1979). "Macroeconomic Strategy and Coordination Under Alternative Exchange Rates," in Rudiger Dornbusch and Stanley Fischer (eds), *International Economic Policy* (Baltimore: The Johns Hopkins University Press).

Helpman, Elhanan and Assaf Razin (1978). "Uncertainty and International Trade in the Presence of Stock Markets," *Review of Economic Studies*, vol. 45 (June), pp. 239–50.

Hendry, David and Neil Ericsson (1990). "Modeling the Demand for Narrow Money in the United Kingdom and the United States," International Finance Discussion Papers No. 383 (Washington, D.C.: Board of Governors of the Federal Reserve System, July).

Hickman, Bert and Lawrence Lau (1973)., "Elasticities of Substitution and Export Demands in a World Trade Model," *European Economic Review*, vol. 4 (December), pp. 347–80.

Hicks, John (1937). "Mr. Keynes and the 'Classics': A Suggested Interpretation," *Econometrica*, vol. 5 (April), pp. 147–59.

Hirschman, Albert (1945). *National Power and the Structure of Foreign Trade* (Berkeley: University of California Press).

Hirshleifer, Jack (1966). "Investment Decisions Under Uncertainty: Applications of the State-Preference Approach," *Quarterly Journal of Economics*, vol. 80 (May), pp. 252–77.

Holtham, Gerald (1984). "Multinational Modelling of Financial Linkages and Exchange Rates," *OECD Economic Studies* 2 (Spring), pp. 51–92.

Holtham, Gerald and Andrew Hughes Hallett (1987). "International Policy Cooperation and Model Uncertainty," in Ralph Bryant and Richard Portes (eds), *Global Macroeconomics* (New York: St. Martin's Press).

Hooper, Peter (1984). "International Repercussions of the U.S. Budget Deficit," International Finance Discussion Papers No. 246 (Washington, D.C.: Board of Governors of the Federal Reserve System, September).

Hooper, Peter, Richard Haas, Steven Symansky, and Lois Stekler (1983). "Alternative Approaches to General Equilibrium Modeling of Exchange Rates and Capital Flows: The MCM Experience," in L. Klein and W. Kreller (eds), *Capital Flows and Exchange Rate Determination* (Vienna: Springer-Verlag), pp. 29–60.

Horne, Jocelyn and Paul Masson (1988). "Scope and Limits of International Economic Cooperation and Policy Coordination," *International Monetary Fund Staff Papers*, vol. 35 (June) pp. 259–96.

Hughes Hallett, Andrew (1986a). "Robust Policy Regimes for Interdependent Economies: A New Argument for Coordinating Economic Policies," Discussion Paper No. 151, Centre for Economic Policy Research (London).

Hughes Hallett, Andrew (1986b). "Autonomy and the Choice of Policy in Asymmetrically Dependent Economies," *Oxford Economic Papers*, vol. 38, pp. 516–44.

Hughes Hallett, Andrew (1987). "International Policy Design and the Sustainability of Policy Bargains," *Journal of Economic Dynamics and Control*, vol. 10 (Winter), pp. 467–94.

Hughes Hallett, Andrew, Gerald Holtham and G. J. Hutson (1989). "Exchange Rate Targeting as Surrogate International Cooperation," in Marcus Miller, Barry Eichengreen, and Richard Portes (eds), *Blueprints for Exchange Rate*

Management (London; San Diego; Sydney and Toronto: Harcourt Brace Jovanovich, Academic Press) pp. 239–78.

Johansen, Leif (1982). "A Note on the Possibility of an International *Equilibrium with Low Levels of Activity*," *Journal of International Economics*, vol. 13 (November), pp. 257–65.

Johansen, Søren (1988). "Statistical Analysis of Cointegration Vectors," *Journal of Economic Dynamics and Control*, vol. 12 (June/September), pp. 231–54.

Johansen, Søren and Katarina Juselius (1990). "Maximum Likelihood Estimation and Inference on Cointegration – With Applications to the Demand for Money," *Oxford Bulletin of Economics and Statistics*, vol. 52 (May), pp. 169–210.

Jurgensen, Philippe (1983). *Report of the Working Group on Exchange Market Intervention* (Washington, D.C.: U.S. Treasury).

Kalai, E. (1977). "Proportional Solutions to Bargaining Solutions: Interpersonal Utility Comparisons," *Econometrica*, vol. 45, pp. 1623–30.

Kalai, E. and M. Smorodinski (1975). "Other Solutions to Nash's Bargaining Problem," *Econometrica*, vol. 43, pp. 513–18.

Kaplan, Jacob and Günther Schleminger (1989). *The European Payments Union: Financial Diplomacy in the 1950s* (Oxford: Clarendon Press).

Kehoe, Patrick (1989). "Policy Cooperation Among Benevolent Governments May Be Undesirable," *Review of Economic Studies*, 56 (April), pp. 289–96.

Kemball-Cook, David (1992). "Learning About Rival Models," London Business School Discussion Paper 05–92.

Kenen, Peter (1988). "Exchange Rates and Policy Coordination in an Asymmetric Model," Centre for Economic Policy Research (London), Discussion Paper No. 240, May.

Kenen, Peter (1991). "Exchange Rates and Policy Co-ordination in an Asymmetric model," in Carlo Carraro, Didier Loussel, Mark Salmon, and Antoine Soubeyran (eds), *International Economic Policy Coordination* (Oxford: Basil Blackwell), pp. 83–107.

Keohane, Robert (1984). *After Hegemony: Cooperation and Discord in the World Political Economy*, (Princeton: Princeton University Press).

Keynes, John (1937). "The General Theory," *Quarterly Journal of Economics* (reprinted in D. Moggridge (ed), *The Collected Writings of John Maynard Keynes*, vol. XIV (London: Macmillan, 1973).

Klein, Lawrence (1950). *Economic Fluctuations in the United States, 1921-1941* (New York: Wiley).

Klein, Lawrence, R. J. Ball, A. Hazelwood, and P. Vandome (1961). *An Econometric Model of the United Kingdom* (Oxford: Basil Blackwell).

Klein, Lawrence and Arthur S. Goldberger (1955). *An Econometric Model of the United States, 1929–52* (Amsterdam: North-Holland).

Knight, Frank (1921). *Risk, Uncertainty and Profit* (New York: Houghton Mifflin).

Kreps, David (1990). *Game Theory and Economic Modelling* (Oxford: Oxford University Press).

Kuh, Edwin, John W. Neese, and Peter Hollinger (1985). *Structural Sensitivity in Econometric Models* (New York: Wiley).

Kydland, Finn, and Edward Prescott (1977). "Rules Rather than Discretion: The Inconsistency of Optimal Plans," *Journal of Political Economy*, vol. 85 (June), pp. 473–91.

Kydland, Finn and Edward Prescott (1982). "Time to Build and Aggregate Fluctuations," *Econometrica*, vol. 50 (November), pp. 1345–70.

Laidler, David (1985). *The Demand for Money: Theories, Evidence, and Problems*, 3rd edition (New York: Harper & Row).

League of Nations (1920). *Report of the International Financial Conference* (Geneva: League of Nations).

Lennblad, Anna (1991). *Desirability and Time Consistency of Monetary Policy Games*, Ph.D. Thesis (Institut Universitaire de Hautes Études Internationales: Geneva)

Levine, Paul and David Currie (1987). "Does International Macroeconomic Policy Coordination Pay and Is it Sustainable?: A Two Country Analysis," *Oxford Economic Papers*, vol. 39 (March), pp. 38–74.

Lipsey, Richard (1960). "The Relation Between Unemployment and the Rate of Change of Money Wage Rates in the United Kingdom, 1862–1957: A Further Analysis," *Economica*, vol. 78, pp. 168–72.

Litterman, Robert (1984). "Forecasting and Policy Analysis With Bayesian Vector Autoregression Models," *Federal Reserve Bank of Minneapolis Quarterly Review* (Fall), pp. 30–41.

Lucas, Robert (1972). "Expectations and the Neutrality of Money," *Journal of Economic Theory*, vol. 4 (April), pp. 103–24.

Lucas, Robert (1973). "Some International Evidence on Output-Inflation Tradeoffs" *American Economic Review*, vol. 63 (June), pp. 326–34.

Lucas, Robert. 1981. *Studies in Business-Cycle Theory* (Cambridge, Mass.: MIT Press).

Lucas, Robert (1976). "Econometric Policy Evaluation: A Critique," in *The Phillips Curve and Labor Markets*, vol. 1, of Carnegie-Rochester Conference Series on Public Policy, edited by Karl Brunner and Allan Metzler (Amsterdam: North-Holland).

Lucas, Robert (1986). "Principles of Fiscal and Monetary Policy," *Journal of Monetary Economics*, vol. 17 (January), pp. 117–34.

Machina, Mark (1987). "Choice Under Uncertainty: Problems Solved and Unsolved," *Journal of Economic Perspectives*, vol. 1 (Summer), pp. 121–154.

McKinnon, Ronald (1984). *An International Standard for Monetary Stabilization*, Policy Analyses in International Economics, 8 (Washington: Institute for International Economics).

McKinnon, Ronald (1988). "Monetary and Exchange Rate Policies for International Financial Stability: A Proposal," *Journal of Economic Perspectives*, vol. 2 (Winter), pp. 83–103.

McKibbin, Warwick and Jeffrey Sachs (1986). "Comparing the Global Performance of Alternative Exchange Arrangements," *Brookings Papers in*

International Economics No. 49:1–62 (Washington D.C.: Brookings Institution).

McKibbin, Warwick and Jeffrey Sachs (1989). "Implications of Policy Rules for the World Economy," in Ralph Bryant et al. (eds), *Macroeconomic Policies in an Interdependent World* (Washington, D.C.: International Monetary Fund).

McKibbin, Warwick and Jeffrey Sachs (1991). *Global Linkages: Macroeconomic Interdependence and Cooperation in the World Economy* (Washington, D.C.: Brookings Institution).

Marris, Stephen (1985). *Deficits and the Dollar: The World Economy at Risk* (Washington D.C.: Institute for International Economics).

Martinez Oliva, Juan Carlos (1991). "One Remark on Spillover Effects and the Gains from Coordination," *Oxford Economic Papers*, vol. 43 (January), pp. 172–76.

Martinez Oliva, Juan Carlos and Stefan Sinn (1988). "The Game-Theoretic Approach to International Policy Coordination: Assessing the Role of Targets," *Weltwirtschaftliches Archiv*, Band 124, Heft 2, pp. 252–68.

Masson, Paul (1992). "Portfolio Preference Uncertainty and Gains from Policy Coordination," *International Monetary Fund Staff Papers*, vol. 39 (March), pp. 101–20.

Masson, Paul and Adrian Blundell-Wignall (1985). "Fiscal Policy and the Exchange Rate in the Big Seven: Transmission of U.S. Government Spending Shocks," *European Economic Review*, vol. 28 (June–July), pp. 11–42.

Masson, Paul, Steven Symansky, and Guy Meredith (1990). *MULTIMOD Mark II: A Revised and Extended Model*, Occasional Paper No. 71 (Washington, D.C.: International Monetary Fund).

Meade, James (1951). *The Balance of Payments* (London: Oxford University Press).

Miller, Marcus and Mark Salmon (1985). "Policy Coordination and Dynamic Games," in Willem Buiter and Richard Marston (eds), *International Economic Policy Coordination* (Cambridge: Cambridge University Press).

Miller, Marcus, Mark Salmon and Alan Sutherland (1991). "Time Consistency, Discounting, and the Returns to Cooperation," in Carlo Carraro, Didier Laussel, Mark Salmon and Antoine Soubeyran (eds), *International Economic Policy Coordination* (Oxford: Basil Blackwell).

Minford, Patrick. S. Marwaha, K. G. P. Mathews, and A. Sprague (1984). "The Liverpool Macroeconomic Model of the United Kingdom," *Economic Modelling*, vol. 1, pp. 24–62.

Mitrany, David (1966). *A Working Peace System* (Chicago: Quadrangle Press).

Modigliani, Franco (1977). "The Monetarist Controversy: or, Should We Forsake Stabilization Policies?" *American Economic Review*, vol. 67 (March), pp. 1–19.

Morgenthau, Hans (1973), *Politics Among Nations: The Struggle for Power and Peace* (New York: Knopf).

Mundell, Robert (1960). "The Monetary Dynamics of International Adjustment Under Fixed and Flexible Rates," *Quarterly Journal of Economics*, vol. 74 (May), pp. 227–57.

Mundell, Robert (1962). "The Appropriate Use of Monetary and Fiscal Policy for Internal and External Stability," *International Monetary Fund Staff Papers*, vol. 9 (March), pp. 70–77.

Mundell, Robert (1963). "Capital Mobility and Stabilization Policy Under Fixed and Flexible Exchange Rates," *Canadian Journal of Economics*, vol. 29, pp. 475–485.

Muth, John (1961). "Rational Expectations and the Theory of Price Movements," *Econometrica*, vol. 29 (July), pp. 315–35.

Myerson, Roger (1979). "Incentive Compatibility and the Bargaining Problem," *Econometrica*, vol. 47 (January), pp. 61–73.

Myerson, Roger (1984). "Two-Person Bargaining Problems with Incomplete Information," *Econometrica*, vol. 52 (March), pp. 461–87.

Nash, John (1950). "The Bargaining Problem," *Econometrica*, vol. 18, pp. 155–62.

Nelson, Charles, and Charles Plosser (1982). "Trends and Random Walks in Macroeconomic Time Series: Some Evidence and Implications," *Journal of Monetary Economics*, vol. 10 (September), pp. 139-62.

Niehans, Jurg (1968). "Monetary and Fiscal Policies in Open Economies Under Fixed Exchange Rates: An Optimizing Approach," *Journal of Political Economy*, vol. 76, pp. 893–920.

Novshek, William and Hugo Sonnenschein (1982). "Fulfilled Expectations Cournot Duopoly with Information Acquisition and Release," *Bell Journal of Economics*, vol. 13 (Spring), pp. 214–18.

Nye, Joseph (1968). *International Regionalism* (Boston: Little Brown).

OECD (1979). "The OECD International Linkage Model," *OECD Economic Outlook, Occasional Studies* (Paris: Organisation for Economic Co-operation and Development, January), pp. 3–33.

Obstfeld, Maurice (1988). "The Effectiveness of Foreign-Exchange Intervention: Recent Experience," NBER Working Paper no. 2796 (December).

Osborne, Martin and Ariel Rubinstein (1990). *Bargaining and Markets* (New York: Academic Press).

Oudiz, Gilles and Jeffrey Sachs (1984). "Macroeconomic Policy Coordination among Industrial Economies," *Brookings Papers on Economic Activity*, No. 1, pp. 1–75.

Oudiz, Gilles, and Jeffrey Sachs (1985). "International Policy Coordination in Dynamic Macroeconomic Models," in Willem Buiter and Richard Marston (eds), *International Economic Policy Coordination* (Cambridge: Cambridge University Press).

Papell, David H. (1989). "Monetary Policy in the United States Under Flexible Exchange Rates," *American Economic Review*, vol. 79 (December), pp. 1106–16.

Perron, Pierre (1988). "Trends and Random Walks in Macroeconomic Time Series," *Journal of Economic Dynamics and Control*, vol. 12 (June/September), pp. 297–332.

Phelps, Edmund (1990). *Seven Schools of Macroeconomic Thought* (Oxford: Clarendon Press).

Phillips, A (1958). "The Relation Between Unemployment and the Rate of Change of Money Wage Rates in the United Kingdom, 1861–1957," *Economica*, vol. 25 (November), pp. 283–99.

Phillips, Peter (1990). "To Criticize the Critics: An Objective Bayesian Analysis of Stochastic Trends," Cowles Foundation Discussion Paper No. 950 (New Haven: Yale University, July).

Putnam, Robert (1988). "Diplomacy and Domestic Politics: the Logic of Two-level Games," *Industrial Organization*, vol. 42 (Summer), pp. 427–61.

Putnam, Robert and Nicolas Bayne (1987). *Hanging Together: Cooperation and Conflict in the Seven-Power Summits*, revised and enlarged edition (Cambridge Mass.: Harvard University Press).

Putnam, Robert and Randall Henning (1986). "The Bonn Summit of 1978: How Does International Economic Policy Coordination Actually Work?" *Brookings Discussion Papers in International Economics*, No. 53 (Washington D.C.: Brookings Institution).

Putnam, Robert and Randall Henning (1989). "The Bonn Summit of 1978," in Richard Cooper, Barry Eichengreen, Gerald Holtham, and Randall Henning (eds), *Can Nations Agree? Issues in International Economic Cooperation* (Washington D.C.: Brookings Institution).

Roemer, John (1988). "Pitfalls of Nash Bargaining Theory in Economic Contexts," University of California, Davis, Working Paper 284.

Rogoff, Kenneth (1985), "Can International Monetary Policy Coordination be Counterproductive?" *Journal of International Economics*, vol. 18 (May), pp. 199–217.

Sachs, Jeffrey (1980). "Wages, Flexible Exchange Rates and Macroeconomic Policy," *Quarterly Journal of Economics*, vol. 94 (June) pp. 731–47.

Sachs, Jeffrey (1983). "International Policy Coordination in a Dynamic Macroeconomic Model," NBER Working Paper No. 1166, July.

Sachs, Jeffrey (1985). "The Dollar and the Policy Mix: 1985," *Brookings Papers on Economic Activity*, no. 1, pp. 117–97.

Samuelson, L. (1973). "A New Model of World Trade," *OECD Economic Outlook, Occasional Studies* (Paris: Organisation for Economic Co-operation and Development, January).

Sargent, Thomas (1973). "Rational Expectations, the Real Rate of Interest, and the Natural Rate of Unemployment," *Brookings Papers on Economic Activity*, no. 2, pp. 429–72.

Sargent, Thomas (1979). *Macroeconomic Theory* (New York: Academic Press).

Sargent, Thomas and Neil Wallace (1975). "Rational Expectations, the Optimal Monetary Instrument and the Optimal Money Supply Rule," *Journal of Political Economy*, vol. 83 (April), pp. 241–54.

Savage, Leonard (1954). *The Foundations of Statistics* (New York: John Wiley).

Schwartz, Anna (1988). "The 1987 U.S. Stock Market Crash," *Economic Affairs*, vol. 8 (February/March).

Shapiro, Carl (1986) "Exchange of Cost Information in Oligopoly," *Review of Economic Studies*, vol. 53 (July), pp. 433–46.

Shiller, Robert (1981). "Do Stock Prices Move Too Much to Be Justified by Subsequent Changes in Dividends?" *American Economic Review*, vol. 71 (June), pp. 421–36.

Simon, Herbert (1956). "Dynamic Programming under Uncertainty with a Quadratic Criterion Function," *Econometrica*, vol. 24 (January), pp. 74–81.

Simpson, Thomas (1984). "Changes in the Financial System: Implications for Monetary Policy," *Brookings Papers on Economic Activity*, no. 1, pp. 249–65.

Sims, Christopher (1980). "Macroeconomics and Reality," *Econometrica*, vol. 48 (January), pp. 1–48.

Sims, Christopher (1988). "Bayesian Skepticism," *Journal of Economic Dynamics and Control*, vol. 12 (June/September), pp. 463–79.

Solomon, Robert (1976). *The International Monetary System: An Insider's View* (New York: Harper & Row).

Stein, Arthur (1983). "Coordination and Collaboration: Politics in an Anarchic World," in Stephen Krasner (ed.), *International Regimes* (Ithaca: Cornell University Press).

Stevens, Guy, R. Berner, Peter Clark, Ernesto Hernández-Catá, Howard Howe, and Sung Kwack (1984). *The U.S. Economy in an International World: A Multicountry Model.* (Washington, D.C.: Board of Governors of the Federal Reserve System).

Stock, James and Mark Watson (1988). "Variable Trends in Economic Time Series," *Journal of Economic Perspectives*, vol. 2 (Summer), pp. 147–74.

Taylor, John (1985). "International Coordination in the Design of Macro-economic Policy Rules," *European Economic Review*, vol. 28 (June–July), pp. 53–81.

Taylor, John (1979), "Estimation and Control of a Macroeconomic Model with Rational Expectations," *Econometrica*, vol. 47 (September), pp. 1267–86.

Taylor, John (1980). "Aggregate Dynamics and Staggered Contracts," *Journal of Political Economy*, vol. 88 (February), pp. 1–23.

Taylor, John (1989). "Policy Analysis with a Multicountry Model," in Ralph Bryant et al. (eds), *Macroeconomic Policies in an Interdependent World* (Washington, D.C.: International Monetary Fund).

Tinbergen Jan (1939). *Business Cycles in the United States of America 1919–1932* (Geneva: League of Nations).

Triffin, Robert (1960). *Gold and the Dollar Crisis* (New Haven: Yale University Press).

Turnovsky, Stephen, Tamer Basar, and Vasco d'Orey (1988). "Dynamic Strategic Monetary Policies and Coordination in Interdependent Economies," *American Economic Review*, vol. 78 (June), pp. 341–61.

van-der-Ploeg, Fredrick (1988). "International Policy Coordination in Inter-dependent Monetary Economies," *Journal of International Economics*, vol. 25 (August), pp. 1–23.

Vives, Xavier (1984). "Duopoly Information Equilibrium: Cournot and Bertrand," *Journal of Economic Theory*, vol. 34 (October), pp. 71–94.

Volcker, Paul and Toyoo Gyohten (1992). *Changing Fortunes: The World's Money and the Threat to American Leadership* (New York: Times Books).

Von Furstenberg, George and Joseph Daniels. *Economic Summit Declarations, 1975–1989: Examining the Written Record of International Cooperation.* (Princeton N.J.: International Finance Section, Princeton University).

Von Neuman, John and Oskar Morgenstern (1953). *Theory of Games and Economic Behavior* (Princeton: Princeton University Press).

Wagner, Harrison (1988). "Economic Interdependence, Bargaining Power, and Political Influence," *International Organization*, vol. 42 (Summer), pp. 461–83.

Wallis, Kenneth F. (1988). "Empirical Models and Macroeconomic Policy Analysis," in Ralph Bryant et al. (eds), *Empirical Macroeconomics for Interdependent Economies* (Washington, D.C.: Brookings Institution), pp. 225–37.

West, Kenneth (1987). "A Standard Monetary Model and the Variability of the Deutschemark-Dollar Exchange Rate," *Journal of International Economics*, vol. 23 (August), pp. 57–76.

Williamson, John and Marcus Miller (1987). *Targets and Indicators: A Blueprint for the International Coordination of Economic Policy*, Policy Analyses in International Economics, 5 (Washington: Institute for International Economics).

Index